The Spirit of Labor

The Spirit of Labor

Hutchins Hapgood

Introduction and Notes by James R. Barrett

University of Illinois Press

Urbana and Chicago

First paperback edition, 2004
Introduction and notes © 2004 by the
Board of Trustees of the University of Illinois
All rights reserved
Manufactured in the United States of America

P 5 4 3 2 1

∞ This book is printed on acid-free paper.

Library of Congress Cataloging-in-Publication Data
Hapgood, Hutchins, 1869–1944.
The spirit of labor / Hutchins Hapgood ; introduction
and notes by James R. Barrett.— 1st paperback ed., 2004.
p.   cm.
Originally published: New York : Duffield & Co., 1907.
Includes bibliographical references
ISBN 0-252-07187-5 (pbk. : alk. paper)
1. Labor unions—United States. 2. Labor Movement—
United States. 3. Anarchism—United States.
I. Barrett, James R., 1950– II. Title.
HD6508.H25   2004
331.88'0973—dc22   2003021635

TO MY FATHER

CONTENTS.

CHAPTER

	Acknowledgments	ix
	Introduction by James R. Barrett	xi
I.	Early Youth	23
II.	On the Road	35
III.	Injustice and Love	54
IV.	The Age of Reason	75
V.	Trade-Unionist	94
VI.	Meeting the Employer	119
VII.	The Radicals	138
VIII.	Organizer	167
IX.	Delegate to New York	189
X.	Chicago Spirit and Its Cause	210
XI.	Social Amenities	220
XII.	Argument With Boss	235
XIII.	An Anarchist Salon	262
XIV.	Politics in the Federation	293
XV.	The Intellectual Proletariat	323
XVI.	Some of the Big Men	348
XVII.	Their Points of View	375
XVIII.	A Ripe Letter	401
	Notes by James R. Barrett	411

Acknowledgments.

———

MY LATE friend Steve Sapolsky first drew my attention to this fascinating book. Steve had a great love of books, and he knew a good one when he saw it. He thought *The Spirit of Labor* should be introduced to a broader audience of scholars, students, and working people in a new edition that placed Hutchins Hapgood's picture of the labor movement and working-class intellectual and cultural life in their broader historical context. Early-twentieth-century Chicago presents a particularly compelling background for such a study, and I can think of no one who knew more about Chicago during the historical moment Hapgood evokes here than Steve. I have done my best to rise to meet his standards.

Steve was a great friend and colleague, and an important influence on my own intellectual development—and that of many others in Chicago, Pittsburgh, and well beyond. His years of research on working-class life in Chicago were not only a source of nearly unlimited information, but also of

Acknowledgments

great stimulation for many scholars in our own work. His healthy skepticism of all dogma kept us honest. In this and in other ways, Anton Johannsen, the subject of *The Spirit of Labor,* reminds me of Steve. Steve's research efforts, especially the work he did late in his life on the use of slave labor by German corporations in the World War II era, showed us ways to make our own work socially useful. Steve died in Schenley Park, Pittsburgh, in August 2001 for reasons we are all still trying to understand. I would like to dedicate this new edition of *The Spirit of Labor* to Steve, who had precisely this spirit. In many ways, this is his book.

For their reading and comments, I would like to thank Jenny Barrett and Kathy Oberdeck, and for his research assistance, Tom Mackaman. Laurie Matheson and Rebecca Crist facilitated the project at the University of Illinois Press and the University of Illinois Research Board provided support for a research trip to the Beinecke Library at Yale. Dave and Marty Montgomery opened their home to me and discussed Steve and Anton during my visit.

—Jim Barrett

Introduction.

James R. Barrett

———

ON A LATE spring day in 1905 Hutchins Hapgood walked into the saloon in the Briggs House Hotel, a hangout for Chicago labor activists. He was looking for someone he had never met, only imagined. "Before I went to Chicago, I had in mind what I wanted to find," he later recalled. "I felt certain that, somewhere in that turbulent world of labor, there must be a man who stood at the center of all the converging elements and who was at least dimly conscious of the development of a labor philosophy. I felt certain I would recognize him if I came into contact with him."[1] He found that person in Anton Johannsen.

Hutchins Hapgood and Anton Johannsen inhabited very different worlds at the beginning of the twentieth century. Born in Chicago in 1867 and raised in the Mississippi River town of Alton, Illinois, Hapgood traced his family back two centuries to the Massachusetts Puritans. In fact, his father, a progressive businessman educated at Brown, was the first Hapgood to have left Petersham, Massachusetts, in many generations. With ancestors on both sides in the American Revolution, one a Tory and the other a revolutionary who served in the Continental and United States Congresses, Hutchins Hapgood could hardly have been more deeply rooted in American myths and traditions. He graduated Phi Beta Kappa near the top of his class at Harvard. At a time when a small minority of Americans went to high school, Hapgood went on for a master's degree and then taught English at Harvard and the University of Chicago. His subsequent life, one of literature and leisure, he spent settled variously in Greenwich Village, Dobbs Ferry, New York, Tuscany, Provincetown, and Key West, when not traveling around the world. Hapgood's brothers were equally remarkable. William Powers Hapgood launched the Columbia Conserve Company, a cooperative factory, in Indianapolis and dedicated his life to a range of reform causes. Norman Hapgood built a successful career as a progressive journalist.[2]

Yet Hutchins Hapgood was that rare bird, a well-educated WASP elite who questioned not only his own privilege but the system on which it rested. In his writing and in his personal life, Hapgood looked toward a new kind of society based more on human worth than personal privilege. For a generation he remained at the center of radical intellectual life in the United States. A central figure in both Mable Dodge's Greenwich Village salon and in the Provincetown Players, Hapgood was a close friend and collaborator of playwrights Eugene O'Neill and Susan Glaspell; writers Floyd Dell, Theodore Dreiser, Sinclair Lewis, Upton Sinclair, and Sherwood Anderson; artists Alfred Stieglitz and Georgia O'Keeffe; and journalists John Reed, Louise Bryant, Lincoln Steffens, Anna Strunsky Walling, and Walter Lippmann.

Like so many turn-of-the-century workers, Anton Johannsen was an immigrant. His father, a roofer with little education, fled the rural poverty of Germany for the small-town poverty of Clinton, Iowa, where he first worked as a brewery teamster and then prospered briefly as a saloonkeeper. With little formal education, Johannsen left school early and went to work in a brick factory and, later, a window sash and door factory. He left town on a boxcar at the age of eighteen and educated himself while tramping around the country and working at a variety of jobs. It was this travel and the people he met while doing so that provided him with what might be called a "blue-collar cosmopolitanism"— a tolerance of, even an interest in, that which was different, new. In this at least, his attitudes actually paralleled Hapgood's. "Life on the road," Johannsen concludes here, "with all its chance meetings with many men and ways of living makes one tolerant of everything except tyranny" (54). At the end of the nineteenth century Johannsen settled down with his wife and children in Chicago, where he earned his living by day in a woodworking shop, led his local union, and became active in the city's labor federation and anarchist circles. Like Hapgood, Johannsen was driven by his own "spirit of protest" which pressed him to consider some broader context for his own life and those of the working people around him.

The Spirit of Labor is thus the product of a rather unlikely collaboration between a bohemian literary radical and an anarchist woodworker. By the time they met in Chicago, however, both men had already made a habit of crossing the kind of social boundaries that separated them. Even in his shop or union meeting Johannsen was the cosmopolitan worker, the one likely to bring in an anarchist book or a free-thought newspaper, to strike up a conversation about the meaning of life or the need for woman suffrage. His intellectual curiosity, his thirst for ideas, drove him beyond his workplace and his union. He might have spent his days making door-frames, but his evenings were likely to include conversations with artists, poets, and influential reformers. Nor were such exchanges simply a matter of the humble worker soaking up ideas from his social betters. What struck Hutchins Hapgood about Chicago, on the contrary, was the degree to which the opposite seemed to be the case, that middle-class and elite people were stimulated by and absorbing ideas from the labor movement. In the university, in the settlements, even in business and professional life, Hapgood noted, the details of daily life "show in a hundred implicit ways the degree to which the radical ideas of the common people have affected all grades of society. . . . Most radicals are either working people or else persons who have come in contact with the feelings and ideas evolved by the laboring class, and have come to express them" (138–39). Surging forward in Chicago and elsewhere at the turn of the century, "the spirit of labor" seemed to pull all else in its wake. For a bright worker like Johannsen, this situation meant, among other things, considerable contact with middle-class and elite "radicals."

Hutchins Hapgood was clearly one of the radical intellectuals drawn by this spirit. Like some other young writers and artists of his generation, he took his interest in the immigrant worker, the street

merchant, and petty criminal "past genteel amuse-
ment to a conviction that meetings with social 'others' might not simply entertain but foster more fully
realized selves."[3] For Hapgood this quest for self-
realization through contact across the class divide
began in 1897 when he took a job as reporter with
the *New York Commercial Advertiser,* edited by the
soon-to-be-famous muckraker Lincoln Stephens.
Journalism was the closest Hapgood ever came to
a vocation, and he worked on and off at it for the
next two decades. Aiming for a newspaper that was
a cut above the common fare, Stephens assembled
a group of talented young writers who recognized
the human drama at work in the city and rendered
it with a literary flair unusual in the mainstream
press. The *Advertiser* was lyrical by newspaper standards of the day. The talented group of young writers around Hapgood and his brother Norman were
drawn by the excitement and beauty they found in
city life. They saw "murder as a tragedy rather than
a crime," historian Moses Rischin writes, "a fire as
a drama rather than police news, pushcart traffic a
vibrant pageant rather than as a nuisance."[4] "Their
observations appealed to an inquisitive public who
wanted to peek across the 'Social Gulf,'" Christine
Stansell concludes, "without actually straying into
the territory themselves."[5] Over the next two de-

cades Hapgood produced hundreds of columns embracing a striking panorama of urban life for various papers in New York and Chicago.

Hapgood was particularly drawn to the Lower East Side, and his wonderful columns evoked the community created there by the burgeoning population of poor Russian and East European Jews. His wife Neith Boyce, also a reporter at the *Advertiser,* convinced him to combine these pieces into *The Spirit of the Ghetto* (1902). Never a great success in its day, *The Spirit of the Ghetto* now stands as a minor classic of immigrant life. In a pattern he often repeated in his early career, Hapgood was able to penetrate the life of the Lower East Side with the aid of native collaborators, in this case the socialist editor Abraham Cahan of the Yiddish *Jewish Daily Forward* and the brilliant artist Jacob Epstein, who produced dozens of drawings for the book.[6] Hapgood shared the proceeds from his 1903 book *The Autobiography of a Thief* with Jim Caulfield, the petty thief whose life provided its substance. He repeated this pattern with the collaborators associated with his next two books involving work across class lines.[7]

The conditions under which Hapgood and Johannsen produced *The Spirit of Labor* tell us a great deal about both the authors and the book.

[xvii]

Hapgood had intended to use Johannsen's life story to capture the energy and pervasive influence of Chicago's organized working-class movement, offering someone like Anton as an archetype of the new working-class radical. He had used this autobiographical strategy successfully in his last book, *The Autobiography of a Thief.* He quickly came up against the clear-cut differences, however, between the genres of bourgeois and working-class autobiography. Hapgood had trouble getting Johannsen to focus on his own story or even getting him slowed down long enough to talk at all. When he did talk, Johannsen wanted to discuss the union movement, politics, and strikes. Such tendencies were typical of worker autobiographers in many countries and suggest the influence of class on notions of self and identity. Whereas Hapgood and other middle-class intellectuals might place the emphasis on the individual and his or her search for the self, workers' narratives tended to be told very differently. They often subordinated the personal to the social and political and described themselves as what one scholar has termed "social atoms"—more or less representative pieces of a much larger whole. Particularly with labor radicals, the self was not the focus of the narrative but rather the movement.[8] There was an individualist anarchism abroad in the early twentieth century, but Johannsen, an ideological eclectic in any case, was clearly drawn by the ideas of anarcho-communism, which emphasized the social and collective over the self and social movements over individual political acts.

At a more practical level, Johannsen was far more concerned with his life in the movement and reluctant to take time away from that for what he tended to view as the bourgeois enterprise of autobiography. "He felt I belonged to another class," Hapgood recalled, "and that my motives were probably profoundly suspect."[9] He absorbed a certain amount from simply visiting with Johannsen and his family and observing him at large in the city, and he was sometimes able to question Johannsen at length in meetings at Hapgood's own room. Such meetings with Johannsen were productive, Hapgood wrote to Neith Boyce from Chicago, but "he is nervous about having to give up many of his trade union meetings. I have many problems connected with him—how to hold him and his interest as well as how to get and use the material." "I can get a good thing from Johannsen," Hapgood concluded in another letter, "if I can keep him up to the work. He is restless, wants to go to his meetings, etc."[10]

For these and other reasons, Hapgood chose a more biographical approach, hoping to place Johannsen in his element and, in the process, bring some notion of the labor movement to middle-class readers. Although Hapgood's book is essentially a biography, extensive quotations from Johannsen convey something of the thinking of a radical worker. It would be a mistake, of course, to assume that these quotations convey Johannsen's unalloyed worldview. Not only did the interviews reflect Hapgood's own interests and biases in the questions he asked and the way he chose to ask them, but the answers themselves come from Hapgood's notes. While these have not survived, it seems that they did not represent a verbatim rendering of Johannsen's words. None of this reduces the value of *The Spirit of Labor*, but it is worth considering when we ask ourselves what the text represents. The two men worked together on the book, but clearly it was conceived and conceptualized by Hapgood. Thus, what he brought to the book was at least as important as what Johannsen brought to it. Hapgood's choices in constructing the narrative can tell us as much about the world of a radical intellectual as they can about the world of a radical woodworker.

One problem with *Spirit* is that Hapgood was so absorbed with Johannsen's and others' personalities that he often failed to provide the broader context required to understand the labor movement.[11] The particular context here is crucial. If, as Christine Stansell suggests, New York was the soul of the bohemian phenomenon of the early twentieth century, then Chicago was "the heart of the radical labor movement in America," as Hapgood recalled in his memoir.[12] Both social reformers like Jane Addams and writers like Jacob Riis and Hapgood himself were moved by the enormous social distance at the turn of the century between the nation's native middle-class population and the ocean of immigrant poor. Nowhere was this social gulf characteristic of U.S. cities in this era greater than in Chicago; nowhere were workers more fully organized or more class-conscious. Throughout the late nineteenth century, the city's diverse working-class communities had created the strongest and most progressive labor movement in the United States. A series of epic political and industrial conflicts, including both the Haymarket Tragedy (1886) and the great Pullman Strike (1894), accentuated the social chasm between the immigrant working class and the city's elites.

The level of union organization and strike activity actually increased in the following decade. In one year, 1903, unions doubled their membership and launched 251 strikes. By September of that year the Chicago Federation of Labor boasted more than

243,000 members, over half of the city's labor force. The breadth of the movement was even more impressive than its size. It embraced not only building tradesmen, railroad workers, and a broad range of unskilled male operatives in heavy industry but also 35,000 female factory workers, scrubwomen, waitresses, and 4,000 of the city's elementary school teachers. The reproduction of class sentiments in the city is suggested by the fact that school children, prominent in many strike photos of the era, organized their own "skilled pupils unions" and strikes in support of their unionized parents and teachers. Union organization and strikes spread throughout Chicago at the turn of the century as the movement passed from an older generation of German, Irish, and native-born skilled workers to the thousands of unskilled "new immigrants" pouring into the city's mills, foundries, and factories. The *Arbeiterzeitung,* the city's main German-language working-class newspaper, declared Chicago the "trade union capital of the world."[13]

While Chicago's movement was extremely impressive, it reflected a broader growth in the size and ambitions of American labor at the turn of the century. From 1897 to 1904, union membership soared from 447,000 to more than two million. The American Federation of Labor tripled in size between

1900 and 1904, and unions also became far more aggressive. The typical number of strikes per year soared from 1,000 to 1,300 in the mid-1890s to almost 3,000 in 1901 and nearly 4,000 in 1903, with an increasingly large proportion of these disputes won by unions.[14]

Chicago was engulfed in class war at the moment Hapgood set out to capture the essence of American labor radicalism in the spring of 1905. The Chicago Employers' Association had launched an all-out campaign against the unions in a bid to rid the city of this "tyranny" and to run the place "open shop." The key target in this offensive was the powerful Teamsters Union. The Teamsters represented the linchpin in the Chicago movement for several reasons. Comprising 35,000 blacks, native-born and immigrant Irish, and workers from a variety of other ethnic backgrounds, they had managed to build an unusually powerful movement by employing their wagons to stop traffic in what came to be termed "street strikes." As historian David Witwer notes, "The nature of the teamsters' trade and the geography of the early-twentieth-century city made non-union wagons vulnerable." Strikebreakers attempting to navigate congested city streets were attacked by large crowds drawn from the city's densely populated working-class neighborhoods. In return, the Teamsters seemed ever-willing to support other groups of workers in sympathy strikes that became endemic in the city around the turn of the century.[15] Doctors at the county hospital labeled the teamster "the roughest, toughest scrapper of the working classes."[16] The Teamsters' power was particularly obnoxious to the city's large merchants. In the spring of 1904 one of them predicted a confrontation between Chicago's militant unions and its increasingly class-conscious employers: "Some day," he declared, "the unions and the business community will have to fight it out to see who owns Chicago."[17]

As the economy dipped and unemployment rose in the summer and fall of 1904, the Chicago Employers' Association launched an ambitious (and quite successful) open shop drive. By July of that year Chicago was convulsed by 92 strikes and lockouts involving 77,000 workers. The net effects were disastrous, particularly in the city's largest factories. Strong organizations of largely unskilled immigrant workers at Illinois Steel, International Harvester, and in the slaughtering plants at the giant Union Stock Yards were completely destroyed. As with the great upsurge at the turn of the century, the decline of the Chicago unions mirrored a national trend. In the face of a massive and well-coordinated open shop drive, from 1904 on union growth stalled, AFL membership actually dropped briefly, and the numbers of workers involved in strikes declined precipitously, with workers tending to lose an ever-larger proportion of those strikes. While employers had launched an open shop campaign in the city's building industry as early as 1900, the cataclysmic struggle for the Chicago unions came in April 1905 during a massive and violent Teamsters' strike. Hapgood did his first round of research in the midst of this dramatic conflict, which highlighted for him and other observers the high degree of class feeling in the city's immigrant working-class communities.[18]

Graham Taylor, a liberal minister and settlement house reformer, was struck by a pervasive and violent class-consciousness that he saw all about him.

> It was the disclosure of the intensity and intolerance of class-conscious feeling prevailing not only among those on both sides who were immediately involved in controversy, but as pronouncedly throughout one whole class as the other . . . our non-union neighbors . . . became as class-conscious, almost overnight, as were the striking teamsters. . . . Men from the sidewalks, women from the tenement-house windows, and even the little children from the playground, cried with one voice,

"Down with the scabs," some of them hurling any missile at hand at the frightened drivers. . . . the "solidarity of labor" extends beyond the membership of unions. . . . on occasion the class-conscious spirit emerges from the whole working class, expressing the personal claim to the job as inviolate.[19]

Jane Addams found that in such situations, "the entire population of the city becomes divided into two cheering sides . . . . Any one who tries to keep the attitude of non-partisanship . . . is quickly under suspicion by both sides."[20] Like Jane Addams before him, Taylor was saddened by what he saw as a form of intolerance. Settlement house reformers like Taylor and Addams dedicated their lives to building social and cultural bridges between immigrant workers and the more "respectable" elements in the city's population. Strikes enlarged the chasm between social classes in a particularly dramatic way. To his credit, Hapgood saw the pervasive class-consciousness of early-twentieth-century Chicago in very different terms. "I was impressed over and over again, when living among the mechanics," he wrote, "with a certain kind of altruism, of a fairly wide-spread emotion of solidarity, akin to the religious; for when men band together in an effort to attain things they deem necessary to their deepest material and spiritual welfare, they are not far from conceiving of the movement, at least in moments of self-conscious-ness, as being from one point of view religious" (109). Even Addams agreed that the "most valu-able result" of the mass strikes involving immi-grant workers was "the expanding consciousness of the solidarity of the workers."[21] The highest prin-ciple in working-class subcultures, Hapgood con-cluded, is that of "organized solidarity." Upon it, all else depended.

* * *

But, as Hapgood demonstrates in *The Spirit of Labor,* if Chicago was the heart of industrial radi-calism, it was also the vital center of a vibrant work-ing-class intellectual and cultural life that shaped not only the lives of the city's workers but also the social, cultural, and political life of the city as a whole. It was at the convergence of this labor and cultural radicalism that Hapgood sought to locate his book. In *The Spirit of Labor* he tried to identify a kind of proletarian modernism. The essence of the "modern," Hapgood believed, lay not in his own group of déclassé radical intellectuals, as many writ-ers at the time and since have assumed, but rather in people like Johannsen and his friends. "I feel he is really nearer the truth of the immediate future than I or any of my leisure class friends," Hapgood wrote to his wife.[22]

Chicago's strong free speech traditions went back to Haymarket and well before, but there were also more recent traditions. Hapgood found that Jane Addams ran "a kind of salon" at Hull-House, "an exchange of ideas where all the surging social conceptions find expression" (213). At dinners and public forums in the old house on Halsted Street one might indeed find some of the leading writers and artists of the day, but they would be rubbing elbows with Women's Trade Union League activists, immigrant anarchists and socialists, and labor organizers.[23] Christine Stansell notes that New York drew off many of the most talented midwestern writers and artists who might otherwise have raised literary and artistic standards in Chicago, but the bohemian scene that remained—and it was an extremely dynamic scene—was much closer to working-class radical politics and culture than its New York counterpart. Chicago's Bughouse Square, Radical Bookshop, and later the Dil Pickle Club seemed to meld bohemian intellectuals and working-class activists, politics and art, more easily than comparable New York venues.[24] These Chicago institutions and others like them were far more open than Mabel Dodge's Greenwich Village salon, attracting many of the era's leading literary lights and artists to spaces they shared with anarchists and socialists and more typical migratory workers.

Drawing on his relationships with Robert Morss Lovett and the novelist Robert Herrick, both friends from Harvard now teaching English at the University of Chicago, Hapgood made extensive contacts among Chicago's intellectual circles and immersed himself in the city's remarkable cultural life. He developed a close relationship with the radical lawyer Clarence Darrow and met with the economist Thorstein Veblen to discuss Veblen's book *The Theory of the Leisure Class* (New York, 1899). He also spoke often with settlement house reformers Jane Addams and Graham Taylor, University of Chicago sociologist W. I. Thomas, and other intellectuals. A regular "lunch group" included Lovett, Algie Simmons (editor of the *Chicago Socialist)*, and writers I. K. Friedman, Raymond Robins, and William English Walling. "In fact," Hapgood wrote to Robert Herrick, "Chicago is full of good humans." While in Chicago Hapgood read Kropotkin's *Memoirs of a Revolutionist* (Boston, 1899), Oscar Wilde's works, and other books "along an anarchist line." But he also had no trouble meeting a range of labor activists including Con O'Shea, president of the Teamsters, a number of other Teamsters, the garment workers' leader Abraham Bisno, and several of the leading figures in the Chicago Federation of Labor, as well as anarchists Ben Reitman, "the Hobo Doctor," Hippolyte Havel, and Emma Goldman.[25]

The radical modernism of Chicago's intellectual elite and professional reformers, the bohemian radicalism of the city's "proletarian intellectuals," the tough idealism of its labor activists, the almost "religious" class solidarity of much of its working-class population—if Hapgood illuminates each of these worlds for us, there is another world that he never penetrated during his time in Chicago, perhaps because he never looked for it. Johannsen cannot be taken for a "typical" early-twentieth-century urban worker, if such a person had ever existed. He was an anarchist radical at a time when most Chicago workers continued to support one of the two main parties, a free-love atheist free-thinker at a time when most working-class families held to traditional values, a sophisticated cosmopolitan in an era when most working-class people organized their lives around their local religious communities and never strayed far from home. Johannsen's story does convey a radical dynamic at the center of working-class life in these years, but it does not capture the everyday experience of millions of immigrant workers and their families.

[xxx]

The rather bewildering ethnic diversity of the city, and others like it, is not apparent in Hapgood's rendering of Johannsen's world. Chicago's broader working-class community was fragmented into literally dozens of ethnic subcultures. Between 1880 and 1930, as the city's labor force grew by 600 percent, a massive migration drew more than 600,000 people from around the world into its shops and factories. By the time of the Great Depression, Chicago had the largest Polish, Scandinavian, Czech, Lithuanian, and Slovak and the third-largest Italian populations of any city in the United States. Even at the turn of the century, Chicago had a substantial African American community; as Hapgood observed, some were integrated into the labor movement, others marginalized by it. The World War I years and the decade that followed saw a new wave of black migrants from the Deep South moving to Chicago, joining the original black community and the "new immigrants" who arrived in the years described in *The Spirit of Labor.* These new black migrants fled to escape the worst aspects of Jim Crow segregation and organized racial violence, and to take advantage of the opportunities for industrial employment that cities like Chicago provided.[26]

What was true in Chicago in these years was also true for many other industrial cities in the North-east and the Midwest—millions of unskilled immigrant workers met black (and, later, Mexican migrant) laborers on the streets and in the workplaces of Chicago and comparable cities. What difference would this have made in Hapgood's telling of Johannsen's story? As early as the time of Hapgood's research and writing, this momentous meeting of immigrant and African American was already breeding cooperation and solidarity in some places and massive conflict in others. In the course of 1904 and 1905, for example, large strikes at the stockyards, among the Teamsters, in the city's restaurants, and elsewhere all involved the vital issue of the integration of black workers along with recent immigrants into the union struggle. In a vital sense, the future of the labor movement in Chicago and in countless other communities throughout the country depended upon the resolution of what the great black intellectual W. E. B. Du Bois called the central problem of the new twentieth century—the race issue.[27] One part of the story Hapgood misses, then, in concentrating solely on the world of labor radicalism and ignoring the marked ethnic and racial diversity of Chicago is the rather compelling tale of the ways in which the city's workers strove to create an ethnically and racially diverse working class movement—both their failures and successes. For

Hapgood, it seems, the central question was one of class and not of race.

Each ethnic community sustained a wide array of religious, cultural, social, and economic institutions, and many immigrant and black workers in Chicago and elsewhere lived their lives within the contours of such networks. Religion was particularly important in many of these communities, yet we find no recognition of this in *The Spirit of Labor.* In a sense, the emphasis on community that made *The Spirit of the Ghetto* such a compelling book is missing here. It is as if Hapgood was so taken with the spectacle of widespread class solidarity that he missed the striking ethnic, religious, and racial diversity among Chicago's workers. How might a consideration of these parallel worlds change our image of working-class life? Is it possible that such communities offered alternative values and perspectives to both those of elite and corporate cultures and also those espoused by radicals like Anton Johannsen?

* * *

For all the social distance between them, Johannsen and his world had a profound effect on Hapgood. "The last two months have meant a great deal to me," he wrote to Neith Boyce in late 1905. "They have made me see the real sadness of things more deeply than I did before and they have removed the last vestige of snobbishness and 'class' feeling that I had. My relations in the past years with thieves, vaudevillians, etc. etc. seem now to me quite unimportant, socially. But these working people and the radical atmosphere in which the thought of the working class results—this seems significant to me in a tremendous, almost terrible way. . . . [They] fascinate, please, sadden, and excite me."[28] Neith Boyce, writing to their friend Robert Morss Lovett, reported in early 1906, "Hutch has been here [New York] five weeks now and has talked steadily for about four weeks. He did have some fearful and wonderful experiences in radical Chicago. When he got here he seemed to feel that he had been rudely torn from the one spot on earth where he really desired to root himself."[29]

His biographer, Michael Marcaccio, traced Hapgood's radical politics to his experience with Johannsen in Chicago. Hapgood had already shown a marked sympathy with common people and outsiders of all kinds and a radical disposition. He was raised by an anti-business businessman father and steeped in an alternative intellectual culture, but until his visit to Chicago he had little sense of either the labor movement or radical politics. Johannsen's world sensitized Hapgood to a working-class critique of modern capitalism and won him over to a support for labor that persisted throughout his life. Writing of the labor ethic he discovered in Chicago, Hapgood recalled in the late 1930s, "my own consciousness and therefore my life was affected by it. I had always sympathized with the underdog. But now I began to give more serious endorsement to the philosophy of those who have not." "As I look back upon my long life," he wrote in 1939 in the midst of a new era of labor insurgency, "I find there is only one faith that burns in me as brightly or more brightly than ever. That is what may be called roughly the faith in the labor movement." As Marcaccio concludes, "Hutchins Hapgood discovered labor in Chicago."[30]

* * *

Their lives after *The Spirit of Labor* suggest the remaining distance between Hutchins Hapgood and Anton Johannsen, the ways in which these two radicals shared deep human experiences, and how their respective class positions determined their futures. Having gathered all of this "human material" in the heart of Chicago's labor and radical communities, Hapgood finished *The Spirit* in New York in 1906 and then read the proofs for the book at a villa in Florence, leaving the slums of Chicago far

[xxxv]

behind. He produced a second book based on his Chicago experiences, *An Anarchist Woman* (New York, 1909), which told the stories of his friends Terry and Marie, working-class anarchists who appear at several points in *The Spirit of Labor.*

Terry and Marie's story represented Hapgood's special interest in the love lives of these proletarian radicals. As Christine Stansell notes, *"The Spirit of Labor* eroticized the subject of labor and the figure of the radical workingman, striking a connection between working-class life and sexual license. Hapgood set out to describe the 'expressiveness' of the American workers and that expressiveness turned out to be, in good measure, a superabundance of sex. The democracy that beckoned across the class line was erotic as well as industrial, a liberalized regime of heterosexual love." Hapgood's account does little to dispel a common confusion about the notion of what has come to be called "free love." A principled position against any legal restraints on individuals' sexual habits, the idea had roots in American reform movements of the midnineteenth century, though it was more common at the turn of the century among immigrant working-class anarchists. Contrary to popular conceptions about sexual promiscuity, it neither prescribed this nor precluded monogamy. The emphasis was on individual freedom in this and other realms of one's personal life. Free love became a strong principle among bohemian intellectuals as part of a more general revolt against bourgeois morality. By his own account, Hutchins Hapgood learned the free love ethic from Chicago anarchists; it was a habit he continued to embrace for much of his life.[31]

Hapgood also continued to write newspaper columns on a vast array of subjects and collected some of these in another book on the "lower classes," *Types from City Streets* (New York, 1910). The *Story of a Lover,* Hapgood's own story of his relationship with Neith Boyce, was not published until 1919, although he wrote it in 1914. An early commercial success, *The Story of a Lover* was confiscated by the New York City Police Department's vice squad. Although the book was ruled non-pornographic, Hapgood attributed its slumping sales thereafter to the scandal. He finished his only play, *Enemies,* which he coauthored with Neith Boyce, in 1915.[32]

From about 1914 until at least the early 1930s, Hutchins Hapgood suffered from depression. He produced little journalism and no major works. It seems likely that whatever tendencies he might have had toward depression and alcoholism were severely aggravated by the death of his eldest son, Boyce Hapgood, in the 1918 influenza epidemic. "For years," Hapgood wrote, "Neith and I were unable in any full measure to live either in work or with our children." While Neith Boyce wrote her way out of her own depression to some degree with *Harry* (1923), a book based on her dead son's personality and life, Hutchins seems never to have recovered from the tragedy.[33] Hutchins Hapgood died on November 26, 1944, and was buried in Petersham, Massachusetts, his family's home for almost three centuries.

Anton Johannsen suffered his own tragedies, but he remained at the very center of the labor movement. He served as state organizer from 1909 to 1914 for the California Building Trades Council, and was indicted along with J. B. and J. J. McNamara of the Structural Iron Workers for a dynamite campaign aimed at anti-union employers in the Los Angeles area. Although Johannsen was never tried for these offenses, the indictment hung over him for two years. The McNamara brothers were placed on trial in late 1911, while labor anarchists David Kaplan and Johannsen's close friend Matt Schmidt fled. Some 80,000 unionists and socialists met in Chicago to protest the indictments. Johannsen traveled throughout the United States, raising funds for the legal case, and Clarence Darrow came to California to defend the brothers in court. Johannsen and workers throughout the country were outraged when the McNamaras confessed to dynamiting the Los Angeles Times building. Convinced apparently that his plea would help avoid further repression of the labor movement, James McNamara later insisted on his innocence. Kaplan and Schmidt were tracked down and sentenced to long prison terms. The trial's outcome ended the prospects for a Socialist party victory in the Los Angeles municipal elections and also led to a precipitous decline in the state's union movement. In the midst of this tragedy, Johannsen's young daughter died; he and his wife buried her in the family's yard.[34] Although he certainly had what Hapgood once called a "dynamiting mind" in terms of his intellectual radicalism, it seemed unlikely that Johannsen was directly involved in the violence. The government apparently concurred, as the charges were eventually dropped.[35]

Still an anarchist, Johannsen spent much of the rest of his life organizing workers. He served as a general organizer for the Carpenters in California from 1914 to 1917 and as an organizer for the Labor Defense Council the following year. He returned to Chicago in 1918, where he worked for seven years as business agent for the Carpenters' district council. During the Red Scare period, 1919 to 1922, he was elected chair of the Chicago Federation of

Labor's Organizing Committee. The federation's president, John Fitzpatrick, trusted and worked closely with Johannsen without regard to politics, as he did with Chicago communists and a host of other radicals in the early twenties. When he last wrote Hapgood in 1933, the liberal Democratic governor Henry Horner had appointed Johannsen to the state's Industrial Commission. "If by chance you ever come to Chicago," Johannsen concluded, "I could probably give you plenty of material for a new edition of the 'Spirit of Labor.'"[36] Toward the end of his life, between 1935 and 1946, Johannsen achieved his highest office in the labor movement, serving as vice-president of the Chicago Federation of Labor.[37] Anton Johannsen died in Chicago and was buried in Waldheim Cemetery—near the monument honoring the Haymarket martyrs and alongside numerous other activists associated with the city's rich history of labor radicalism.

* * *

The Spirit of Labor provides memorable glimpses of the diverse worlds that made up life in an early-twentieth-century industrial city, and it also leaves us with some questions. In what ways was Anton Johannsen typical of workers of his generation? Hapgood conveys a fascinating picture of a manual worker who is at once in some ways representative of other workers in this era, but also profoundly radical in his worldview. More than his manual work, union meetings, and political activity, we also get a glimpse of his domestic domain, his personality, even his emotions—a rare insight into a worker's personal life. Listening to Johannsen's insights about social and personal relations, the state of the world, and various matters of ethics and aesthetics, it becomes more difficult to think of him any longer as simply a pair of strong arms or even a "class-conscious worker"—though this label certainly applies. We are forced to ask if there is an "intellectual history" far beyond what we normally associate with that term, a world of ideas and values created and exchanged in the working-class neighborhoods, factories, saloons, and other common spaces throughout cities like Chicago. And if such a world of ideas and values did exist, how does that change our understanding of life in an industrial city like Chicago?

How representative was Chicago of American cities in these years? In what respects was it unique, and why? Between them, Hutchins Hapgood and Anton Johannsen stress the city's deep and expansive class-consciousness. Chicago might have been unusual, as Hapgood suggests, in the extent to which such consciousness pervaded every aspect of life, but certainly class divisions and working-class organization had become characteristic of American cities by the end of the nineteenth century. What explains the particular resonance of labor and its influence throughout society at this moment in U.S. history? What was it about this period that stimulated such divisions and conflict?

Like our own, Johannsen's world intersected with many others. Such intersections inevitably leave us with questions as well as answers. There is, of course, the world of the trade union activist, racketeer, and reformer. When we leave the experience of the middle-class reformer and try to see these divisions through Johannsen's eyes, they become far more complex than we might have imagined them. You will certainly find corruption in our world, Anton and his friends tell us, but is this corruption comparable to the everyday corruption in a system that destroys the lives of workers and their families?

While working women play a frustratingly minor role in *The Spirit of Labor* (Johannsen's was in many ways a man's world), we get some intriguing glimpses of their lives. How and why were the lives of working women different from those of the male workers around them? Radical women like Marie and Emma Goldman struggled not only to build a new world, but also a new way of life for themselves.[38] In their relations with the men in their lives, as much as in their relations with Chicago's elites, they fought for a place in the world and did so outside the mainstream movement for women's rights. Trade union activists like the teacher Margaret Haley demanded their place in the burgeoning labor movement, but they also demanded that their sisters join this class movement and support male unionists. Most intriguing is Maggie, Anton Johannsen's wife. A "typical working-class housewife" to middle-class observers, perhaps, Maggie turned out to have her own ideas. What were these, and what was her role in the working-class experience that Hapgood strives to capture in his book? What was it that Marie, Maggie, and Margaret Haley had in common, and what was it that separated them from one another?

We are also introduced to the underground world of the "proletarian intellectuals," worker radicals who sought to transform the world through an anarchism that remained embedded in the lives of Chicago's workers. In the late nineteenth century, the city had produced one of the strongest anarchist labor movements in the world. The context for the Haymarket Tragedy of 1886 was a rich subculture of labor radicalism, ranging from trade unionism and the reformist Knights of Labor to Marxist socialism and the anarchist International Working Peoples' Association, a potent force on Chicago's proletarian scene. In the midst of a demonstration during the great May 1886 strike for the eight-hour day, an unknown bomber killed several policemen and workers and touched off a "Red Scare" aimed at suppressing the city's radical movement.[39] The political repression following this tragedy undoubtedly weakened that movement, but *The Spirit of Labor* shows that it never really died. Much smaller, the radical community was vibrant at the moment of Hapgood's visit, and more than its predecessor, perhaps, this turn-of-the-century anarchist movement crossed boundaries of sex, class, and nationality.

Still, Hapgood missed some things here, too. The Industrial Workers of the World (IWW), that quintessentially American radical labor organization, was founded in Chicago the very summer he visited.[40] One might have expected Hapgood to encounter the IWW, a new revolutionary industrial union organization with considerable anarchist influence in its early years, as he made his way in Chicago's labor circles in the fall of 1905. One founder of the new labor organization, Lucy Parsons, was at the center of anarchist activity in the city. Yet Parsons, the wife of Albert Parsons—the

[xliv]

central figure in the Haymarket story—is not mentioned. She personified whatever link remained between the Haymarket movement and the one Hapgood found in Chicago two decades later. One possible explanation for this gap in the story is the existence of rather distinct anarchist subcultures, one focused more on the world of unions and strikes, another focused more on cultural phenomena. In fact, at the moment of Hapgood's visit a major controversy split the Chicago movement between a more culturally inclined group that soon left for the Home Colony in Washington State and a more industrially inclined group centered around Lucy Parsons that continued to work on the city's West Side and to focus on unions, strikes, and working-class politics.[41] Why was Hapgood drawn by some of these Chicago anarchists and not others? What does the persistence of anarchism after the turn of the century tell us about social relations in cities like Chicago? What was it that the anarchists wanted, and how did their goals relate to the broader struggles of the era's workers?

One boundary crossed—in the collaboration that produced this book as well as in saloons and meeting halls around working-class Chicago—was the one that separated Hapgood's "proletarian intellectuals" from people like Hapgood himself. Hutchins

Hapgood and other bohemian radical intellectuals were caught between classes at war in the early years of the twentieth century. Moreover, they were in-between not only in the sense of their divided sympathies and sensibilities, not only in terms of lifestyle, but also in the sense that these "modern radicals" were trying to forge a new way of living and a new way of looking at the world around them. In the decade following the publication of *The Spirit of Labor,* these two subcultures were drawn more and more toward one another—though the overlap between an urban-based bohemian literary tradition and working-class cultural radicalism was always more pronounced in Chicago than in that bastion of bohemianism, New York's Greenwich Village.[42] How did Hapgood's own experiences and values shape his rendering of the radical worker's world, and what does this tell us of the radical intellectuals of his generation? What drew Hutchins Hapgood and some other middle-class intellectuals to a person like Anton Johannsen and his circle of friends? In what sense were this attraction and its cultural context any more "modern" than the cultural forms that had preceded it?

At its broadest level, *The Spirit of Labor* is vital for the way it introduces us to the intersections dividing these various worlds, even as it reflects the

very real boundaries that continued to persist between them.

NOTES

1. Hutchins Hapgood, *A Victorian in the Modern World*
(New York, 1939), 186–87.

2. Hapgood, *Victorian;* Michael D. Marcaccio, *The
Hapgoods: Three Earnest Brothers* (Charlottesville, Va., 1977).

3. Christine Stansell, *American Moderns: Bohemian New
York and the Creation of a New Century* (New York, 2000), 16.

4. Moses Rischin, "Introduction," in Hutchins Hapgood,
The Spirit of the Ghetto, ed. Moses Rischin (Cambridge,
Mass., 1967), viii. For the influence of the *Advertiser* and the
writers around it on Hutchins Hapgood, see also Hapgood,
Victorian, 137–72.

5. Stansell, *American Moderns,* 24–25. On the phenomenon
of Progressive Era reform-oriented journalists "dressing up" to
cross class lines in search of the authentic working-class experience, see Frank Tobias Higbie, "Crossing Class Boundaries: Tramp Ethnographers and Narratives of Class in Progressive Era America," *Social Science History* 21 (Winter 1999):
559–92; Kathryn Oberdeck, "Popular Narrative and Working-
Class Identity: Alexander Irvine's Early Twentieth-Century
Literary Adventures," in *Labor Histories: Class, Politics, and
Working-Class Experience,* ed. Eric Arnesen, Julie Greene, and
Bruce Laurie (Urbana, Ill., 1998), 201–29; Mark Pittenger, "A
World of Difference: Constructing the 'Underclass' in Progres-
sive Era America," *American Quarterly* 49 (Mar. 1997): 26–65.

6. Stansell, *American Moderns,* 24–25; Hapgood, *Victorian,*

141–43; Moses Rischin, Introduction to *The Spirit of the Ghetto,* by Hutchins Hapgood. (Cambridge, Mass., 1967).

7. On the production of *The Autobiography of a Thief,* see Hapgood, *Victorian,* 166–72. The evidence that Hapgood shared his royalties is suggested in a series of correspondence with lower-class collaborators. See, for example, Anton Johannsen to Hutchins Hapgood, Corte Madera, Calif., Apr. 13, 1914, Box 4, Folder 117, Hapgood Family Papers, Beinecke Library, Yale University; Hapgood to Terry Carlin, New York, Mar. 31, 1914, Box 2, Folder 40, Hapgood Family Papers.

8. Reginia Gagnier, "Social Atoms: Working-Class Autobiography, Subjectivity, and Gender," *Victorian Studies* 30 (Spring 1987): 338. This phenomenon is remarkably similar across autobiographies from numerous societies, whatever their other differences. On British workers' autobiographies, see John Burnett, David Vincent, and David Mayall, eds., *The Autobiography of the Working Class: An Annotated Critical Bibliography* (New York, 1984), vol. 1: xvii–xxix; on French and German workers, Mary Jo Maynes, *Taking the Hard Road: Life Course in French and German Workers' Autobiographies in the Era of Industrialization* (Chapel Hill, N.C., 1995), 33; and on Russian workers, Diane Koenker, "Scripting the Revolutionary Worker Autobiography: Archetypes, Models, Interventions, and Markets," 8 (working article in the author's possession). On the problem of personality (or lack of it) in the autobiographies of working-class radicals in the United States, see James R. Barrett, "Revolution and Personal Crisis: William Z. Foster and the American Communist Personal Narrative," *Labor History* 43 (Fall 2002): 465–82.

9. Hapgood, *Victorian,* 189.

10. Hutchins Hapgood to Neith Boyce Hapgood, Chi-

cago, Oct. 9, 1905 (quote); Hapgood to Boyce Hapgood, Chicago, Oct. 7, 1905, Box 12, Folder 363, Hapgood Family Papers.

11. Marcaccio, *The Hapgoods,* 146.

12. Hapgood, *Victorian,* 186.

13. *Chicago Record Herald,* Mar. 26, 1903, 2, Dec. 27, 1903, 6; *The Economist,* Sept. 5, 1903, 299; clippings in Box 86A, Bessie Louise Pierce Papers, Chicago Historical Society; Dorothy Richardson, "Trade Unions in Petticoats," *Leslie's Monthly Magazine* (1904): 489–500; Steven Sapolsky, "Class Conscious Belligerents: The Teamsters and the Class Struggle in Chicago, 1901–1905" (unpublished seminar paper, University of Pittsburgh, 1974), 1–2; David Montgomery, *Workers' Control in America: Studies in Work, Technology, and Labor Struggles* (New York , 1979), 57–58; *Arbeiterzeitung,* Apr. 3, 1903, quoted in Georg Leidenberger, "'The Public Is the Labor Union': Working Class Progressivism in Turn of the Century Chicago," *Labor History* 36 (Spring 1995): 194.

14. Philip S. Foner, *The Policies and Practices of the American Federation of Labor, 1900–1909,* vol. 3 of *History of the Labor Movement in the United States.* (New York, 1973), 27.

15. John R. Commons, "The Teamsters of Chicago," in *Trade Unionism and Labor Problems,* ed. John R. Commons (New York, 1905), 36–64; Sapolsky, "Class Conscious Belligerents"; Georg Leindenberger, "'The Public Is the Labor Union,'" 198–99; David Witwer, *Corruption and Reform in the Teamsters Union* (Urbana, Ill., 2003), 22–28, quote, 22. See also Ernest Poole, "How a Labor Machine Held Up Chicago, and How the Teamsters' Union Smashed the Machine," *The World's Work* (July 1904): 896–905.

16. Poole, "How a Labor Machine Held Up Chicago," 896.

17. William English Walling, "Can Labor Unions Be Destroyed?" *The World's Work* (Dec. 1905): 6955.

18. *Chicago Tribune,* July 31, 1904. On the national trends, see Foner, *Policies and Practices of the American Federation of Labor,* 32–60, especially 59–60. On the Chicago Employers' Association and its offensive against the unions, see Isaac Marcosson, "Labor Met by Its Own Methods," *The World's Work* 7 (Jan. 1904): 4313, and "The Fight for the Open Shop," *The World's Work* (Dec. 1905): 6955.

19. Graham Taylor, *Chicago Commons through the Years* (Chicago, 1936), 118.

20. Jane Addams, *Twenty Years at Hull-House with Autobiographical Notes,* with an introduction and notes by James Hurt (Urbana, Ill., 1990), 109, quote, 131.

21. Ibid.

22. Hutchins Hapgood to Neith Boyce Hapgood, Chicago, Oct. 9, 1905, Box 5, Folder 363, Hapgood Family Papers.

23. Hutchins Hapgood, "Seen from the Outside: An Aspect of Hull House," *Chicago Evening Post,* Mar. 17, 1905, clipping in Box 27, Folder 792, Hapgood Family Papers.

24. Roger A. Bruns, *The Damnedest Radical: The Life and World of Ben Reitman, Chicago's Celebrated Social Reformer, Hobo King, and Whorehouse Physician* (Urbana, Ill., 1987); Stansell, *American Moderns,* 85–86; Dil Pickle Papers, Newberry Library, Chicago; Alison J. Smith, *Chicago's Left Bank* (Chicago, 1953); Albert Party, *Garrets and Pretenders: A History of Bohemianism in America* (New York, 1933), 175–211; and Dale Kramer, *Chicago Renaissance: The Literary Life in the Midwest, 1900–1930* (New York, 1966) all emphasize the bohemian literary angle.

25. Hutchins Hapgood to Neith Boyce Hapgood, Chicago,

May 27, 1905, Box 12, Folder 361, Sept., 1905, Box 12, Folder 364, n.d., 1905, Box 12, Folder 365, Hutchins Hapgood to Robert Herrick, May 22, 1905, Box 4, Folder 104, all Hapgood Family Papers.

26. David J. Hogan, *Class and Reform: School and Society in Chicago, 1880–1930* (Philadelphia, 1985), 3; John Allswang, *A House for All Peoples* (Lexington, Ky., 1971), 17–22; Allen Spear, *Black Chicago: The Making of a Negro Ghetto, 1890–1920* (Chicago, 1967), 129–66; William M. Tuttle, *Race Riot: Chicago in the Red Summer of 1919* (New York, 1970), 74–107; James R. Grossman, *Land of Hope: Chicago, Black Southerners, and the Great Migration* (Chicago, 1989). For the increasing proportion of African Americans in laboring and manufacturing jobs in Chicago between 1900 and 1920, compare the tables in Spear, *Black Chicago,* 30–33, 152–54.

27. W. E. B. Du Bois, *Souls of Black Folk* (Chicago, 1903).

28. Hutchins Hapgood to Neith Boyce Hapgood, Chicago, Dec. 6, 1905, Box 12, Folder 365, Hapgood Family Papers.

29. Neith Boyce Hapgood to Robert Morss Lovett, New York City, Jan. 18, 1906, Box 5, Folder 144, Hapgood Family Papers.

30. Marcaccio, *The Hapgoods,* 141–42, quote, 141; Hapgood quotes, Hapgood, *Victorian,* 207, 581. On the anti-business attitudes in the Hapgood family, see "Intimate Warriors: Portraits of a Modern Marriage, 1899–1944," in *Selected Works by Neith Boyce and Hutchins Hapgood,* ed. Ellen Kay Trimberger, (New York, 1991), 5, 6.

31. Stansell, *American Moderns,* 282–83. For Hapgood's own rendering of his attitude to the free love of the working-class anarchists, what they termed "varietism," see Hapgood, *Victorian,* 202.

32. Marcaccio, *The Hapgoods,* 160–64. There is even some question as to whether the play *Enemies* was written entirely by Neith Boyce. See Trimberger, ed., "Intimate Warriors: Portraits of a Modern Marriage, 1899–1944," 180.

33. Hapgood, *Victorian,* 432–47, quote, 434; Marcaccio, *The Hapgoods,* 194–204.

34. Philip S. Foner, *The AFL in the Progressive Era,* vol. 5 of *History of the Labor Movement in the United States* (New York, 1980), 7–31; Michael Kazin, *Barons of Labor: The San Francisco Building Trades and Union Power in the Progressive Era* (Urbana, Ill., 1987), 205–8; Clarence Darrow, *The Story of My Life* (New York, 1932), 172–84; A. J. [Anton Johannsen] to H. H. [Hutchins Hapgood], Oct. 24, 1911, St. Louis, Box 4, Folder 117, Hapgood Family Papers; A. J. to H. H., Dec. 25, [1912?], Corte Madera, Calif., Box 4, Folder 117, Hapgood Family Papers.

35. Hapgood, *Victorian,* 289.

36. *The American Labor Who's Who* (New York, 1925), ed. Solon De Leon, 116; Kazin, *Barons of Labor,* 299; Anton Johannsen to Hutchins Hapgood, Chicago, Sept. 28, 1935, Box 4, Folder 117, Hapgood Family Papers.

37. *Chicago Tribune,* June 3, 1946.

38. Margaret S. Marsh, *Anarchist Women, 1870–1920* (Philadelphia, 1981); Candice Falk, *Love, Anarchy, and Emma Goldman* (New York, 1984); Hapgood, *An Anarchist Woman.*

39. On the Haymarket events, see Paul Avrich, *The Haymarket Tragedy* (Princeton, N.J., 1984), and on the working-class anarchist movement surrounding it, Bruce C. Nelson, *Beyond the Martyrs: A Social History of Chicago's Anarchists, 1870–1900* (New Brunswick, N.J., 1988) and *The Haymarket Scrapbook,* ed. Dave Roediger and Franklin Rosement (Chi-

cago, 1986). Nelson is undoubtedly correct that the anarchist movement declined precipitously in the 1890s, but Anton's story suggests that an anarchist culture persisted and that anarchists remained an influence in the city's labor movement.

40. The literature on the IWW is voluminous. For an introduction, see Melvyn Dubofsky, *We Shall Be All: A History of the Industrial Workers of the World* (Chicago, 1969), and for a historical view of the organization from within, Fred Thompson and Patrick Murfin, *The IWW: Its First Seventy-five Years—1905–1975* (Chicago, 1976).

41. Carolyn Ashbaugh, *Lucy Parsons, American Revolutionary* (Chicago, 1976), 217–21.

42. For Hapgood's own assessment at the time of the ambiguous class status of the new bohemian intellectuals and their connections with the working class, see Hapgood, "The New Bohemia," mss, Box 28, Folder 64, Hapgood Family Papers.

The Spirit of Labor

Preface.

ON AND off for eight months I looked about in Chicago, for a man. I was more fortunate than Diogenes, for I found a great many of them. But it was a long time before I discovered the one I was looking for, and when I finally laid hands on him, I found him other, though far more interesting, than what I had, like the German metaphysician, evolved from my inner consciousness.

I had had several previous experiences with the "human document"; and had, in journalistic and literary experiments, attempted to present my material in such a way that the type and the individual should be at once portrayed. For this purpose the autobiography seemed the best form. In that way, a whole class with its ideals and conditions might be expressed, and at the same time a definite per-

sonality vividly and sympathetically presented; the man and his environment could
thus speak for themselves.

This method seemed to work very well as a
means of expressing the world of crime, the
world of the stage, or any *milieu* not too com-
plicated and not too important. In my "Autobiography of a Thief," the simple story, in
the first person, of a pickpocket's life, seemed
sufficient to give the reader a fairly complete
idea of the manners, customs and mental habits
of the professional criminal. The material of
professional crime is picturesque, in that it is
exceptional and comparatively unfamiliar.
It is also limited in scope. For all these reasons, the very definite manner of the autobiography is a vivid, central and adequate form
for the artistic expression of this material.

But when I became interested in the laborer, I found the problem a very different one.
At first, indeed, I thought the form of the
autobiography would be sufficient to suggest
the world of the workingman. I imagined

that I should be able to find a man who would occupy a sufficiently typical position and who would be sufficiently expressive to enable me to convey, merely by telling his story, as far as possible in his own words, an idea of the conditions, the ideals and the broad humanity underlying the labor situation.

It seemed to me that I should be more likely to find such a man in Chicago than anywhere else. In the democratic Middle West of the United States the common man is probably more expressive than anywhere else in the world. Labor, there, is more self-conscious and socially, if not politically, more powerful than elsewhere. The proletariat of America, and more especially of the progressive and intensely vital Middle West, is no real proletariat, in the dumb and crushed European sense, but in its hopefulness and early activity, in the breadth of its interests; in its mental joyousness and vitality, seems to have the quality of a Renaissance.

In my search for a man who stood at the

center of the labor world, I therefore went to Chicago, the hot-bed of the Middle West, the place where labor is most riotous, most expressive, where the workingman abounds in his own sense and has formed an atmosphere of democracy extending far beyond his own class. There I at once came in contact with so many vigorous personalities, that I was, for a long time, swamped by the richness of the human material.

I went to their saloons, I visited them in their homes. I was astonished by their practical knowledge of mankind, I was fascinated by their temperament and robustness and joy in life, I was touched by their altruism and feeling of human solidarity. I felt a kind of class sweetness under their rough manners, and also a class rebelliousness, a rebelliousness which could not have arisen if they had not been comparatively well-off, for the necessary energy would otherwise have been lacking. I saw how a new morality was forming on the basis of a new public opinion different from the past public opinion upon which much of present law is based. One rather disagreeable expression of this new morality was the suspiciousness with which for a long time they regarded me. They saw that I was, in their meaning of the word, a parasite: I did not work with my hands. I was therefore a member of the capitalist class, they felt, and would bear watching. One night, early in my Chicago experience, I was set upon in a saloon and slugged by friends of Sam Parks, about * whom I had in all sincerity and friendliness expressed an unfavorable opinion.

This little episode hurt my feelings at the time, and, incidentally, changed the shape of my nose. But, after a few months, when I had come more sympathetically to understand the feeling of the men and the difficulties of the leaders, I saw that I was at least ignorant, if not unkind, when I expressed an absolute, unmodified condemnation of a man like Parks. And, although even now, I do not approve of the manner in which the men in the saloon

expressed their sense of my unphilosophic narrowness, I can realize that their action was
based upon some obscure feelings not entirely
unjust and brutal.

After a time, my friends became less suspicious, and *pari passu* more interesting to me.
But as the richness of the material grew more
apparent, the difficulties in the way of my task
became greater.   The men with temperament
among them were intensely alive, so alive that
"art" seemed to them a mere trivial excres-
cence due to the superfluous well-being of the
capitalist class: and since, in their feeling, literature, history, art, law and religion, as they
are to-day, had for the most part originated
on the basis of an unjust social order, so these
things tended to keep the proletariat enslaved: they tended to cradle the mind and
senses and make man ignobly content with his
bonds.

So that my scheme for a book did not interest them in the slightest—not the real men
among them.   They were too active to take

the contemplative point of view: they thought, but their thought had the unformed and fragmentary character of action. And then, too, as I have said, they distrusted the moral and social tendencies of "culture." They were too genuinely interested in themselves and the "movement" to be able to see themselves as a whole. They lacked variety, and though they talked extremely well about the things that interested them, they became stiff, inexpressive and conventional when I induced them to talk about their lives and their personal opinions. The vanity of a pickpocket, the sense for self-advertisement of a soubrette, easily lends itself to the egotism of autobiography. But the active impersonality and seriousness of a laborer lacks the pleasure in subjective contemplation and in the *recherche* of the ego which is of prime necessity in autobiography.

The world of labor is so big—it has so markedly not only the character of a great human thing, but also connects itself so definitely with history and politics,—it has so many aspects, so many threads, that no one man can possibly stand at the center of it. That is another discovery, which, indeed, I was rather slow in making, and another difficulty in the way of my enterprise. I became deeply interested in one man after another, but in every case I found that either the man was not sufficiently typical of what I imagined the labor situation to be, or that he lacked an interest in my work, or was not sufficiently expressive for my purpose.

At last, however, after being in Chicago for several months, I did meet a man whose temperament and character, and experience, both as a type and as a person, seemed to combine much that I wanted. I remember well the occasion of our first meeting. It was at the bar of the Briggs House. He stood, drinking a glass of beer, and talking with energy and rough irony to a couple of newspaper men, about the teamsters' strike. I was immediately struck with his intellectual vigor, his free, anarchistic habit of mind, and the rough, sweet health of his personality. We had a long discussion about Tolstoi's ideas of "non-resistance," about labor, about life. I found him wonderfully expressive: he excited me most pleasurably, and I made an appointment with him for the next day.

He was too busy for me to see much of at that time. He worked in the shop every day, and his nights were usually given up to trades-union activities, or to "radical" meetings, of one kind or another. Soon after, I left town for the summer. While away, I wrote my friend, told him what I wanted, described as well as I could the work that I had planned, and asked him for his co-operation. He wrote back a good-natured letter of consent; and on the basis of that I returned to Chicago in the autumn and spent there three of the most interesting months of my life.

He lived in Austin, a suburb of Chicago. *
I went to a boarding-house near by, so as to be near him and his family. He was busier than

ever: he was a man of growing importance in the Federation, he still actively worked in the shop, his need of social pleasure was strong and constant, and his "radical" friends and activities were many. When I was with him in the bosom of his family—where I was received with the utmost hospitality,—or in company with his trades-union co-workers, or his "radical" friends, I found his talk always expressive, significant and most interesting.

But I discovered to my disappointment that I could not interest him in my work. He was not at all interested in his autobiography or in what I could make out of it; and it was only when he thought himself working with me that he was comparatively uninteresting. He hated to commit himself to anything, or to feel that, when once he was out of the shop, he need do anything except enjoy his body or his mind and temperament in the way he saw fit. And no prospect of any material compensation as a result of the work had any effect upon him. I found him so thoroughly a man of temperament, that by excess, it precluded the artistic results of temperament.

But, although we did not "hit it off" very well in what we called our work, we got along extremely well together in life. I became almost a member of his family, and came to occupy an acknowledged place in the circle of his radical friends. I grew to be so much interested in many of his companions, male and female, and so thoroughly absorbed and fascinated, that the need of making use of it all seemed very remote to me. My own family, however, beckoned to me from distant New York, and I finally tore myself up by my acquired roots, and departed.

The total result of my Chicago experience was to make me feel that in this work the autobiographical form must be given up. The man and the subject was at once too interesting, too significant and too inexpressive. I was compelled to choose the more circumstantial, comprehensive, if slower, less vivid and less exciting form of biography; to tell about the man, his life, his friends, often quoting his words, but sometimes resorting to my own. The looser and freer form of biography had the advantage of enabling me to bring into the book a good deal in Chicago and its people which is influenced and determined by the character of America's intellectual proletariat; although not immediately belonging to the world of labor.

The Spirit of Labor

The Spirit of Labor.

CHAPTER I.

Early Youth.

ANTON, when I met him in the saloon of the Briggs House, was thirty-three years old—old enough to have experienced a great deal, and young enough to retain the excited point of view about life. He is a woodworker, making the best wages at his trade, and has been in steady employment for some years. That fact, however, has not limited his energy in other ways. Of late he has become an important man in Chicago labor circles, and last autumn was the Chicago delegate to the International Labor Congress at Pittsburg. He is the President of his local union, and in trades-union matters very active in every way. He is an effective speaker, and enjoys an intellectual bout on the floor with any man. He now meets men of all walks of life and finds it interesting to measure his strength with theirs. He derives keen mental satisfaction from contact with local philosophers and "radicals"—and to their meetings he goes as a relief from the more strenuous occupation in trades-union matters.

The contrasts in the life of this workingman have been marked. He began adult life as a tramp, picked up a knowledge of his trade on the road, and came in contact there, also, with the injustice of organized society: this made him think, and laid the foundation of his later radicalism. Love for a girl came in—he had his great adventure—and this took him, eventually, away from the road. Children came, and with them comparative fixity of purpose, and the turning of the man's energy into the deepening of his social and intellectual life. Many leaders in the labor world, starting with sympathy for the "rank and file," lose that sympathy when they become leaders. But Anton has, at any rate as yet, retained the essential qualities of the workingman, although he is endowed with far more energy and brains and character than the average. This is partly due to the fact that he still works in the shop, among the men, and partly to his steadfast refusal to become a "politician" in the movement. In the Federation meetings he is a free-lance, bold, aggressive, terribly frank at times, with a youthful pleasure in shocking his companions, but of sterling honesty and a deep joy in the truth, because it is the truth, the exciting truth, no matter if it hurts, no matter though it be quite out of place. To express what he deems the truth, in season and out, is to him almost an emotional dissipation.

When I met Anton in the Briggs House, his face and manner indicated his character and his experience. He has the powerful body of the young mechanic—not lithe or graceful, but with the strength of a gnarled root. He is short and thick-set, with stubbed and horny hands; his head is a bullet, his brow broad, his eyes large, deep, and kind; his voice big. The lines in his face show a man who has lived roughly: his life on the road was almost as rough as they come. Yet his hard life has not made his face hard. He is rough in manner and in look; and his appearance shows experience. But in spite of the many sordid facts of his life, there is no suggestion of hardness about him. He looks big and open, as he is. The sweetness and the roughness of simple humanity are in his face. And he meets men in this spirit—often with brusque roughness, but always with the essential respect for others that sweetness gives.

This man was born abroad: as is the way with the typical American workingman. His home was in Germany, in Schleswig-Holstein. His father was a house-roofer, a jolly fellow who liked to drink too much and who caused his family much trouble. He was a fat, round person, a great story-teller, and great as a father, for he had twelve children, of whom eight died, through neglect, for the mother was forced to go out working, and the children were left to themselves. She washed for the farmers in the neighborhood, often not returning home till 2 o'clock in the morning, and going away to work again at 6.

When the father went to America, to find a home for his family, the oldest sister was glad to see him go. He was in the way, she thought. The wife cried, when he went, and Anton prayed, for Anton was the only earnest Christian among the children. "When mother was out working," he said "I always waited till she came back, no matter how late it was, so that I could say my prayers, before I went to sleep. At that time I accepted everything that the preacher said. I imagined that his every remark was the essence of the Holy Ghost."

He was a loving child, and by nature and education had the patience and reverence that is part of the laborer's character. "I was very happy," he said, "when I could bring my mother some pennies. I used to sing for them, on the farms." It was the custom for the children to stand at the back-door to beg for the dinner that they were to take to school. In the fall of the year, the farmers killed hogs, and the children begged part of the meat, and took it home. On New Year's eve the children would go around the village, singing, for coins and baked things. Anton was a favorite on that night, for he was a good singer, and had, as he said, "an unlimited amount of gall."

He went to the parish school where he "learned religion," as he put it, and a little mathematics; also to swim, as that was a part of the program of the government, to train the boys for soldiers. He also learned to take a beating with equanimity.

For the grown people in that village had

many superstitions. One was a strong belief in the need of beating little children. Anton's father, mother, sister and school-teacher all beat him with great frequency. "My father was good-natured," he said, "but bad whiskey drove him to this brutality. In spite of my religious tendencies, the slightest error or mistake on my part would mean a sound thrashing. The effect of the rod was to make me want revenge, but not at that time so much as later, for I thought I was born to work and slave and be beaten—that was the fundamental doctrine of the Bible, as it was conveyed to me."

Another superstition was the universal belief in witches. The parents "grafted," said Anton, "on this superstition, using it as a club to keep us indoors at night. I imagined I saw witches everywhere, and used to turn it to account by frightening other children. I remember getting under the house and making horrible noises. I didn't see why I should not make use of the witches, if my parents did. But they objected to my graft, and my sister beat me with a soup-bone."

One of the most vivid memories from his childhood was of the insufficient food. Many is the time he went hungry to bed, because there was nothing to eat in the house. At the best, the bill of fare was dry bread and potatoes, salt lard and tallow in place of butter. Once a year, "on Christmas, when the birth of Christ was celebrated," he interjected, satirically, "we had butter and white bread." Meat was to be had only when the farmers were killing. The mother used to go out early in the morning for craw-fish, and would also gather driftwood for the fires.

After the father had been away two years, the family followed him to Clinton, Iowa, where he had settled. They were only four then; the other children had died. The only doctors in the village were the druggists and the preachers, but probably the children would have died anyway, from poor food and neglect. "I was glad," said Anton, "to go to America, for I thought I would not need to beg there, and that I could get enough to eat."

"I enjoyed the trip across the ocean, for I got extra food from the steward for doing dirty work. The grub was awful filthy, but there was enough of it. One day I went without my extra rations, because I fell downstairs with a dozen bottles, and the cook thought he ought to discipline me. A boy finds a moral teacher wherever he goes. This world is said to be a bad one, but as for me I find virtue everywhere, more's the pity.

"After nineteen days we reached New York, very lousy from our steerage experience, and landed in Castle Garden. The first thing I noticed was a negro. I had never seen one before, and I thought he was the devil. But he told me his color was due to the climate, and that I would soon be as black as he was. As my youngest brother had been very ill on the voyage, the doctor in New York sent him and mother to a hospital for ten days, and the other children to an orphan asylum. In this place they put us through a course of gymnastics: we had all the exercises except stomach exercises. The food, indeed, was little and bad. Here, too, I got my regular beatings. I began to think that I was owned by the whole world and that everybody was good but me."

When they reached Clinton, Iowa, they found the father there doing much better than he had done in Germany. He was driving a beer wagon for a German brewer, and was a great favorite with his employer, who weighed four hundred pounds and enjoyed the father's jokes. "Father was naturally a great jollier," said Anton, "and that kind of a man gets along in America." The brewer drank a keg of beer every day and soon "died of avoirdupois." Anton's father then became bartender and afterwards saloon-keeper, and prospered, because he told good stories and knew when to treat and when to extort payment.

In this American town Anton went to school more or less for two winters; and acquired there the reputation of a bad boy. "The spirit of protest," he said, "which is now developed to a considerable extent, began to stir in me. Whenever the teacher asked me why I was tardy, I told her the truth, and the other boys lied. So I was beaten and the other boys were not; and this seemed to me unjust. One day the school-teacher beat my little brother, and I attacked the teacher, and the stove fell over on us. Father took my side, and rescued me from this affair. A few months before Easter, when I was preparing for confirmation, the teacher and the minister asked me, with a view to finding out the effect of the religious teaching, what I would do with my wife, if she were negligent in the household affairs. I replied promptly that I would run away. On another occasion I insisted there were witches in the town. The teacher said there were not. But as I had seen them with my own eyes, and as my parents had told me these things existed, I thought the teacher was a liar, and told him so."

Finally the school became too warm for him, and he left and went to work in a brick yard at twenty-five cents a day. This was his first experience as a workingman. He was then twelve years old, and worked ten hours a day, at turning and hacking brick, hard work, but he became the best turner in the yard. He was a favorite with the boss, for when work was slack he peeled potatoes for the employer's wife. "I did this for a couple of years, but my industry had no effect on my boss. He took it as a matter of course. Wasn't I getting twenty-five cents a day?"

Although Anton's father was working steadily at this time, his mother still went out to wash, and his sister worked as hired girl. He had no holidays but Sunday, and so his life, at twelve years of age, was almost all work. "I don't think," he said, "that any one of my family enjoyed life; I am sure I did not, as a child. Perhaps my father did, for he drank heavily, and always had a good story to tell." The father was the only one of them who lived the life of the temperament. At least, he belonged to the poor man's club, and often talked eloquently to the men in the saloon.

When he was fourteen, Anton went to work in a sash and door factory, where every man and boy had his place like a machine. He worked there on and off for eight years, making window frames and nothing else. It was monotonous work, and he learned little from it. "If I had never run away from home," he said, "I would never have become a mechanic. The work there was too monotonous, and the men took no interest in the boys and did not teach them anything. I got fifty cents a day for ten hours' work, and after six years was getting only a dollar a day. But at that time I did not think much about the wages. I wouldn't have minded if it had not been for the monotony of it. I became awfully bored, which always happens to me when anything lasts too long."

When Anton was sixteen, there was a strike, under the auspices of the Knights of Labor.

It did not involve his shop, but he at once felt in sympathy with the purposes of the strikers. It was a mob strike; the strikers were not organized and they lost. This was the first strike that came to Anton's attention. "But I felt at once," he said, "that the other fellows were in reality our enemies, and were trying to get all they could out of us and give us as little in return as we would accept.

"Under the circumstances, I felt justified in killing as much time as I could without being discharged. The monotony of the employment and the greed of the employer took all interest away from the work. So I organized a number of boys into a kind of entertainment society. We built a watch-house in the shop, and while one boy acted as the look-out, the others played cards, during the work hours. We kept this up for months, but I was finally caught and laid off a day. My father threatened to thrash me if I didn't get my job back. At that time my father was running the saloon and I sometimes used to tend bar for him in the evening. I was to do so on that night, as the old gent was uptown. Instead, I left home without saying good-bye to anybody, got in a box-car half loaded with shelled corn, and in a few hours I was in Chicago. I was then eighteen years old."

CHAPTER II.

On the Road.

Now began a period of wandering, often interrupted by brief returns to his family in Clinton. He became one of the large class of nomadic workingmen, so to speak, who are as much hobo as laborer; indeed, many of * them more so, as they work only in order to earn enough money for a "front," a suit of clothes, and then restlessly pass on.

On this first trip he was in Chicago only a short time. He boldly pretended to be a mechanic, but was discharged for incompetency a few days after finding his first job. He then washed dishes in a restaurant for a night or two, but dropped this for a magnificent position on a railroad at $1.40 a day—high wages for him, who lived at the time on 25 cents a day. The old feeling of monotony interrupted this lucrative work, and, after three days, he quit—and did not get his money.

Beating his way to Burlington, he worked

eight days as a woodworker, but was discharged: he was not yet a mechanic. But each time this happened, he was a little wiser: knew a little more of his trade. Conditions were slightly different in each shop, there was greater variety than in the monotonous work at Clinton, and, as time went on, he learned.

At Burlington he lost his watch, as well as his job, and was "broke." Then he begged, for the first time, and took another step towards membership in Hoboland. Previously to begging he had lived for two days on watermelons that had burst and been thrown away. At this time, he was very much discouraged. He was willing to work, and saw the utter lack of sympathy in the people he met. He felt particularly the jealousy of the mechanics, who refused to teach him anything. He perceived that he was thrown entirely on his own resources, and as he is naturally generous and kind himself, he felt this coldness deeply.

He managed to beat his way in a box-car to Cedar Rapids, and thence home, to Clinton. His trip had not been a spectacular success, but, when he reached home, he was, he said, "as proud as a peacock." He felt he was a hero and had been almost around the world.

But the good people of Clinton "gave him the laugh" for coming back so soon. "I stood in the saloon," he said, "and tried to brag to the other boys, but they could not see it that way."

He had been away two months, and was glad to get back; but the ridicule of the boys and the need of work sent him away again in four or five days. Without saying anything to his family, he boarded another box-car and was off for Council Bluffs.

In the box-car he met a tramp with a philosophic turn of mind. He was a mechanic and had had some good jobs. After Anton heard this man talk, he vaguely felt that his life in Clinton had been a narrow one, and that he had had no real opportunities there. Dimly it seemed to him, too, that his misfortunes, somehow, were more profound and radical even than that. "I didn't know anything about Socialism," he said. "But I liked the talk of that tramp. He made me feel that I had been deprived of opportunities, that I had been denied the right to live. The spirit of protest grew stronger within me, though I was not clear yet about anything. Even as early as this I began to think that Christianity was a humbug and that I had been hoodwinked.

This tramp talked to me about unions, and I felt the leaders must be heroes, all spotless."

At that time Anton had never been to a union meeting, had never read a book, not even a newspaper, and had never had a real companion. The first "intellectual" man he met was this box-car friend of his—this hobo-mechanic who had a sprinkling of Socialistic ideas. The civilizing influence that "radical" ideas have upon the entirely uneducated laborer is marked: a fact that will be abundantly illustrated in the course of this narrative.

"This box-car," he said, "seemed to me Paradise. My friend the Socialist talked like an angel, and we sang the song 'Playmates Are We.' He was a Carl Marx man, and was friendly to unionism, for at that time there was not so much antagonism between Socialism and trades-unionism as there is at present." Anton traveled with the hobo for several weeks: they beat, begged and worked their way. When waiting for a train, they built a fire, slept or talked, or fried steaks and prepared coffee. The Socialist talked all the time, and, although Anton has forgotten everything definite that was said, yet he still regards this man as his first friend.

"I remember," he said, "that he was neat in his dress, and that he carried soap and towels with him in the box-car—the only clean tramp of my acquaintance. He also used to beg often for a wash instead of a cup of coffee."

Anton tried to find a job at Council Bluffs. He dropped into the Universal Exchange, a saloon, and after being cheated by the saloon-keeper, got a tip which led to a $3.50-a-day position. He hired out as a first-class mechanic, "on my gall," as he put it. When the foreman saw what he was like, he paid him only $2 a day, but that seemed very big to Anton. He held this job only a short time, as usual. One day he was making hand-rails for fancy stairs, and, being "not even a second-class mechanic," got excited when the boss was looking on, and spoiled two feet of a rail. "The boss grabbed me by the neck and took me to the office. He was so mad," said Anton, "I thought he would kill me; but he had the kindness to pay me $5 for three days' work. So he did not cheat me much."

The proprietor of a restaurant where Anton ate had taken a fancy to him, and when he lost his job in the factory, he got another as a waiter. Anton was a jolly singer and dancer, and pleased the wife and daughter of the proprietor, who offered him $8 a week and board to stay with him. "It was easy work," said Anton. "But it was monotonous, and the two women, who were ugly, made love to me. After a while, when they thought they had claims on me, I found that monotonous, too. So I jumped on a box-car and went to Omaha."

He took a trip South at this time, passing rapidly from town to town, from one job to another, from periods of begging and "bumming" to brief periods of work. If his natural restlessness was thus being intensified, there was the compensation that he was rapidly learning his trade. He was a quick, intelligent boy, and he thinks he learned more from these widely varying jobs than he could have done through any careful system of apprenticeship. During his wandering period of seven years the longest stay he ever made was four months, at Fort Worth.

Sometimes he was discharged because of incompetence, more often because of his "independence." Frequently he left because the work became monotonous, and he desired to pass on. When he had a few dollars in his pocket and a fairly good suit of clothes, it was hard to keep him at his job.

"You are better treated at the beginning," he said. "While a stranger you get more recognition. They treat you with courtesy, at first. But familiarity breeds contempt. You wear out your welcome. When that stage came, I generally moved. When I heard the train whistle, my heart throbbed, and I wanted to go. In the spring of the year I couldn't sleep at night for thinking of the road, and when the train pulled out, I generally got the fever and went with it."

He came to know the "road" well, learned to beg with skill, and met many hoboes and "yeggs." What he learned from them helped him to the art of handling men which he is now turning to account in his trades-union activity. "What one learns from the yellow and the black will help you a lot with the white," he quoted.

Workingmen who are engaged in any unstable work, such as printers, bricklayers, and those working at railroad construction, often become hoboes. They are not the real tramps, whose technical name is "yegg." The latter have concluded that it does not pay to work. To do so is dishonorable. They therefore despise the hoboes, and will have nothing to do with them socially. They are the aristocrats of the floating population— more truly aristocrats than the aristocrats at the top, for they can lose nothing: nothing worries them, and they are more exclusive than the Four Hundred.

Anton was often snubbed by these "swells" of the road. From motives of curiosity he attempted to become intimate with them, but they would have little to do with him. Once, when nearly starving, he met some yeggs sitting about a fire and eating. They refused to share their food with him. "Why don't you go to work?" they asked, contemptuously. Then they threw the victuals in the fire, deliberately.

"Those yeggs interested me," said Anton. "But I never had a desire to be one of them. I couldn't see their philosophy. They were too cruel, too hard-hearted. They care for nobody but yeggs. Solidarity among them is absolute. They admire good thieves and prostitutes, but even these are not admitted to the inner circle. Their feeling of caste is awful. It is much worse than that of the capitalist class. Like the capitalist class, they are careful of their manners, too. They will steal if they get a chance, but they won't beg at the back door. They won't take the hand-out, nor apply for work; nor will they wash dishes or saw wood for a breakfast or an old coat. There is only one way that a yegg can honorably beg. He may size a man up and tackle him in the street for money. He uses the money for a place to "flop," in a lodging-house. If any is left over, he will buy alcoholic stimulants, but not food. That is disgraceful, to spend money for food, in a city. If he really needs a meal, he will try for a "chase-in"; he will beg a meal ticket, which is much more readily given away than a piece of money.

"The yegg will have nothing to do with women. He prefers boys, and in this way, too, he is like some aristocrats. Sitting around their fires, or smoking their snipes (tobacco picked up from the streets and re-rolled) in a lodging-house room, they talk of the kids they have met along the road: praise this one's begging powers, that one's crookedness, another's strength as a hold-up man—or

[43]

they tell of having met Phil Yegg in such a place, Omaha Shin in another; and discuss where the bulls (police) are most hostile. They do not rush the can in the saloon, as the hoboes do, but they sit together in the back room of the lodging-house over a glass of beer, and smoke their snipes. As long as there is money in the crowd, there is no question of who pays. As their taste for social pleasures is identical in each one, there is no need of one man having more money or spending more than another. In this respect, they are Socialists or Communists.

"The yeggs are well taken care of by the politicians. They go to places where they are absolutely safe, such as some of the resorts presided over by Hinky Dink and Bathhouse John, in Chicago; Bucket of Love, in St. Louis; The Three Brothers, in New Orleans, or Sailors' Home, in New York. Saloonkeepers and politicians have no regard for hoboes, but they know that yeggs are powerful because of their solidarity. A yegg never forgets an affront, and his boycott is everlasting and complete: it spreads like wildfire throughout the world of the road."

One day I went with Anton to hear him

make a speech on tramps before the Social Science League, a Chicago organization of "radicals." After describing the habits of the yeggs, he made the following interesting application:

"Whether we like or dislike the tramp, the fact is he is here and is just as I have described him. His aim in life is to escape labor, to be a parasite. He makes a profession of that. It is as dishonorable for him to go against the rules of his profession as it is for a preacher to work in a factory, a lawyer on a farm, or a doctor behind a saloon bar. The yegg is very similar to these other professional men. While the one is supposed to serve justice, the second to uplift morals, and the third to preserve the health, the percentage of those who confine themselves to these principles is so small that it is almost invisible. The spirit of commercialism has been a most potent factor in prostituting these professions. The spirit of commerce appears to me very largely directed to reaping the benefits produced by the labor of others. He who is the most cunning among the lawyers is considered to be the greatest. He among the preachers who can spellbind the best, attains to the most salary;

[45]

the doctor who can give the best reasons for proving that artifice is better than nature, is the most successful. The yegg has these same characteristics. He is a cunning and shrewd thief; and he plays on the emotions of others, when he tells the wayfarer a hard-luck story; the fundamental motive is always to escape labor. The yegg very seldom criticizes the methods of his fellow yegg. And this same respect for the graft of the profession we see in the ranks of lawyers, doctors and preachers."

This speech was made long after Anton had ceased to be a tramp. But he began, at this early stage in his career, to form some of the ideas which he was so fond of expressing at a later time. He was not long on the road before his religious ideas began to grow a little vague; not that he had become definitely sceptical as yet, but that this side of him received no longer any nourishment. One seldom meets a religious man on the road, or one who has respect for the law. They feel the necessity of opposing the law, because the law opposes them.

While in the South, on this trip, our hobo did meet one religious man, but his religion took an industrial turn. He was called Preacher Bill, and he was a confirmed hobo. He would sit for hours and argue about politics and industrialism. He was a great agitator, and was called "Preacher" because of the enthusiasm and emotion he felt for the cause of the workman and of the outcast.

These budding ideas, or rather feelings, for they lacked the definiteness of ideas, made it easier for him to beg and to lead a rather hard life than it would have been otherwise. He became a good "bummer," clever at getting a dinner or a suit of clothes. I found out, from my own intimacy with him and his associates, that he certainly "has a way with women"; it is not a very gentle way, but it is effective, and this served him on the road. One day he hid his overcoat, his hat and his coat, and then went to a house and begged for some clothes, which he intended to sell. The good woman, after a few minutes' talk, gave him a breakfast, a suit of clothes, underwear, collar, ties, shirt, shoes, and some money for a hat.

"Women like to be sympathetic," said Anton. "That is the way they get their graft."

After this good luck, Anton got a shave, bought a hat, dressed himself well, and went to see his chum, who did not recognize him. With this new suit of clothes "as a stall" he went to New Orleans, where, some circus men having got into trouble, he on his arrival, was rounded up as a stranger, and, in spite of his good clothes, put in jail, and given only half a bologna sausage to eat. But it was as good sleeping there as in a box-car. The jail, indeed, is one of the hotels of the hobo. The next morning he was discharged by the magistrate, and with him a yegg, who had been "rounded up" at the same time, and whom he had met in jail. This yegg did Anton the honor of liking him, and conducted him to Houston, Texas, to a headquarters of hoboes and yeggs. Here numberless hoboes were controlled by a few yeggs, who spent the hoboes' money and ate their food, but gave them nothing in return.

Then he and his friend the yegg went to San Antonio, where they met a bricklayer, a careless hobo, who had a job at the time, at his trade, and was making good money. He had just drawn his wages—$35; it was Saturday night, and as he liked the two strangers, he took a box-car with them, and they all went to Mexico. He and Anton treated the yegg as a king. The bricklayer gave him all his mescal, a kind of whiskey, which the yegg liked, but which Anton found better adapted for "killing lice than for drinking." It was on this Mexican box-car that Anton discovered the true reason for the yegg's friendship for him. It was a reason which made Anton use a knife, in order to defend himself, and which determined him and the bricklayer to separate from their distinguished companion.

They made their way to Laredo, and there, as in other Mexican towns, they found that a little bad whiskey would bring them whatever they wanted. For a drink, they could get, in exchange, food and a bed so large that it contained the Mexican's wife and daughters, as well as themselves. It was not necessary to beg in Mexico. There the people are so poor that they give whatever they have.

A man who comes from the States is well treated in Mexico. It is known that he is a better workman than the natives. So when Anton arrived in Monterey, without a "front," thinking he would go to work, under favorable circumstances, he and the bricklayer stationed themselves before a restaurant. The first man tackled was pleased with the young

woodworker, gave him a meal, and a job at
$5 a day. The bricklayer obtained employ-
ment at $12 a day. This seemed like clover
to them both, and the bricklayer staid on. So
would Anton have done also, had it not been
for an accident. One day he was careless with
a machine and nearly killed a Mexican. He
realized the danger, jumped a box-car and
made for the States. He dropped off at the
first Texas town—Beaver—ran for the first
house he saw and was hospitably received by
a young widow, who in return for some gar-
dening, gave him money, clothes, and the best
of food. He staid with her four days, and his
motive for going was an indication of his popularity with the sex. "I didn't want to stay
there for good," he said.

"I never had much trouble with the
women," he remarked, not complacently, for
he is not given to that, but in his matter-of-fact
way. "I remember one time I was working in
Hammond for three weeks, because I wanted
a front to go to New Orleans. After I got
together a few dollars, I started, with a contractor, for the big city. We struck the town
on the night of a masquerade ball; and we
went there on a lark. I was a good dancer,

and met a young girl who introduced me to her friends. The contractor presented me as the superintendent of the plant at Hammond. We met the girl's five sisters, brother-in-law and mother. I suggested a supper, but a common place was not good enough for me, so I told them to take us to the swellest restaurant in town. The contractor feared he would have to pay the bill and sneaked away. We went to a fine French restaurant, and I had the meal of my life, with all kinds of expensive wines. I didn't pay a cent. They insisted that I was the guest. I made a mash on the little girl, and escorted her home; went to dine with them the next day, and the old lady offered me a job in her clothing store at $50 a month. I nursed it along for a while, for I was stuck on the little girl. But I couldn't keep up the game, as I had no trunk, no resources, and had to lie every minute. So I skipped."

On virtuously leaving the young widow at Beaver, he went to Corpus Christi, where he arrived the day before Thanksgiving. In accordance with his general custom, he stood before a restaurant, for a "chase-in," and there met a man who was justice of the peace and the leader of a band of minstrels. "When I told him I was a theatrical man," said Anton, "he was interested, and gave me a dollar. He took me to the stage manager, whom I told I had been stranded at Meridian. I passed myself off as a character singer and a black-face comedian. 'Come up and rehearse,' he said, and gave me shirts, collars and ties. At the five o'clock rehearsal I was there, but as I knew nothing whatever about music, I told them I was very sensitive to my accompaniment, and that I must sing without music. I passed the examination, and was engaged for that night's performance. When the time came for me to do my act, I went on and sang without music. I had been introduced as a stranded actor, and I took the house. I sang 'On the Bridge at Midnight,' and I had $14 thrown at me from the audience. After the show, the minstrels crowded around me and wanted me to stay two weeks, and would pay my restaurant bills, washing, etc. The story went around the town like wild-fire. They more or less got on to me, and called me 'the hobo-king.' That night we went around the town serenading, followed by a big crowd. I sang under a banker's window. He invited us in, gave us drinks, cigars, and handed me a ten-dollar bill. I sang at the theater every night. A lady in town took up a collection for me, and this brought me in $15. A printer made 500 copies of my songs, and I sold them for about $20. A little Spanish girl made love to me and gave me a shell fan. I was a hero, the town was off the main line, and that is one reason why they liked my line of theatricals. That's the first time I ever was an actor. I wish I had stopped then. But I tried it once more, a few weeks after that, in San Antonio. I was with a bum crowd of show people. One of them ran away with the money and the audience threw potatoes at the rest of us. We had to run away without our trunks, to avoid being lynched."

CHAPTER III.

Injustice and Love.

IT WAS not long after this theatrical experience that Anton was arrested for the second time. It was this second arrest that filled him with the bitter feeling of social injustice. "Life on the road," he said, "with all its chance meetings with many men and ways of living makes one tolerant of everything except tyranny." And in the case of this second arrest, he felt he had come in contact with tyranny in its ordinary and commonplace, and, therefore, particularly damnable, form.

It was at Fort Worth, Texas. He had worked in the town before, and was well acquainted there, but as he was now on the tramp, and accompanied by two other hoboes, he did not want to be seen by his acquaintances. He and his two companions were eating lunch in a lodging-house near the stock yards, when a drunken man invited himself to partake of the food. He fell into a stupid sleep, and while in that condition was robbed of seven or eight dollars by the two hoboes. A boy, who had been sent for some whiskey, returned at the moment of the robbery, and reported the affair to the police. Anton and the two hoboes were arrested on a charge of larceny. The boy had said that the two hoboes had taken the money, and that Anton had had no share in it. But the police arrested him anyway as an important witness, and they also suspected that he was in with the others. A religious man for whom Anton had worked, and who regarded him as immoral but honest, secured a lawyer for $25, money for which Anton wrote a letter home.

"I was approached by the police," said Anton, "and told that if I would 'tell the truth' I would be released. In that town they get so much for every conviction; and if the police and prosecuting attorney could get my evidence against the other two, they were willing to let me off. But I didn't see it that way. I considered it blackmail on their part to threaten me with prison for a crime I had not committed, unless I would peach on the others. Besides, I did not think these two hoboes had done anything they ought to be put in prison for. They relieved the drunken man of some money that was doing him harm. It did not seem to me as bad a crime as the authorities were guilty of in their action against me."

The judge declared that there was not enough evidence against Anton to indict him, yet it would be well to hold him as a witness against the others. This, too, seemed to our hero an arbitrary and unjust proceeding. In the meantime, he was in jail with his companions. Money had come to him from his family, and with this money he was to pay the lawyer. The latter visited them in jail and said the State's attorney had agreed to make it a county fine; that if they pleaded guilty they would only be fined; if not, they would be kept in jail until October, and then tried. Anton and his companions therefore pleaded guilty, and Anton paid all costs.

"It was very repulsive to me to do this," he said. "I was weak in letting them blackmail me in this way, but I didn't want to stay in jail so long and then have a good chance for from two to five years in the penitentiary."

For three days before the money came, Anton was forced to work on the county road, chained and guarded with a carbine. When he was released, they gave him nothing for his three days' work. He went to Fort Worth and tried to get the fine remitted. After he had paid the lawyer and the costs he was without money, and could borrow nothing from the judge, the lawyer or from the women who had performed religious ceremonies in jail. But a negro loaned him $3—which he afterwards paid back—and with this he went to Weatherford, Texas, where he found a job and worked hard to save some money, with revenge in his mind. He worked ten weeks and saved $100. During that period he did not spend a cent for beer or smoking tobacco; for nothing except the bare necessities.

At the end of that time he bought a suit of clothes ("you can do nothing with Christian people without a front," he said) and returned to Fort Worth. He went to the newspaper office, and offered the editor forty dollars to print his story of the arrest, and how the authorities had urged him to plead guilty. But the editor refused, of course. "This experience," he said, "pushed me on far towards thinking. I began to believe that justice is a farce, and worse than a farce."

Anton is very emotional about this episode,

not merely because it formed a step in the evolution of his social opinions, but because it marked a very important step in the development of his love affair. "It pushed him on," as much towards "the great adventure," as towards "thinking."

Little Maggie had been in love with him, as she admitted to me, since she was fourteen years old. She was a house-maid in his mother's family, a German girl, intelligent and capable, full of life. She has played a much more important part in her husband's life than falls to the lot of most women, great as that part usually is.

"I loved him at once," she said to me one night, as she and I were sitting over her excellent tea, her three children playing happily on the kitchen floor, and her husband away on important Union business. "I used to pray God to protect him while in those dreadful box-cars. He never staid in Clinton long, and while he was away other boys paid attention to me, and I kept company with some of them. But as soon as Anton turned up from one of his tramps, I dropped them all and flocked back to him at once. I certainly did like my tramp. My mother tried to get me to make up with some of the respectable boys who wanted to marry me. One of them was a Minister of the Gospel, but I couldn't see him for long."

It seems that the vagabond did not violently return this devoted girl's affection for a long time. He was busy "seeing the world." But when he was in jail at Fort Worth he fell to thinking about his real friends, and little Maggie came up in his mind and senses. He was twenty-one at the time, and had often been back home for a flying trip. During these brief visits, he had seen much of Maggie and had regarded her as his "steady." But now, in jail, he fell in love with her, for the first time. He put the case to me, as follows:

"When I was in jail I was very lonesome and homesick. I grieved considerably, and Maggie came up always in my thoughts. She had been told by her family that I was a vagabond. She thought she ought to suppress her feelings for me and keep company with somebody who was more polite and steady. She had thrown over a good many, for my sake, but she did try to like a young preacher who never smoked or drank anything stronger than lemonade. I thought of this preacher, now, in jail, and I did not like the idea of him. So I wrote Margaret an appealing letter. That letter was a pathetic confession. I never wrote that way to any one else, and never but once to her. Jail and thinking had made me tender. I wrote it with absolute feeling. I felt it was a crime to be in jail, guilty or not, for I was brought up that way. So I wrote to her, really for sympathy. I asked her to overcome the prejudice against me. I promised to lead a better life and asked her to be my wife.

"When she got the letter she was sick in bed with pneumonia. The preacher went to see her every day and took her flowers. He never swore, but he chewed gum. She was so ill that she thought he was very nice and kind. He had a good education, but no wisdom, executive ability, or originality. He was a man, who, while very much in love with Margaret, did not possess the strength or wisdom to temper his feeling with moderation. That is necessary if you want the woman to return your love."

"He was anxious to run after me," explained Margaret, interrupting her husband's narrative, "and so he made himself less attractive."

Maggie is a psychologist, too.

"She answered my letter," continued Anton. "She did not know I was in jail, but thought I was sick in a hospital. She wrote that my letter had affected her deeply—so much so that her mother and the preacher noticed it. I think they read the letter, but she won't admit that. Sick as she was, she wrote me, and stated that she was keeping company with the minister. While she couldn't love him, she might learn to like him, and she would always be a dear sister to me. Her letter was pretty strong, and it made me lose hope. I suppose I did not know much about the women, then. If I had, I would have known that I could have butted in."

And he did "butt in" a few months later, as we shall see. He was to go home for a double triumph—the great one, that over the minister, and a minor one over two fellow workmen who had treated him badly when he was working at Fort Worth, Texas, at a time previous to his jail experience there.

There were two young men in Clinton who had been schoolmates of Anton's and had worked fourteen years in the shop where Anton had his first job in the wood-working line. They had not been advanced in position or wages, and were discontented, so they wrote to Anton in Texas, and asked him to get them a job. He wrote them to come, but when they arrived, he found it was not so easy to secure a job; for they were far from being good mechanics. Anton had learned more about the trade in two or three years of knocking around than they had learned in fourteen years in Clinton. He was then being paid $18 a week for nine hours' work a day, while they had not even dreamed of a nine hour day and their best wage had been $12 a week. They knew that Anton had shown no marked ability in Clinton and they thought they would do at least as well as he when they went to a more favorable locality.

As he could find them nothing at Fort Worth, he advised them to go to Dallas, where the opportunities in the trade were much greater. They did not have the nerve to go alone: they were borrowing money from Anton at the time, and wanted to "stick." So they asked him to go with them. "They were home people," said Anton, "and so I picked a quarrel with the foreman at my shop, and got fired."

No sooner had Anton been discharged, than

one of his friends tried for the vacant place! "But he didn't know how to ask for anything," said Anton, "he was too shy. I balled him out, but overlooked it and went with them to Dallas."

At that city they tried for a job every day, sleeping in the woods at night. Each man covered a certain section of the city, and they met to report at a certain hour. On the second day Anton found positions for two men, one at $2.50 and one at $2 a day. Both he and the man who wanted his job at Dallas worked at the moulding machine, and these jobs therefore fell to their lot. His friend claimed the job at $2.50 a day and Anton agreed to it. It was with the understanding that he should pay 25 cents a day more towards supporting the third man than Anton paid.

The two went to work in the cotton gin mill. As Anton had had some experience in that variety of work, he made an impression on the foreman and soon succeeded in getting a job for the third man at $1.75 a day. But this other noble companion of Anton's was dissatisfied because he got less than Anton and wanted to quit. So Anton fixed it with the foreman so that his friend might have his own place.

This was done, and Anton looked for another job for himself, and soon found one at $18 a week. Then both of his friends became jealous at once.

In the meantime, they were writing letters to friends in Clinton, boasting that they got $18 a week. Anton finally got tired of his provincial companions and went alone to Houston, and then to Galveston, worked a week, and then back to Houston, where for a time he was out of a job. Here he had another experience with man's proverbial gratitude. He came across a person whom he had met on the street months before in Palestine, out of a job and "bumming" it. He was ragged, "broke" and hungry. Anton got him a breakfast, a drink, and a job in the same factory where he was working at the time. This fellow was a good mechanic and he soon showed the foreman that only one man was necessary, so Anton was discharged.

When Anton met this man later at Houston he (Anton) had no position and little money, while the other held a good position. "I thought I would test the man," said Anton. "So I asked him to give me a supper and a bed. He apologetically said I could have supper but couldn't stay over night. I went to eat with him, but with the spirit of revolt I insisted on paying for the supper. When he saw that, he got friendly, and took me to a saloon. I bought him whiskey and beer, and then before a big crowd of hoboes and yeggs I gave him a d— roasting, gave it to him good and plenty, and he actually cried."

Anton wandered around several months and after having his jail experience in Fort Worth he returned to Dallas, where his so-called friends were. One of them had lost his job and they both wanted to go home. They did not like the world, found it cold and forbidding, and thought Clinton was big enough for them. "And it was," said Anton.

He, too, longed to go home. He thought he had lost Maggie, but he wanted to make sure, and besides he had not seen his family for a long time. So the three "bummed" their way together. Anton wrote to his brother, through whom he had learned of scandalous letters his "friends" had written home about him, and told him where to meet them. He wanted someone to see these fellows in their ragged shape, hoboing it, so that it might be known at home how they had lied in their boasting letters. They met, and the brother "balled them out for fair," and they were disgraced in the town.

When Anton reached his father's house, he found a conspiracy on foot to get him married. His father was succeeding in the saloon business, and as his mother's early experience with hardship had made her a superb economist, the family had saved some money and consequently their ideas of respectability had developed. The thought of their son Anton leading a careless and godless life on the road was disagreeable to these good people. His mother had had her eye on little Maggie for a long time as a good wife for her son. The girl was very industrious and this represented all the virtues in the eyes of the old lady.

Anton showed plainly that he had been "on the bum." His clothes were "not nice," as he put it. The first thing his mother did was to give him a new suit. It was the 2nd of July, and they intended he should make a good showing at the Sunday School picnic on the historic Fourth. So his father gave him $4, his mother $2, one brother $2, and his other brother $2. His sister also contributed $2. With $12 and a new suit he felt he could make a magnificent showing on the 4th. When the day came, the entire family bundled into the old carriage and rumbled off to the picnic.

Maggie was at the picnic, with her fiancé, the minister. Anton thought her more beautiful and desirable than ever, but he felt she was not for him. He was determined, however, to show that he was alive anyway, and that he came very near being "it," as he explained it. So he sang a German song, to the great delight of the crowd, and then proved himself the best talker in the place. He had had a wider experience in life than any of the others, and his anecdotes were full of raciness, his jokes were lively and up-to-date. Besides he was looked upon as a little immoral by the German Lutherans, and this, if nothing else, fastened the attention of everybody upon him.

He addressed no word to Maggie, but he soon perceived that she was listening. This gave him confidence, and the show of indifference. He began to see that the feeling she had had for him might be on the point of coming back. Two or three little German girls, who admired this man who was so well-dressed, so generous in his way of treating and so confident and varied in his talk, asked him where he was going that night. He replied in a loud tone, that he was going to the German ball.

Maggie heard him, and decided to be there, too. In the meantime Anton's mother had given him an additional $2, so Anton turned up at the ball, where the admission was $1 and the beer free, prepared to make "an awful showing," as he put it.

"I had a certain amount of wit," he said, "was a good dancer and attractive to their taste. The spirit of dignity would not allow me to make any approach to Maggie."

He did, however, include her with several other girls and fellows in a magnificent and sweeping invitation to go with him to a wine room; where, at Anton's expense, they had beer and lunch.

"This made me a big fellow," he said. "It overcame the tendency in the town to say that I was broke. They guessed, when they saw me spend the coin."

One of the girls passed the word to Anton that Maggie was "all right." On this hint, the young tramp asked Maggie for a dance; and when they had returned to the hall and were waltzing, he asked Maggie if she would write a different letter now from that she wrote three or four months ago.

"The coquettish answer came so quickly," he said, "that I was surprised. She said she did not need to write now, but could tell me all about it. So I escorted her home from the ball, and that settled it."

The next day, Sunday, Maggie had an engagement with the minister. She kept it, but brought him the sad news, and told him she would be his sister. In the evening, Anton called, and was received very coldly by her father and mother, who preferred the man who did not swear, drink or chew anything but gum.

"But now," said Anton, with a touch of pride, "they think I'm all right. When I smoke in the house now, her old father says he used to be just as bad, and when I drink, he says, 'Boys will be boys—that was the way with me.' Now they are interested in me, they cannot see anything bad in what I do."

A few months later, Anton and Maggie were married. When he went for the marriage license, he did not have a cent in his pocket, or anywhere else. They lived, at first, with his parents, but soon Anton had a chance to go into the saloon business.

"A brewery was interested in me," he said. "As I was talkative, and had met many men and knew how to get along with them, they thought I would make good, if I did not give away too many drinks."

He started in a business that had been closed up six months, and for which he had to drum up a new trade. The first month he ran $20 behind, the second month he made $60 over all, and the third month he cleared over $125. He understood the tramps and rough element and knew how to treat them. On the night his son Alfred was born, there was a very rough crowd in the saloon, headed by a desperate fighter, a bull-headed Andrew. Anton made them a little speech, told them about the great occasion, and said he would treat them to music, cigars and cock-tails until midnight, with the understanding that if there should be a row, they would abide by his decision. They drank a gallon of whiskey and half a barrel of beer and then began eating the glasses. But there was no fighting.

"The news that I could manage a bunch like that traveled like fire," said Anton. "I made an impression on the brewers, and the biggest toughs in town began to respect me. I had learned to deal with men on the road, and it helped me in the saloon business just as it helps me now in my trades-union activity."

A certain kind of rough delicacy is a quality marked in Anton's character. The brewer was a stingy fellow who never wanted to treat, and who insisted on having only his own beer sold. That was a handicap to Anton, for he often was forced to say that he did not have the beer called for. One day this rich brewer dropped into the saloon when there were fifteen or sixteen men there, drinking.

"He bought a bottle of beer," said Anton, "and treated me. I felt sore that he didn't call up the boys, so that I could introduce him as a good fellow and help the business. So I treated the crowd and said, sarcastically, 'Mr.—'s brewery cannot afford to buy.' This galled him so that he spent ten dollars in treating, but when the boys were gone, he called me down hard. But a friend of his, who was with him, said I was right commercially."

Soon after the business was recognized as a success, a young fellow, son of the widow who owned the saloon, wanted to get hold of it. So his mother raised the rent on Anton, who, understanding the reason for it, got angry and refused to renew his lease. Repentance came almost immediately, but it was then too late, and he was again out of a job. And now he had a wife and child. He had the satisfaction, however, of knowing that the business soon ran down and that the widow went bankrupt.

Anton was forced to go back to the old furniture factory, at $1.50 a day. It was very irksome to him to work for so little, after holding so much better jobs throughout the country. It hurt his pride, but the man is not vain, and he recognized it as a necessity. But when summer came, and work was slack, he was laid off. He then "got the fever again," heard the whistles blow, and in spite of his wife and child, jumped on a box-car and was off for his last tramp. His father wanted him to pay his way, but this seemed to Anton a pure waste of money.

It generally takes a long time for a radical change to come about in a man—if it ever does. Anton loved his wife and certainly the experience of marriage tended even then to make him steadier. But it needed more interests than those of family life to hold him closely in one place. Those interests came at a later time in Chicago: and in this combination of activities which have made him an integral and useful member of his society, his family plays an important and interesting part. To be sure, he needed a job, but his going South just then was perhaps due as much to the remains of a vagabond temperament as to necessity.

He left Maggie in a difficult and trying position. During the time that Anton was in the saloon business they had lived in a little cottage where Afred was born and where they had had plenty. With her skill in management, industry and intelligence, they had been decidedly well off and quite independent. But now she and her child had to live again with her husband's family. And she had the proverbial difficulties with her mother-in-law. As Anton's father became more prosperous he grew steadier in his habits, and did not drink so much. But Anton's mother kept up the habit of parsimony even though it had ceased to be a necessity. She was practical and helpful, gave Anton and Maggie the clothes they needed and met all her duties and the necessities of life. But life had been so hard for her, that she did not understand the pleasant aspect of things: she was tyrannical and fussy and gave in a way that brought no pleasure, as Maggie put it. She was one of those unfortunate women who do their duty so sadly and constantly that they receive no affection from their own children and incur the active dislike of all others who are connected with them. Whenever Anton sent money to Maggie from the road, his mother locked it up for safe keeping and doled it out as necessity required. She was determined that nothing should be wasted. Her part is the part played by many a poor man and woman who have been the mainstay of a family but even thereby have deprived themselves pathetically of most of the lovable qualities.

CHAPTER IV.

The Age of Reason.

ANTON'S last trip on the road was in most respects similar to its predecessors. He worked at anything he found: waited at table, washed dishes in boarding houses, worked at his trade, gambled and "bummed"; spent a night at ease in a Pullman car which was empty, and had to jump in the morning when the train was going fifteen miles an hour; found many sympathetic ladies, and few good jobs; met yeggs and hoboes, and imbibed more of the philosophy of the road. An anarchistic miner, with a gift of gab, made an impression on him. But, at that time, Socialism and anarchism were only names to him. The words stirred his blood, but meant little.

A hobo always wants to move rapidly. He has no engagements and no place to go, but he is always in a hurry. So he sometimes rides on the trucks of the passenger trains, though it is dangerous and uncomfortable.

In the box-cars, he is more comfortable than the bloated millionaire travelling in his parlor-car; for there the tramp can lie down and smoke. But he is generally so restless that he objects to the slow speed of the freight train.

So Anton hurried on from place to place. The thought of his family made him even more restless than before. He was anxious to get a job, but when once secured it did not seem good enough for him. And, indeed, he was now forced to take positions which he formerly would have sneered at. When a man wants a place badly, he is generally paid less than when he is indifferent. At New Orleans he was hired at $1.50 a day, eleven hours, by the same foreman who had formerly paid him $3 a day; and now he was a skilled mechanic.

"I was treated with this same generosity wherever I went," he said. "You see, I was not yet a Union man."

Yellow fever and the fear of quarantine drove him from this job. While "on the bum" he was introduced by a policeman to an employer as a man out of work. The employer volunteered to give him a position at

$1.50 a day, for 11 hours' work. He didn't dare to refuse, as otherwise the policeman would have jailed him as a hobo.

"Certainly," he said, sarcastically. "It's work I want, not wages, like all other men."

He turned up at the mill for work, "just for curiosity," as he put it; worked twenty minutes, went to the W. C. and forgot to go back. On the street he met the policeman, who thought he possessed a gift for gab. "I jollied him along," said Anton, "convinced him that I was a good fellow, and after I had listened a long time to his wit, he advised me to leave town. Instead, I went into a saloon and began singing to a lot of steamboat men. For this I was arrested as a disorderly character, and taken before the magistrate. I made my plea straight, and so the judge felt I was a hardened criminal, and sentenced me to the stone pile. I ran away, but was caught and served my ten days. The law doesn't like music, apparently. But it is hard on a man to have to remember that the law has nerves. When I got out, I jumped on the night Flyer and as we pulled out I saw four policemen watching to see if there were any hoboes on the train. I yelled the most insulting things

I could think of; we were going at full speed, and had just turned around a block, and at the curve was a house of ill-fame from the windows of which two women of the town looked down and enjoyed my jokes. They, too, hated the police."

As the train passed through Whitecastle, Louisiana, he saw the large sign of a sash and door factory, so he dropped off, to try for a job. The first man he met was an outcast from the richest family in Clinton. "He was an aristocrat, and when at home used to run around with the free element and drink," said Anton. "But when he was thrown on his own resources he quit the booze and with me at Whitecastle, he drank only soda." Through this young man Anton got a good job in the sash factory and was enabled to send money home, but after a few weeks, yellow fever became general in Louisiana, and the factory shut down. A shot-gun quarantine was in force and Anton found himself out of a place and unable to leave town.

Under these conditions, all he could do was to amuse himself and wait. Books and even newspapers were unknown to him. He did not read at all. At a later time, he seems to have rejoiced in his ignorance of classical culture. "My mind was not prejudiced," he said. "I was not mis-educated. I was not burdened with a common school education. I was unperverted and radical ideas could take a firm hold on me."

What he learned, he learned from experience; and his experience during the period of quarantine was largely that of a town loafer. He "hung around" the hotel bar and billiard room and played pool, at which he was an expert. He worked about the hotel and that, with what he could make at pool, gave him a living. On one occasion he had instructions from his backers to lose the game. At first, he allowed his opponent to distance him, but the boasting of the latter and the applause of the crowd made him forget that his backers wanted him to lose; and he won by a close margin. In consequence, he received only $2.50 out of the $50 stakes, and all the sports were down on him. They thought he had won because enough "considerations" had not been offered him. He was unable to secure another game during his stay in the town. The proprietor of the hotel gave him, however, another chance, and put him in charge of a saloon that was patronized by negroes. "There," said Anton, "I had a chance to make ten dollars a day, but my sympathy got the best of my judgment. It was easy to graft there off the drinks, polo, lunch, showing favors about the women, etc., but my lack of courage and my sympathy for the coon made it impossible for me to succeed, although I was very anxious to send money home."

This man never expresses ordinary snap-shot condemnation of the ordinary immorality. It is in his eyes so closely connected with property and the class-standards developed from it, that moral indignation seems out of place to him. But when it came to the point, he was unable to do the human harm to somebody that cheating or theft involves.

The morning after the first frost, the quarantine was raised. There was a general jubilee and Anton sang songs and made a speech. Then he took a train, on his way home, but as he was broke and hungry, he dropped off at the first town, for a bite. A woman put him to work cutting wood; he sawed wood for 1½ hours; she then called him to breakfast which consisted of 2 biscuits. a cup of coffee. and a little bacon.

" I was mad enough to choke her," he said. "She then asked if I had enough. 'Too much,' I replied. 'Enough to last me a week.' I avoided wood piles after that."

This lady was a Christian and wealthy. The next morning Anton begged a meal, at the house of some working people. The woman cooked for him some sweet potatoes, plenty of bacon, two eggs, two or three cups of coffee, butter and biscuits. The contrast impressed him. On the basis of a full stomach he found a planing mill and began to think the world was his again. The proprietor hired him at $2 a day. Anton worked there three months and sent home $45 of his wages. On Xmas day he spent two dollars in fruit and candy and took the present to the family of the working woman who had given him so good a breakfast when he was in need. He continued his way home, but at Belleville, Illinois, came one of his most unpleasant experiences. It was winter and the snow was deep. He was sleeping in a rolling mill, over the boilers. The men in the mill thought they would have some fun, and took some waste, saturated it with oil and lighted it. The heat scared him and awakening suddenly he thought the whole building was on fire. Without taking his shoes, which he had used as a pillow, he jumped down, eight feet, and rushed out in the snow, bare-foot. He went into four different stores in the town, but they all refused him shoes. Finally in another rolling mill he secured some shoes and a place to sleep. In the morning when the crews were changed, he was discovered asleep by the son of the superintendent. He and his father landed on the sleeping hobo and nearly pounded the life out of him, "for no reason at all."

"I had a strong feeling," said Anton, "that I ought to kill them. I started to do it twice, but I thought of my wife and child. The employees put me wise and I could easily have settled them, but my courage failed me. I ought to have done it. I am still sorry that I didn't do it. When I got home, I told my friends I had fallen off the train, to account for my bruises."

That was Anton's last hobo experience. His wife "seemed good" to him, when he returned; and although, at times since then, he has heard the whistles blow and his blood has been stirred with the strange eloquence of the sordid road, the attraction has never been strong enough to make him break loose.

"I returned to Clinton," he said, "a family man and a sceptic, though not yet a free-thinker. Hobo-life and experience with men has taken the old faith out of me, but I had not yet got any philosophy as a substitute."

His first duty was to find a job. He was forced to "humiliate himself" by asking for a position in the old factory where no boy could learn a trade. The foreman referred him to the owner; he had been discharged so often and had made so much trouble that he would not hire him on his own responsibility. The owner gave Anton a lecture, told him that since his father and brothers had worked there he (Anton) ought to settle down. Incidentally, he spoke of his own brother, who was running for congressman. Anton understood, and promised to settle down. "I wanted a job," he said, "but it didn't influence my vote."

Maggie was overjoyed when she found that Anton had a position in the town, although his wages were only $1.35 a day. They moved into a hut with a little yard where they could plant their own potatoes. The floor in the kitchen slanted, but they paid only $3 a month rent.

"I made it look cute and nice, anyway," said Maggie. And I can well believe her. For the first time I had the pleasure of taking my Sunday dinner with her, Anton and the children (there were three of them, then; this was several years later than this point in the story), I was at once struck with the cleanliness and well-being of the entire household. Maggie had no one to help her; she did all the cooking and house-work, kept her children healthy and perfectly clean, the house as neat as her snow-white apron, the garden productive and attractive, and set as good a plain table as has been my good fortune to know. In addition to all this, she did outside washing and did it well (for this also I can vouch, for she did mine!). Her work did not seem to oppress her in the least; she always had plenty of temperament left over to take an interest in her husband, his friends and affairs, and to do a little reading on her own account. She often went out to socials, and sometimes ran into the house of a neighbor for a good gossip. So, when she told me that the little hut in Clinton where the family lived for a year was clean and neat, I readily believed her.

Anton worked steadily in the old shop for a year. It was a happy, domestic time. A little girl was born, and, on his small wages, everything went well. The energy he had saved from the strenuousness of life on the road, went into more definite intellectual life. "The spirit of protest"—a phrase of which he is very fond, grew stronger in him. He regretted that there were no unions in the town, in his trade of woodworking, which was the largest industry in the place. But his organizing talent had not yet developed; there had been no opportunity for it.

There was an old man named Greenhill working in the factory. Years before he had met Robert Ingersoll in Chicago and had been   * much impressed. Ingersoll's clear, though limited and narrow human scepticism, had struck old Greenhill as the last word. With this as a starter, he began to read "radical" books. He subscribed to the *Free Thought*   * *Magazine* and *Truth Seeker,* and Tom Paine's *Age of Reason* was his Bible.

Greenhill saw that Anton was ripe for these ideas, and at odd times in the shop, he undertook the younger man's education. The little thing that started the ball rolling was a copy of *The Truth-Seeker.* Greenhill dropped it, in the "W. C.," "accidentally on purpose," and Anton read it there. It contained a cartoon attacking the principle of the Spanish-American War. As Anton was opposed to the war, he subscribed to the magazine. In this way it was that he discovered Greenhill to be a "free-thinker," and their intimacy began.

"It was rather hard on Maggie, at first," said Anton. "All our folks were Lutherans, and she thought I was going to the devil. But she tolerated it. I got the magazine every week and Greenhill began coming to the house. We talked about astronomy and Darwin, and it was exciting, I can tell you, to begin to get some little idea of the way things really are. Greenhill felt most people were still monkeys. Finally he showed me Tom Paine's *Age of Reason.* This was the first book I ever read through, and I read this book many times. I used to read it aloud to Maggie in the evening, and she got as much interested as I was. We referred to the German Bible and found the absurdities and contradictions that Paine pointed out. I loaned it once to a Catholic who liked it so much that he never returned it. I wish I had the old book now. My father thought it was awful.

"I began to hate the Church and its doctrines. I never let an opportunity pass to hurt the feelings of the people in that God-ridden town. There was a young fellow in the factory who was studying to be a minister. He ran his machine next to mine and we used to argue while at work. He tried to argue me out of free thought, but I had him skinned to death. I laughed at him, and it hurt him. I hated him because of my disappointment; for it was a disappointment to have everything go up in smoke. I told him it was the God-idea that had kept the workers in darkness and ignorance and poverty. Maggie followed me in these ideas like a child."

"No!" said Maggie, indignantly, "I led the way."

"The world," continued Anton, without paying any attention to his wife's remark, "is dominated by fear; and religion is its strongest weapon. Tom Paine proves that. He goes about it in such a mild way: it is grand. He does not get excited, but he is uncompromising. 'I believe in one God and only one,' he starts out. 'I have hopes of happiness beyond this life.' As for me, I have hopes of happiness in remaining dead. My hopes are so strong that they overcome the fear of not remaining dead. It is immaterial whether I die soon, or late. I am all right as long as the factory whistle doesn't blow; but when it blows and it is time to go home, I am miserable."

"That is what he calls satire," said Maggie.

Whenever Anton talks philosophy, and he does so constantly, he becomes merry. He likes expression for its own sake. On Maggie's remark, he said, stroking his son's head:

"Alfred is not a sentimentalist, like Maggie. He is cold-blooded and stands by his father instead of his mother."

"My passion for investigation along economic lines was strong at that time," continued Anton, "and I became interested in Socialism. I met a Jew who ran a second-hand shop—a man who would rob his next door neighbor. He was a Socialist soap-box orator. I used to listen to him argue Socialism, for at that time I was a listener and not a Butinsky. I had very little to say, but I was very vindic-

tive when I met a religious man. As a boy
I had been very religious, and now I was as
extreme in the other direction. The foreman
tried to lecture me and show me the evil of
my ways. Also, a young minister used to
advise me to read something useful, such as
bookkeeping, instead of Tom Paine.

"But I didn't care about them. I liked old
Greenhill, although he was a narrow-minded
man. His time was devoted to the interest of
killing God, and this tended to side-track him.
He was also a free-lover and a subscriber to
Lucifer. He had been married three or four
times. He was a good mechanic, and if he
had not had these ideas he might have been a
foreman. Foremen are generally ignoram-
uses. They know nothing about philosophy,
sociology, or economics. They feel it an
honor to be in the Church, and are nearly all
religious."

Anton, on being offered 30 cents a day
more, went to another factory in the same
town, and moved to another house, near his
new working place. He grew "more talkative," as he expressed it, among the workmen.
He began to feel his intellectual superiority
to the rank and file, and tried to think, and

to teach them something about the conditions of labor. He soon had the satisfaction of "breeding discontent among them," and the foreman began to look upon him as a nuisance. One day he had a big boil on his neck, and Maggie was ill with cramps in her feet. So Anton did not reach the shop till noon, and was discharged. This he felt to be unjust, after they had induced him to leave his old place and go to the expense of moving. He realized his being late was only an excuse. He had done his work well—he was now a fair mechanic—but he talked too much among the men.

Anton determined that he would have a verbal understanding with his employer. The desire to "ball people out" with whom he had quarreled is very strong in this expressive workingman. So one Saturday he waited for the employer on the road, and, on meeting him, insisted that he should explain the discharge. He did not reply, but swore out a warrant of assault and battery against Anton, who was taken before an old justice of the peace.

"The justice was satisfied," said Anton, "that the charge of assault and battery was not justified. He sympathized with me, but this man was a boss, and part owner of the factory. So he made me sign a document pledging myself not to molest the boss, and he fined me $5 besides. My father was very angry, and wanted me to prosecute the man, but my respect for the law was already so low that I gave the idea no consideration; but the next day I went by the employer's fine house. It was Sunday, and he was sitting on his veranda. I balled him out for fair. I talked so loud that all the neighbors could hear. I explained to him how he took the bread out of the mouths of women and children. I told him I was going to Davenport to work, and that if he queered me there by a boycott I would kill him. I am now boycotted in Clinton. I could not get a job there to-day, because of my agitation years ago."

After ten or twelve days in Davenport, where he could obtain no satisfactory job, he returned to Clinton, with the determination to take his family to Chicago. That would give him a larger field, and he knew that he could get nothing in Clinton. It was exciting, too, the idea of settling in the big city.

So it was decided, and this decision made

Anton's mother very anxious that his little girl should be at once baptized, before she was beyond the reach of salvation, in distant Chicago. Maggie wanted to please the old lady, and so Anton consented, somewhat against his principles, and he went to engage the minister, a German Lutheran preacher.

"He invited me into his—studio, I believe he called it. I told him my mission. He asked me my name, place of birth, names of parents, and what Church I belonged to. I was quick and proud to tell him I belonged to none. 'Why?' he asked. 'I don't believe in it,' I said. He was horrified and shocked, arose and said he knew I must be a bad man. I told him he had no reason to think so. He said he had every reason. 'You are a damned liar,' I said, in his own studio, where he might have studied, if he had been so disposed. Then he wanted to know why I desired to have the child baptized. 'I am more tolerant than you,' I said. 'I want it baptized to please my mother.'

"I had started to go, but he asked me back again and tried to argue with me. He turned over many pages in the Bible, and I pointed out the contradictions, as Tom Paine had taught me, and laughed. He was shocked, but talked three mortal hours. I admired his perseverance. He asked who was the godfather, and when he found that Maggie's father was a Christian Scientist, he objected, but the objection was not sustained. At first he refused to come, but when I said I would get an English preacher, he consented to help us out.

"The night of the christening there was a little beer in the house, and the wife was on eggs all evening for fear I would start an argument with the preacher. I wanted to stand by the beer keg and drink as a protest, but Maggie would do anything to avoid trouble. After the ceremony, the preacher called me out, for a talk. I gave him mother's money for the christening—$3. He was pleased and gave me a book called *'The Word of God and His Enemies.'* I suggested his taking along with him Tom Paine's *Age of Reason,* but he said he would just as lief have the devil in his house. I remarked that the devil is more tolerant than God, and always has been. I was too prejudiced even to read his book."

CHAPTER V.

Trade-Unionist.

IMMEDIATELY after the christening, Anton went to Chicago alone, to find a job, and establish a home for his family. He took with him his entire capital, consisting of one dollar and thirty-five cents. He found employment the first day at Carbon Brothers, Union and Twenty-seventh streets. He was then reduced to thirty-five cents, had no money for board or for tools. They put him on the molding sticker, which is his favorite job. Working next him was a Union man, who did not ask him to join the Union, and paid no attention to him. He was apparently afraid that Anton would make a showing and was jealous. This man, as Anton afterwards discovered, was a prominent "lusher" in the Union, and thought more of himself and of whiskey than of the good of the cause. On this, as on many other previous occasions, Anton had the opportunity to reflect on the lack

fact, his peaceableness has never been marked. He can be very sweet and generous, but neither in temperament nor in philosophy has he the virtue of patience and endurance of what he deems unjust or churlish.

He was assistant "straw" boss in the shop, which, as he put it, "is next thing to nothing," but which nevertheless marked an advance in his trade and the consideration with which he was regarded. The foreman was "a conceited Irishman, generally drunk." Once, when he was off for two weeks, Anton was put in charge of his department, at wages of $2 a day. Another department foreman received $2.75 a day. "He was," said Anton, "an obedient slave to the interests of the concern. If a man went to the toilet he would go after him and make him hurry. He was not a member of the Union, and had no interest in anything except the work and his wages. He was a narrow-minded man. I had no use for this kind of foreman, but I had to deal with him when I was in charge of the other department. One day he told the superintendent that some things had not been properly made, and put the blame on me. The superintendent started to raise Cain, and I flew off the handle and swore. The superintendent pulled off his coat, and I got out of my overalls. Then he discharged me. But, when he got down stairs, he was cooler, and evidently wanted me to ask to be allowed to come back. 'You ought to apologize,' he said; but I could not see it that way. I told him he ought to treat all men with consideration, and that there was as much logic in mine as in his. When he found I wouldn't stay, he wrote me a good letter to a factory on the North Side, highly recommending me. But that shop had no Union scale, and was a ten-hour shop. So I didn't go there."

He was out of a job for several weeks. Every day he went to the Union headquarters, looking for work. It was in the winter time and he was very short of money. He was compelled, like the vast majority of workingmen, to buy coal by the basket, and thus pay more for it than the rich man does. On New Year's Day there was no coal in the house, and it was bitterly cold. Fortunately, the next day, when it was 8 degrees below zero, he found a job and went to work in a shop that was "open to the air, but closed to the scab." In this Union shop he received

$2.25 a day for nine hours' work, good money for him at that time, but he could not get along with the boss, whom he described as "an intolerant, brutal bastard," and left to go into a non-union shop at $1.75 a day and ten hours' work.

The immediate cause of his rupture with the boss of the Union shop was a dispute about extra wages. He had worked an hour and twenty minutes overtime, but was paid for only an hour. Anton kicked for more, and the boss told him to go to the conventionally hot place. 'Complain, if you like, to your old business agent,' he said. I replied that I would go to the Police Station instead and have him indicted for larceny to the amount of 50 cents. Then he got mad and threw a half dollar at me, and said, 'Take it and git out.' I sarcastically asked him to have a drink. While I worked in that place I thought the earth was not so big a Paradise as some philosophers make out. Indeed, soon after, this factory burned down."

Very unpopular factories sometimes have this habit of going up in smoke.

In the non-union shop, where he was getting only $1.75 for long hours, Anton did not feel himself much better off. "It was a rush place," he said. "Instead of running 15,000 feet, I ran 50,000 feet on the machine. I was too strong for that kind of a job and quit in two weeks."

His brother married at this time, opportunely for Anton, whom he invited to visit him in Clinton, so Anton and Maggie and the children made a trip home. Maggie staid on for several weeks, but Anton was soon back in Chicago, after a job, which he found at the Union Headquarters. "The official head scrutinized me, as he always did new men, to see if I was a victim of alcohol. There are many mechanics who drink, and they, of course, are often laid off. The firm had sent word through the walking delegate that they wanted a sticker hand, and that job was offered to me. The man whose place I got was a drunkard. He had not showed up for several days, and when he did come back to the shop, he asked the boss to lend him a quarter to get a drink. He was an excellent mechanic, but that was too strong, and he was discharged."

The scale at this Union shop was $2 and eight hours, and Anton, feeling well off, wrote Maggie to come back. He arranged to meet her at the train, but it was the night when the district council met, and he was beginning to be deeply interested in debates. He gradually learned to take the floor. "At first I did not have much confidence in myself. Since then I have accumulated too much." On this particular night he was to meet a business agent, a radical, courageous man, whom he liked. So Maggie and the children slipped his mind: if not, he thought they could take care of themselves. When he returned to the flat at 11 o'clock he found all Maggie's bundles in front of the door. She did not have a key, and had to go with the children to a friend's house for the night!

"Anton," she said, "is an interesting husband. He is very fond of me and the children, but he likes to talk so much at the Union that it makes him sometimes forget everything else."

It was perhaps just as well, for Anton, during Maggie's absence, had quarreled with the landlord, and on that night all the things were packed up, ready to be moved the next day. "He was a mean bastard," said Anton, "and told me all the fault was with the Unions."

So they moved to a little flat of four rooms over a grocery store, for which they paid six dollars a month.

From this time, which was in 1900, Anton's activity in the Union grew rapidly. From the start, he assumed a critical attitude. "I was always suspicious," he said, "of those who had more authority than the others. I was naturally an anarchist, in the sense that I distrusted all authority, though I did not know it, at that time. I had, however, begun to call myself a Socialist. I was too emphatic about it, and made enemies."

After he had been in the Union about six months, he was approached by several members and ran for the position of delegate to the district council of the woodworkers.

"I was willing to be a delegate," he said, "yet I felt I could do more good by being closer to the rank and file and remaining free to criticize. I had a suspicion, like a good many other members, that the district council was not too honest. This was largely a mistake, and was educated into me as it was into all Socialists by the Socialist press and propaganda. At that time all Socialists' papers bitterly attacked all labor leaders and called them grafters and fakirs. In my enthusiasm I thought the Socialists could not be wrong; and so I suspected the honesty of the central organization. But I thought I might be of service, though not very popular, in the council, and so I ran for the position and was elected by an overwhelming plurality. For weeks I had attended the meetings regularly. The men saw in me a peculiar, rough honesty, and workingmen like that. I knew men, and felt instinctively that it was best to appeal mainly to the manhood in a man. Any injustice, no matter how small, seemed to me of the greatest importance and to constitute a big question for consideration. This attitude, natural to me, was popular with the rank and file, and so I was elected.

"I felt very important for some time, and thought I would make them all Socialists. I understood nothing about politics, at that time, and did not know how to scheme. I always acted extemporaneously, and the next meeting, perhaps, I wanted to retract what I had said or done. I did not go to the caucuses, but I learned from experience. I was so fierce and bold and frank that I was looked upon as a danger to machine rule. I was under no obligations except to the rank and file who elected me.

"After I had been a delegate for some time, I discovered that a large majority of the delegates were as honest as I, but I also saw that they were more or less helpless. Some, indeed, were unscrupulous at times, not knowing whether to advance their own interests or the interests of the majority.

"There were two prominent walking delegates who represented two very different kinds of men, and there are many of both kinds in the Unions. They were always fighting each other. One was a crafty politician without any convictions, except the need of holding his job and feathering his nest; and the other was a man who believed in the rights of man, who loved men, and who worked for them. He was an anarchist. This man had been chased out of Germany, where he had been in the Reichstag, and in New York had spent a year in Sing Sing because of a speech he made at the time of the hanging of the Chicago anarchists. He was a vigorous, positive character, and never spoke in the council without success. He was, and is, physically and mentally strong.

I liked him for his hearty way, his courage, and his love for men.

"The politician, his rival in the council, was a thin fellow physically and mentally, though very clever. He was also a positive character. He was a cunning dodger who sometimes believed in resorting to the jack-knife. I was informed by the anarchist that this politician went to the Bohemian district and made a speech in favor of a certain judge. I was disappointed to think that a man who claimed to be a Socialist, and was active in the trades-union movement, would support a Democratic judge. As I was in doubt as to the correctness of the story, I went to him directly and asked him point blank if the story was true. He admitted that he had made the speech, and wanted to know who told me. I finally told him that my informant was the walking delegate, his rival in the council. Then the politician told me how it came about. The judge in question had been very lenient in cases involving strikers, pickets, violence, etc., and in the matter of fines, and there were reasons to believe that he would continue this favorable attitude, if our walking delegate would speak for him and solicit for him the political support of the working-men. So the judge's friends had first gone to a man high up in the affairs of the International, a man deeply respected and admired by all parties. He had refused to make the speech—or, in fact, to make a speech for any judge. This thin politician was then approached, and he consulted the respected leader who had refused. 'Do as you please,' was the reply. 'I am not Anthony Comstock.' He then consulted his rival, the anarchist, who said: 'It is more important for you to use your own judgment than to do right.'

"This was a very characteristic reply of this anarchist member of our council. Every woodworker knows this man. I love him. He is a positive, heroic man, who does not like graft and theft, but who knows there are worse things. And that the kind of honesty that is harped upon by the reformers is often the most insidious wrong to the workingman. This man refuses any undue luxury: he will not drink champagne because it is too expensive and unnecessary. He has high ideals, and is an extensive reader along his line. He never went to an English school, but he knows how to say 'I give a damn' in the most expressive and independent way. He can go to any strange town and arouse an ordinary meeting with more lasting enthusiasm than any man of my acquaintance. Once I heard him, when a general organizer, make a speech at a town in Wisconsin. Previous to his speech, he had read the town's directory, picked out the names of the men whom he thought could be reached, and wrote them postal cards. The character of each man he judged largely by his nationality—Swede, Pole, Irish, German, etc. He represented on the postal cards that the meeting was social and involved no responsibility to join the Union, and no fear of losing their jobs. Then at the meeting he picked out the men he could use. He had been attacked in one of the local papers as an anarchist, and in a speech to the meeting he said, in reply:

" 'They call me an anarchist. I give a damn for that. I admit I be an anarchist. The only question is, what kind of an anarchist. The Mayor of St. Paul—am I dat kind of an anarchist? Mr. Rockefeller—dat kind of an anarchist? Mr. Big Business Man, who buys the law to help his business—dat kind of an anarchist? If I am dat kind of an anarchist, dey ought to chase me out of town. But den dey can't, for den I have too much influence. But do dey mean anodder kind of anarchist? Do dey mean by anarchist a pioneer in de labor movement? Is dat de kind dey mean? If so, den I am an anarchist, and glad of it.'

"That's the man who replied to the thin politician that it was more important for him to act independently than to ask advice about something he ought to know. The thin man thought that his rival, when he told me about the speech supporting the judge, ought to have given me the reasons; and he wanted me to speak against his rival in the council. But I refused to do so. I told him, however, that if the opportunity came I would roast him (the thin delegate), and that would give him an opportunity to explain his position. He had to be content with that. I got this opportunity at a later time, as we shall see."

I myself have met this labor politician, whom Anton speaks of above. And the difference between him and Anton is remarkable. It does not lie in the latter's nature to change fundamentally. No matter how "wise" he is becoming about political and other methods, he remains at heart a workingman. This is much more than can be said of many of the other leaders. They are, as he said, roughly divided into two classes—the enthusiast and the politician.

I was impressed over and over again, when living among the mechanics, with a certain kind of altruism, of a fairly wide-spread emotion of solidarity, akin to the religious; for when men band together in an effort to attain things which they deem necessary to their deepest material and spiritual welfare, they are not far from conceiving of the movement, at least in moments of self-consciousness, as being from one point of view religious. The point, indeed, always comes in the affairs of men where selfishness, when the interests involved are of the deepest moment, becomes to a certain extent altruism. If we strive to attain small things for ourselves, our action seems selfish; but if we strive for the highest good to ourselves, our deep egotism is sympathetically called altruism and assumes an emotional relationship to religion.

The best men in the rank and file of the laborers have this feeling partly unknown to themselves, and they make many sacrifices to it. In the case of the leaders, however, the situation is different, in large measure, and not so inspiring. I have no doubt that many of them are honest men—most of them are honest as far as money is concerned—but some of them still seem to be workingmen at heart, with an emotional interest in their class. Anton is one of these, and so is his friend, the anarchist agitator.

Corruption is a subtle thing; one not always easily recognized by the uncasuistic man. To keep clear of wrong requires intelligence of a high order, as well as good will. And the labor leader is subjected to temptations of a kind not easily seen as temptations. By virtue of these he often becomes far less fundamentally attractive than the class he represents.

Several sets of circumstances bring about this degeneration, for it is degeneration, of the labor leader. As he acquires the feeling of power, he tends to adopt some of the worst methods of politics, and encourages the growth of a public feeling often extra-if not anti-legal. Several men in Chicago have said to me things which indicated an apologetic, or even exculpatory, attitude towards leaders convicted of bribery and other forms of graft—a kind of sentimentalism, rather than sentiment for the cause. They often acquire a rather unscrupulous willingness to adopt the unjust methods of their opponents. Demanding fairness and charity, they are often inclined to show little of these qualities. I have seldom met a class of men who are, in some ways, as narrow-minded and as prejudiced as the typical labor leader of the "political" type. *

But this is not the worst. Narrowness, suspiciousness, an eager tendency to accomplish good results unscrupulously, if necessary, this is natural enough to men of little preliminary training and not often of the best natural quality—for the best men do not, as a rule, come to the top. And the essential justice of the cause outweighs mere money dishonesty, if the spirit be otherwise right.

But, worse than all these in its results, is the moral change due to a different standard of life. The labor leader lives well. He spends well. He drinks, and develops the luxurious needs of the class he is combating. "I must spend 50 cents for my lunch, at the very least," said an admirable carpenter to me. He gets in a habit of mind where he will no longer work at his trade, even if he gives up a position which ought to be merely temporary. He becomes a "professional" leader. Like the "professional" politician, he tends to become inferior morally. He loses sympathy with the class from which he has sprung. Living no longer as they do, he no longer genuinely feels their needs. On the contrary, he is likely insensibly to attempt to live still better, insensibly drifts in feeling into the class supposedly hostile to the class he officially represents.

He loses seriousness, temperament. I have often talked with men in the rank and file who fascinated me with their idealistic earnestness, their simplicity and pathetic honesty; but among the leaders temperament and seriousness are more rare. I find the easy, good-fellowship characteristic of the small politician, but little that suggests the virtues of the laborer. There is nothing Millet-like about many of them.

The importance of the laborers' representatives remaining laborers at heart is obvious. Otherwise, the organizations would become in time as aloof from the real interests of the laborers as the bureaucracy of Russia is aloof from the interests of the peasants.

I have seen on many occasions a crowd of labor leaders standing before a bar and spending money recklessly for drinks—many dollars would be spent by each man in the course of one evening in this way.

They have the false ideals of drinking, "treating," of doing things on a "big scale," characteristic of the rich young college buck or man-about-town. This is hardly the spirit which tends to preserve what is idealistic and humane in the labor movement.

It is a case similar to what has, in the matter of the Russian-Jewish idealists, frequently come under my notice in New York. These people, many of them, came to America with the finest ideals, with devotion to the cause of humanity, with a love for Tolstoyan doctrines, and with vividly "temperamental" expressiveness and earnestness. Soon, however, when they began to "get up" in the world, they lost their interest in the "movement," and men who had been simple or prophetic workers for a cause became merely practical and personally ambitious, in a small manner. It seems the way of the world.

No one condemns this kind of labor leader as bitterly as do the real workingmen, whether they belong to the rank and file, or whether they are themselves leaders, but leaders still emotionally devoted to the "movement"—men like Anton and his friend, the anarchist walking delegate and organizer. They do not condemn the "politician" so much because of any "graft" he may be guilty of. This is not so common as is generally supposed, although being spectacular and sensational it is what usually is emphasized in the newspapers and in novels which are dependent on the exceptional, the bizarre, on "high-lights" for their effects. They rightly feel that occasional theft is not so important as the emotional backsliding from the cause. They realize that men like Parks may be good men, in the sense that they keep warmly disposed to the interests of their class; and the fact that such a man might be inclined to "steal" from the class whom they regard as robbing the workingmen in general, does not seem to them to be of any great moral moment.

The great virtue is the virtue of fidelity to one's constituents. And that is, indeed, the origin of all social morality—to live up to the best public opinion with which you have come in contact—whether that public opinion be with or against the existing law.

One night I met in Chicago a man who well illustrated the deepest morality of a certain class. He was a criminal and an outcast from every society except the society of thugs and vagabonds—no man in any class would tolerate him. But he had been brought up as a member of the working class, and, although he had lost his position in that class, yet he had retained the most essential of its virtues, its feeling of organized solidarity and its hatred of the "scab."

At first I was inclined to think that this Chicago criminal was the worst human being I had ever known; and my acquaintance among people officially labeled "criminal" is considerable. He talked about his deeds in a natural, off-hand way. One could see that the opportunity to talk pleased him, though it was against his sense of form to show any undue exhilaration or emotion.

At first, he seemed a little doubtful, a little

hesitant, not having made up his mind whether I could really appreciate him or not. But when he had hazarded a few bolts, and found that I was apparently unmoved, he launched complacently forth in a description of his acts. He poured them out impersonally, calmly, yet with obvious pride.

He had originally been a workingman; and even now he takes a job when there is nothing more lucrative to do. And he still has friends among the honest laborers, who, although they do not approve of his ways, sometimes use him, according to his account, to "smash" a scab or two. He has been very useful to some of the violently inclined among the labor unions. But this, although there was some money in it, was after all a labor of love. It enabled him to function naturally, and also to do a good turn to society. It seemed a small thing, even to me, who at that time was unfamiliar with a certain set of ethics, in comparison with some of his other exploits.

These exploits are largely unmentionable. His mode of life has not been "nice" at all. He has not only "done" people openly in broad daylight on State street and other thoroughfares, but he has been effective in the expedition of other people, men and girls, to another world. His treatment of the women in this and other respects has been abominable. In this connection, a certain method of making money which he has occasionally adopted does not look well, even when merely thought of.

He told me these things with great assurance, without enthusiasm, without circumlocution. He did not seem to feel the necessity of delicacy in expression. His countenance is open and frank, and his blue eyes are innocent and he talks right on.

At first I had been guarded in what I said to him. I did not wish, for several reasons, to imply any disrespect. I knew that there was such a thing as honor among thieves, although personally I have found it only with the help of a microscope. I am convinced that it represents what the German thinkers call "a vanishing moment," only. However, after he had revealed pretty thoroughly his ways, I felt it was no longer necessary to be guarded. Here, apparently, was a man whom it was impossible to insult. He probably had no sensibility.

So, among other things, I asked him if he had ever been a "scab" or had worked for the corporations. For a moment he looked as if he would strike me. But all he did was to throw up his hands, and say in a deeply hurt tone:

"Oh, no. I may be bad, but I'm not as bad as that. That is against my principles."

I pacified him as soon as possible. I said I did not understand. Even yet, I had not fully realized the strength of the social law: "Thou shalt not be a scab." Public opinion that can so deeply influence the code of a man like that is indeed a real thing. To him it was the first and only commandment. Without that he would have been utterly lawless and utterly lost, utterly without principle. His morality was the deepest morality of his early companions. They, of course, had other virtues, but only the essential virtue remained with him. And to that he seemed true.

CHAPTER VI.

Meeting the Employer.

A STRIKE, which had been on, over the eight-hour day, for several months, gave Anton the opportunity he had been looking for, to bring before the council the matter of the thin politician's speech. At that time the eight-hour day held in thirty-two of the Chicago shops, while in the fourteen unorganized shops the working time was nine hours. The employers of the thirty-two eight-hour shops felt they were competing at a disadvantage with the nine-hour shops, and sent a request to the Union to appoint a conferring committee. They desired the men to send a committee of six, to talk the matter over with the employers' committee of the same number, and see if they could not arrive at a settlement, and stop the strike.

The men, at the meeting of the council, passed a resolution to appoint a committee to meet the employers; and the thin politician and Anton were two of those elected to serve. Anton at once arose, and protested against the thin politician being on the committee.

"He is unworthy," said Anton, in his speech before the council, "of serving on such an important committee. He, at one time, in his official capacity as walking delegate, made a speech in favor of a certain judge in the Democratic party."

The thin politician was on his feet immediately with a sweeping denial, and a demand for the name of Anton's informant.

"I gave the name," said Anton, "and then he and the anarchist, who was present, thrashed the matter out. There is more to this later on, but for the time the thin politician was sustained as a member of the committee. I had satisfied my conscience, however, and had kept my promise."

The strike of the woodworkers had begun several months before the conferring committees had been formed. The trade agreement, entered into two years earlier, provided for a nine-hour day, $2 minimum scale of wages, absolute closed shop, apprentice system, and the inauguration of the eight-hour day on

Meeting the Employer.

February 1st, 1900. All the factories, with a solitary exception, had agreed. The men demanded a ratification of this agreement, but the bosses insisted on going back to the nine-hour day. They were willing to pay for the extra hour, but the men felt it was important to maintain the principle of the eight-hour day. The employers felt themselves stronger than they had been. for at that time there was going on a building trades lockout, and it looked as though the men would be defeated, and if the trades were defeated it would be a blow to the woodworkers.

Anton worked at the time just previous to the strike in the sash and door factory of C. E. Petersen, who was "a monument in the Employers' Association," and he was also active in politics. A little while before the strike, Petersen called a meeting of his men and made them an address, an account of which is thus given by Anton:

"He told how much the trade had lost as the Unions had got more privileges, but he did not tell how he had been able to build his factory larger and larger. He told how he had charitably built homes for his employees, but he did not dwell on the rent he charged them. He did not fail to tell them that in case of a strike he had the power to put them out of their homes, but that he was too good to do so. At the close of his lecture he said he liked his men and would love to pay high wages and maintain the eight-hour agreement and keep closed shop, but that, unfortunately, if Bryan was elected business would be paralyzed and he would be unable to keep his agreement. He asked the men to give an opinion. They all sat silent, as the rank and file always will, so I spoke up and informed him that all of his men had voted in favor of the old agreement, which provided for an eight-hour day, at a certain date. I told him that all of the men were satisfied with their employer and their wages; that Bryan's election was almost impossible, and that, if he were elected, it would make no material difference, that the political parties were all alike.

He had referred in his speech to the business agents as 'the hoodlums downtown.' I assured him the men had not listened to the 'hoodlums,' but if they had they would have accepted the nine-hour day instead of being against it. As it was, they had taken the reins in their own hands and voted against the nine-hour day.

"Petersen did not like my attitude. He thought I was a Butinsky. He started to go away, and met the thin politician, who had been in the meeting and had heard himself referred to as a 'hoodlum.' But Petersen extended his hand cordially, and so did the walking delegate, and I set them both down as hypocrites. I used this to advantage when the strike came on in impressing the men."

At the beginning of the strike, Anton had been made captain of the pickets. "I was fearless," he said, "and I also had enough discretion for the position. My duty was to tell the rank and file of pickets what to do. They were to watch the shop, inform all scabs that a strike was on, and show them what their obligations to the community were. They must persuade these men by peaceful means, if possible; but they must be persuaded: they must see the light. Often the only way to make them see the light was to make them fear something more than they feared going hungry."

The strike in Anton's shop lasted only a few weeks: the men lost, and when Anton appeared for work, he was politely informed there was no place for him; but when wanted he would receive a postal card. He knew he would never be wanted.

It was after the strike in the shops remaining out had lasted several months that the employers had called for the meeting with the men's committee. Petersen, Anton's employer, was there, and a Mr. Von Platten, who said the first word for the employers.

"We feel," he began, "that as the strike has lasted so long, and as some of the shops have accepted the nine-hour day, our shop cannot grant the eight-hour day; if we did, we could not compete in the trade. We should have to close our mills and get out of town."

"I got up," said Anton, "and made for Mr. Petersen. I remarked that I, as one member of the committee, felt no confidence in the committee of the employers; that I questioned their sincerity, and their honesty. At this one of the bosses, a good man named Lockwood, grew very indignant, and said his honesty had never before been questioned. I was waiting for a little incident like that, so I apologized and said that perhaps my remark was too sweeping; that I, as a matter of fact, referred to one member of the committee, Mr. Petersen. I then balled him out. I told the committee that I had been in his employ before the strike; that he had had a meeting with the men and had told them he was satisfied with the attitude of the organization, and would keep his agreement, but that he now wanted to break it. Mr. McKinley had been elected, and Bryan defeated, and now there was no reason why Mr. Petersen should not keep the old agreement, according to his own statement. While I was speaking Mr. Petersen was nervous and excited, and the other bosses were tickled. Petersen said I had misunderstood and misconstrued him. I said: 'Mr. Petersen, it is too late now. Your men voted for Mr. McKinley. If they had known how you would act, they wouldn't have voted as they did.' This incident gave me great satisfaction.

"The result was that our committee made out a report recommending a nine-hour day. This I refused to sign, as I had been so instructed by my local. Yet I felt the position of the bosses was peculiar, because of the nine-hour day being already accepted by some of the shops. When, in the meeting of the

Union, they applauded my opposition to the nine-hour day, I got up and foolishly said that, while I voted in accordance with their instructions, I wanted no applause, for I thought they had better accept the inevitable and consent to the nine-hour day. There was a storm of disapproval at that. It was far from popular, and was the beginning of my internal fights in our Union."

The issue was left to a general referendum vote, and the nine-hour day accepted by a small majority; and so the strike was lost to the men. The nine shops which had been lost went back to ten hours, and, as always after a lost strike, the membership of the Unions dwindled and there was pretty general discontent. All the officers who had been in power during the strike were defeated in the next election, except the thin politician, partly because his local was the biggest in the city, and partly because he had trimmed successfully during the fight.

The anarchist organizer had, during the strike, been outspoken against the folly of holding out at this time for an eight-hour day, when the conditions of organization did not warrant it. He was therefore very unpopular. After the men had returned to work, a charge was trumped up against him—that he was short $24 in paying out strike funds. He handled, during the strike, from $2,000 to $5,000 every week. For this man to steal $24 seemed to any one who knew his character an utter impossibility. But the rank and file are extremely suspicious of their leaders. Sometimes they have good reason to be, but they are generally unreasonable, even when right, and in this case they were unreasonably wrong.

A trial board of five was appointed to try this burly, honest and vigorous man. But the board did not have the courage to find either for or against him: they were afraid to acquit him, because of the popular prejudice, and they were too fair to find him guilty. So they recommended that the council should decide. Anton made a vigorous fight against the cowardice of this trial board; and the council re-committed the decision back to the board, which again showed an incapacity to decide. The council then discharged the board and elected another. When the anarchist was summoned before this second board, he did not appear, knowing that the proceedings were out of order. He made as an excuse his being absent from the city on the business of prosecuting three Union men for scabbing. The board tried him, with him and his witnesses absent, and brought in a verdict of guilty. Anton, in the council meeting, fought vigorously against the illegitimacy of these proceedings. The President of the council left his chair to state on the floor his belief in the insufficiency of the evidence on which the conviction rested. In spite of that, this President voted, when it came to the roll-call, in favor of sustaining the decision of the board. Only four or five members of the council had the courage to go in the face of popular feeling and vote against a decision that was unjust and irregular. The power of the crowd is strong enough in the country's politics, but this case would indicate an immediate reference to popular passion in the affairs of the Union that is quite as strong as anything in our general politics.

The defendant appealed from the Woodworkers' Council to the General Council, which reversed the decision and ordered a new trial. A trial board of three, one selected by the Woodworkers' Council, one by the General Council, and the third elected by the two appointed, found the anarchist organizer innocent of the charge, and he was acquitted.

Anton has a great deal of sympathy for the rank and file. He thinks their emotions can be trusted, but not their intelligence. The unscrupulous demagogue or the hypocritical reformer can lead them with ease, if he is willing to observe their unreasoning passions. Here was a splendid man, who had for years labored in their interests, and yet whom they suspected of having stolen twenty-four dollars!

He had, indeed, early in his American career, refused to have anything to do with trades-unionism: he was a fiery Socialist, and always spoke from a soap box or in the shop. But when he gave up Socialism, because of its "intolerance," and became a theoretical anarchist, he started in to work for the Unions, with the "general strike" as his slogan; and knocked fiercely at the ballot and at the efforts of the Socialists to get hold of the Unions and lead them into politics. He made one of the most important speeches against the Social Democratic party: a general attitude that has now become the slogan of the American Federation of Labor, where the Socialists are very unpopular.

This anarchist was a splendid organizer; he organized the first interior finish shop in America, and being in New York when the woodworkers started to organize in Chicago, they sent to New York for him. Three years later, the same Union that sent for him wanted to run him out of town, because they thought this devoted man had misappropriated $24! At an earlier time he had resigned as business agent, because of the hostility of the Germans, whose clannishness he had opposed. Immediately after his resignation the Union lost 2,000 members by a foolish strike. They went out when they were not strong enough. It was, as Anton put it, "a strike of enthusiasm. They struck just because their cause was just—and that's no reason to strike at all."

After that strike, this anarchist organizer made a proposition to return to Chicago and take hold and help the Union to recover its membership, but on the condition that he be placed in a position of absolute autocracy. The organization would not accept that. "I also opposed it," said Anton, "though I admired the man immensely."

"I admired him especially because he was a fire-brand, and yet because of his usefulness and originality was tolerated in the Federation. He never takes the floor till he is ready to fight. I have heard him shout, over and over again, to the President: 'You must do this. You shall do this.' He is an autocrat by nature, but he hates injustice and intolerance. He bluffs the ordinary workingman. The crooked man is afraid of him. Yet he does not expose the politicians if they help the work of organization. That is the main thing. But they fear him because they know he has only one purpose. It may seem queer that an anarchist should be so much of an autocrat. But this man is an individualist, and that is why he is an autocrat and an anarchist. In organizing he would prefer to pay one man $100 a week than ten men $10 a week, if the one man was active. He works for the mass, but he does not believe you can work with the mass. I have not met a strong man in the trades-union movement who would not admit anarchism as an ideal—and yet every strong man is an autocrat.

[131]

"Sometimes I love to see a machine or a man working hard. And I love to see this man talk. When he is speaking he sweats like a Polar bear in mid-summer. He calls his wife 'Mike.' She is an old German woman who cannot speak English. He is very kind to her, gives her money regularly, and won't look at another woman. Yet she feels she is a martyr, because he is away on the road so much, organizing. He consoles her by pointing to his victories: how, after many years' struggle, he always comes out on top. He thinks this ought to satisfy her. He will never forgive you if you step on his corns. He will only talk about trades-union-ism or anarchism. Maggie likes to have a man talk to her, or at least look at her, but he won't. You can generally trust a man like that. No man on earth can get a secret from him. His great object is the movement. He never votes, always says 'damn the rank and file,' but really works for their benefit."

Anton was rapidly losing his interest in Socialism. He was probably influenced a good deal by the general spirit in the Unions which was averse to making the movement a political one, based upon a distrust of politics in general. It is likely, too, that the striking and picturesque figure of this anarchist organizer made a deep impression on him. One of his deepest passions is an abstract love for toleration, and this he seemed to see in theoretical anarchism. His growing experience in the actual affairs of organizations had made him distrust government, and at the same time feel the necessity of it. This tended to give him that balanced, psychological attitude that is never consistent, but usually intelligent, and which he associates practically with philosophical anarchism. He saw that politics was too likely to determine the actions of the leaders and folly that of the rank and file.

"At this time," he said, "I was still a Socialist, but a rather uncertain one. My Socialist friends were surprised because I felt I could not endorse a man purely and simply because he was a Socialist. He must have unionism and manhood and good-fellowship, too. They could not understand my motives for doing things. They thought I ought to look on Socialism as something holy. They were so narrow that I began to question their philosophy. I began to be sceptical about Socialism, just as I had been sceptical about religion and politics. I saw that Socialism, too, was political, and liable to the same narrowness. I championed the anarchist organizer before I knew him, and when I came to meet him, his ideas took a strong hold on me. My attitude for justice hurt me with the Union, for a time. After the fight in the council I found considerable opposition. I invited great disfavor because I was foolish enough to stand for only what I knew to be right, and for a time I lost ambition in that direction. I had assumed that the central organization was capable of greater things, but their treatment of this sincere man sadly disappointed me.

"I saw that politics were more predominant than reason. I saw that the central body was controlled by politics and the rank and file by sentiment and emotion. I had more tolerance for the sentiment than the politics. So I stuck to the man and went to every meeting and was again elected as a delegate. By degrees I came back to my old standing, but I came back a sceptic, not trusting anything, but hoping for everything. One incident that made me so as much as anything was a deal I learned of, proposed by the thin politician to my friend the anarchist. I will not say what it was, but it was a proposal not altogether honorable. The anarchist told him that under no circumstances would he be willing to do anything of that kind; that while he was as much dissatisfied with the damn rank and file as anybody, yet it was the only thing worth working for. The other man felt cheap to have made a proposition which assumed that the anarchist was as corrupt as he. I got wind of the matter, and, as on a former occasion, I went to the thin politician and told him that I could not sit as delegate in a council representing the rank and file unless every delegate knew this story about the chief business agent, in whom the rank and file put its trust. I insisted that he should tell the council, and he promised to do so, but many months passed and he did not do it.

"There came an election of business agents and I was a candidate. I was defeated. I stood purely and simply on the emotional side, thinking at that time that honesty and good-will were all that were necessary to be business agent. The thin politician was re-elected, and I waited patiently for him to make the statement I had required of him.

But he did not do so. So, when the board of business agents reported that they had selected this man as the chief business agent, I got up in the council and protested, and objected to his being chief business agent until he made a statement to the council about a story that had been circulated. You could have heard a pin drop in the council that night.

"He got up and told the facts, partly admitting that he had been guilty of a breach of confidence towards the organization; but he made a kind of threat to me. He said I had used my knowledge of the affair as a knock against him in the election, and that if I undertook any such knock again he would knock me, threatening physical force. I wouldn't stand for the bluff; I got up and said that I had been absolutely fair with him: I had gone to him directly with the story and not to anyone else. If he had heard that I was 'knocking' him, he ought to have come directly to me, and asked if it was true. He then grew angry and said if I did not keep my mouth shut something would happen. I then informed him I was his superior, both mentally and physically. There was no man in the council, I said, who could make me keep my mouth shut by reason of a threat. I branded as a lie the charge that I had circulated stories about him, and challenged him to produce a single witness in evidence of the truth of what he had said."

These experiences tended to disgust Anton with political organizations, and the Socialists, of whom one was the thin politician, seemed to him to be as ready for deals as any one else; not that he so much objected to a deal practically, it was rather a matter of temper and mind with him. He wanted something more admirable and attractive, less small and sordid. He saw that these organizations of workingmen had some of the same drawbacks that obtain in the larger organization of society with which he had come in disagreeable contact as a tramp.

CHAPTER VII.

The Radicals.

IT WAS at this time that Anton came in contact with the Chicago Liberal Society. It was composed of atheists, free-thinkers, "radicals" of all kinds. The word "radical" is a common one in Chicago. In it a great deal of what is most significant to-day of the Middle West of the United States, and of what is most progressively American, is embodied. It is a vague word, implying extreme democracy, implying also an attitude of criticism towards many of the institutions founded on a capitalistic order of society. It is a much more "respectable" word in the Middle West, or at any rate in Chicago, than in the East. Not only in labor circles and in out-and-out of Socialistic and anarchistic groups does one often hear this word used with approval, but also in the university set, in the social settlements, even in business and professional life. The newspapers, to a limited extent reflectors of the people's temper, show in a hundred implicit ways the degree to which the radical ideas of the common people have affected all grades of society.

Wherever there is a lack of cultured training combined with vitality and vigor of feeling and thought, there are likely to be societies half-baked and on one side ridiculous in character — pseudo-scientific, spiritualistic, — based upon a strong but not definitely worked out spiritual life. In Chicago there are innumerable clubs and societies of this kind. Masonic Temple is supposed to be the seat of a hundred religious or emotional, scientific or social faiths. The basis for all these faiths is the labor situation. Most radicals are either working people or else persons who have come in contact with the feelings and ideas evolved by the laboring class, and have come to express them.

The Chicago Liberal Society was a society of this kind. Anton was thoroughly in a frame of mind to enjoy a gathering of this sort —it gave an opportunity for the emotional needs of the workingman to assume an intellectual and scientific shape, no matter how crude and imperfect. In the Unions it was all business or definite struggle of one personality against another; it was good to escape from these inexpressive, serious gatherings and go to hear a lecture or some philosophical aspect of the labor or social situation. Anton, with his keen senses, his keen intelligence and his love for debate, thoroughly enjoys himself in these gatherings. In them there are, of course, many of the "long-haired, anæmic, over-gentle sort. Into these Anton likes to stick pins. He sympathizes with many of their ideas—he feels that through them he and his class are being expressed, and he enjoys thoroughly the more intelligent ones among them, but he sees their limitations. He is keen in the detection of shams, and when he finds himself dealing with a tender imbecile of the "radical" variety he is like a bull in a clover field: his voice becomes loud and his words are rough. Maggie cautions him not to break loose—but she wouldn't love him so much if he didn't!

One of the first of Anton's experiences with the Chicago Liberal Society was a lecture by
* Clarence Darrow. Anton immediately perceived that here was a man voicing many of the sentiments and "protests" that he had

vaguely felt. In another field this tended to have the same influence on his critical faculty as the reading of Tom Paine's *Age of Reason.* Darrow, indeed, is a man wonderfully typical of one aspect of the life of the Middle West to-day—dreamer, practical man, lawyer, politician, friend of labor, friend of women, friend of literature and of experiment! A rich personality, often distrusted, generally inconsistent in all but humanity, too complex to be philosophic, but a gathering point for all the "radical" notions of the time. Significant, indeed, it is of Chicago and of the Middle West, that a man like this can flourish and occupy a position of respectability and practical importance. In some communities he would be merely laughed at; in others he would be forced to become an out-and-out Bohemian. But in Chicago this interesting man is pretty nearly appreciated at his proper value; for, although he is regarded as "dangerous" by the ultra-conservative, and as "crooked" by the pure idealists, and as "immoral" by the inexperienced ladies of blue stocking tendency, he occupies, nevertheless, a position of sufficient respectability to enable him to work and live to the best advantage.

[141]

Interested as Anton was in these gatherings, it did not prevent him from exercising his critical faculty. A little before the lecture which meant so much to him, a member of the local Union of which Anton was the President, died, leaving a widow and six children in absolute destitution. While he was ill, he received $4 a week benefit for thirteen weeks before his death. His widow received $75 for his burial. This was barely enough for that purpose. She asked Anton to assist her in raffling off her husband's tools. In the Union meeting he, as chairman, called for a voluntary committee for this work. The result was $87.75 for tools worth about ten dollars. Then Anton went to the shop where the deceased had worked, to try to get some money from the employer. He himself had worked there soon after his arrival in Chicago and had been discharged, so it was with some pride that he introduced himself as the President of Union 67. The employer recognized him and was at first inclined not to give him an audience.

"But I knew he was a Jew," said Anton, "and I immediately branched into philosophy and put in my opposition to Christianity. So he wrote me out a check for $25 for the widow. I went to her with this money and also the raffle money; found her in three little miserable rooms in Halsted street. The six children were lying and walking all over the floor, and the baby was in a chair alongside the tub where the mother was washing. She cried when I gave her the money.

"While I had been engaged in selling the tickets, I appeared at the Masonic Temple one night where a lot of the bug-house cranks and free-thinkers had got together to expose their irreligious matters in a religious way. [Anton himself often talks in a way that makes him subject to his own satire.] It was the Chicago Liberal Society, now dead, and was composed of men and women of Lofty Ideals. I felt sure that these people would assist me in such a worthy cause. The Church would not, though the widow had been a member for years. She had neglected to send the children to Sunday School regularly, for the Sunday School does not want children who have not good clothes. So poverty kept the children home and when the father died, the Church would do nothing.

"The Free-thinkers, however, I thought

would do something. I had been a member of the Society for some time, had taken part in the discussions and was known. I spoke to the President and the trustees and asked them to let me have the floor to explain the circumstances and ask the audience to contribute. That was a more effective way than to ask each one separately and would save time. The President ran a book store, and that was really the reason why he was a member of the Liberal Society. He wanted them to buy his books liberally. That was the only liberal thing about him. So he told me that he would like to accommodate me, but there were other things more important. They would not let me have the floor and I was horribly disappointed. My spirit of protest became aroused again, and I wondered if there was anything right anywhere. I went around among the members and sold about twenty tickets. I waited for an opportunity to make an exposé of their hypocrisy. They made a display of being opposed to the Church because it enslaved humanity, but when it came for them to show any superior feeling, they failed to make good."

Anton perceived another instance of human

weakness and self-interest in this matter of the tools. An affectionate Irishman won the raffle. He was a common laborer, not a member of the Union. Finding that most of the important tools were missing, he thought he had been "done" and went indignantly to Anton, and scolded him: said he had thought better of the Unions than that. Anton went to the woman, who cried, and said that a member of the Union Committee had picked out the best tools and intended to keep them. They were fortunately still in the house, and Anton, after telling the woman not to let the tools be taken away, went to the man who had tried to steal them. This man was always suspicious of the honesty of the Union officials.

"I balled him out," said Anton, "and told him I would prefer charges against him in the Union, if he took the tools. Then I went to the Irishman from whom I wished to hide the guilt of our member, in order not to disturb the man's sympathetic inclinations toward Unions. I told him a mistake had been made and he would find the tools at the woman's house. He was tickled to death. I did not expose our member in the Union meeting on account of his wife and children. He was an awful ugly fellow, a brutal shaker-hand. He was so meek morally that he imagined he was strong and tried to roast everybody else on the score of dishonesty."

The lecture of Mr. Darrow's which made so great an impression upon Anton was on "Crimes and Criminals" and seemed to the workingman to be much nearer the truth than the current ideas on the subject. After his lecture, Mr. Darrow announced the coming
* of Prince Kropotkin, who was to lecture before the Society; he was to speak on Modern anarchism.

"I was still a Socialist," said Anton, "but a wavering one. I had a strong appetite to understand anarchism, and I was eager to hear this lecture. But yet I could not resist the opportunity to protest. Mr. Darrow requested that a certain woman present should sell tickets for the event, and the chairman put the request before the Society. I arose and forced recognition from the chair and said:

"Mr. Chairman, while I have no objection to granting the request of Mr. Darrow for a purpose of this kind, yet I feel inclined to protest against this manner of granting special privileges. When I requested the privilege, a few weeks ago, of saying a few words to the Society, to induce them to help a poor woman, the floor was denied me. I feel certain that my mission was far more urgent and necessary than the intellectual luxury of hearing Mr. Kropotkin; although it would not have brought as much honor to the Society. I stand here and say that I think our President is as much a hypocrite now as ever.'

"Then came the gavel, but I continued, and said: ' I'll be glad to hear Kropotkin, and, although I desire to expose the hypocrisy of the President of the Liberal Society, I am still capable of being unselfish enough to hope that he will remain President as long as he is engaged in the book business.'

"He blushed. I was so unruly and crude and unrefined that it put him in a difficult and peculiar position. After the meeting I went to the secretary and told him to take my name off the list of membership. I told him I was opposed to the Church because of its hypocrisy; and that if I belonged to a Society that had a hypocrite for its President, I too would be a hypocrite. A man is a man, after all, whether he is the President of the United States or only the President of the Liberal Society. They are very much alike. The Society is dead now; it broke up because of being split into factions and everybody seeking places of honor, money and graft. The Society was like the Unions, the Churches, and everything else. It is the same old story."

Anton, however, was very anxious to hear Kropotkin, and to have the workingmen hear him, so, one evening coming from work, he went to Mr. Darrow's office and asked him for tickets. Mr. Darrow was interested, gave him twenty tickets and asked him to try to get the workingmen to go to the lecture. "Sell them if you can," he said; "if not, give them away. No need to make an account." Anton succeeded in interesting several Union men, and when the night of the address came, the laboring world was well represented. Anton's account of the lecture is as follows:

"Mr. Darrow introduced Kropotkin with the remark: 'In Russia they exile their prophets. In this country we hang them. [This was in reference to the execution of the Chicago anarchists.] He then gave an account of Kropotkin's life, said he had been offered the world if he would suppress his inclination to champion the masses against the classes. He was of the aristocracy of Russia and could have been prominent in the government, but he preferred to cast all this aside.

"Then the old gentleman spoke, to a packed house, in every chair there being a copy of *Free Society*. I was terribly interested, for he dwelt on something new and very sympathetic. He told of the waste of energy there is in labor, more wasted than profitable labor. He emphasized strongly the great waste of labor in making the implements of war, which is government murder. He spoke of the principles of anarchism and socialism and sketched the history of the struggles of the working classes in Europe. He stated that the American workingman ought to be thankful for the opportunities here in land and timber and natural resources; that the soil seemed to contain all that was necessary for life, vigor and happiness. He thought that if the workingmen in America were as energetic in efforts for freedom as they were in Europe, they ought here to be more successful. If the American workingmen failed, they themselves would be largely responsible for it, he said. He made a strong point against the British government because of the war with the Boers. Here the applause was great, and Mrs. Potter Palmer and other conservative people who were there clapped their hands. But right after the applause, he made a similar remark about Uncle Sam's treatment of the Philippines. The audience continued to applaud, but with not so much vigor. He then said it was very easy for Americans to criticize the government of Russia; but when you attack the government in the land in which you live, you are then regarded as an anarchist. This speech made a deep impression upon me, and I became far more interested in anarchism.

"I took home with me a copy of *Free Society*. I was interested in it, and decided to investigate. Kropotkin's lecture had been so great a contrast to what I had heard of anarchism. I thought anarchists were all red-handed devils. I had the common conception. I saw advertized in *Free Society* Jean Grave's *Moribund Society and Anarchy* and I went to the editor of *Free Society,* Mr. Isaak, and bought copies of this book to distribute among my friends. I went by the house several times before I got courage to go in. I thought there might be bombs in the house.   Finally I went in and met Isaak's son, who is hard of hearing.   I imagined he might only be pretending deafness, and that he was dangerous.   He invited me to go up-stairs to see his father, but I was suspicious, and thought it was a trap.   So I bought twelve copies and went away.   I found out afterwards that they were much interested that a workingman should come voluntarily.

"I took these twelve copies of Grave's book to the Union meeting and distributed them. They began to call me an anarchist.   I was rather proud of it.   At that time I was President of my local and had to sign a document favoring the building of battleships by Union men.   This act was repulsive to me even then, even from a Socialist standpoint.

"A member of the Machinists' Union, an anarchist, asked me why I signed it, if I didn't want to.   I couldn't tell him.   I couldn't explain my position to him, any more than I can explain life.   I was President of the Union and it was important to extend Union principles everywhere.   Life is so made that nothing can be consistent it seems.

"Yet if we never try to be consistent, we are

certainly no better than grafters; not that grafters are necessarily very bad."

Anton now began to attend the meetings of the Philosophical Society. At first he was almost afraid to say "good evening" to them, as he thought they represented an astonishing amount of learning and intelligence. But, as he gradually took part in the debates, he found it a good school. It helped him in the Union meetings, to make his points. In these philosophical meetings, he felt he was learning something; while in the meetings of his Union the main considerations were practical and warlike—measures by one class against another. Maggie always insisted that Anton went to the Unions to have a good time. This is only partly true; I have often seen him in a position where he gave up the opportunity of going to the Masonic Temple and exciting himself temperamentally and intellectually in debate, for the calmer, more business-like and generally quite unexciting Union meeting, which he regarded as his duty.

A few months after Kropotkin's talk, Anton became what he calls "an anarchist." With him, this faith is an attitude of mind, the expression of general class unrest, rather than definite affiliation with a group or any definite philosophical tenets. In this respect, Anton is typical of a great many of the more intelligent and active laboring men. The extent to which emotional anarchism obtains among the mechanics is very great. Many men who occupy a conservative and important position in the Unions are at heart what they call anarchists. One of the high officers of the American Federation of Labor took occasion, during the meetings of an International Labor Congress, which took place some time after the period of this narrative, to reprove Anton because of the boldness with which he gave expression to anarchistic principles on the floor of the meeting. "We are all anarchists," he said, "but what's the use of shouting about it?"

A few nights following the death of President McKinley, Anton was attending a meeting of the Union. After the meeting, Anton and several other officers went, as usual, to a saloon. They talked about the assassination, Anton, an enthusiastic Socialist, and a sceptical Scotchman who never committed himself. While they were talking and drinking, a stranger who seemed to be under the influence of liquor came up to them and asked a pointed question as to what they felt about the assassination. The Socialist, who was a Swede, said: "Well, I don't know. I sorry he dead, but I sorry he capitalist." The stranger then asked the Scotchman, who replied: "My God, I was just going to ask you. What do you think?" Then the stranger put the question to Anton, who "was rather sceptical as to the justification of his butting in." But he replied: "I would have as much and perhaps more sympathy for my neighbor if he were killed than for McKinley. I should feel sorry for his wife and children."

This reply did not suit the stranger, and he cried out that Anton was an anarchist. There was great confusion in the saloon and it looked like a fight, until the Scotchman gave the stranger the signal of the Masonic Order, and then it was all right.

Anton had become sufficiently known as an anarchist to make Maggie nervous about what might happen to him, in the excitement following McKinley's assassination. So she burnt up the copies of *Free Society,* Jean Grave's book and some Socialistic papers; fearful that her husband might be arrested.

Anton "was disappointed," as he expressed
it, at this, for at that time, in the first flush of
his anarchistic faith, he would have welcomed
arrest. At a later time—now—he is much
cooler about all theories. Now that he is
more of an anarchist, in the sense of being
more of a sceptic, he is far less of a propagandist. He is now as sceptical about anarchism as he is about any other system of
running the world's affairs successfully.

Even at that time he felt the logical difficulties of his faith; for with him it was a
faith, just as his early religion had been. "I
had difficulties," he said, "in calling myself
an anarchist and yet not being able to justify
my position theoretically. I saw that system
and force were necessary: that we had to employ both these things in the Union, and yet
it did not affect my feeling. Anarchism cap-
tured my fancy for it seemed the strongest
protest against economic and social injustice.
It seemed more humane and sympathetic than
anything else."

Vague as his anarchism was, it seemed to
get him into trouble; first with his family;
then with the law, indirectly.

"I was lacking in tact," he explained, " told

my position to a young man from Clinton who was visiting in Chicago. When he went back to Clinton he told everybody I was an anarchist. My brother wrote me I would soon be a victim of the hangman's noose, and he appealed pathetically to me to change my ways. He had no effect on me, whatever, for I felt I was far above him in every way. Mother, too, wrote me. She seemed to think that I would be in the pen and that this was the logical result of a hobo's career. I was very sorry that mother thought I was an anarchist, according to her conception of the word. As for my brother I wrote him and showed him where he got off at. I gave him several quotations from the Bible and told him that if he carried these out he would be an anarchist, too. They felt sorry for Maggie, had it all fixed that I would die a dog's death, but it has as yet failed to materialize.

"At this time, I was always out with my neighbors. I was always discussing unionism, socialism and anarchism. I used to bore people terribly and they didn't like me. I was brutally frank, and the police, at this time, as before and since, were disagreeable to me. One afternoon I saw a large crowd at 59th

Street and Center Avenue and I discovered three policemen roughly arresting two young fellows. One of them was intoxicated and used rough language, but this did not seem to me sufficient cause for arrest. I said sarcastically, ' It seems to require three policemen to arrest two kids.' One of the policemen, who was drunk, grabbed me and said: 'Come along and I'll teach you a lesson.' So they put me in a patrol wagon and wouldn't let me notify the wife, and took me to the police station. The crowd held an indignation meeting but it came to nothing through lack of organization. I noticed, when in the police station, that one of the young fellows, who was the son of a State Senator, received a great deal of consideration. He was not booked, but was sent home. I was booked for disorderly conduct, and I and the other fellow were put in jail.

"I finally got telephonic connection with a Union saloon-keeper and asked him to get me out. In the meantime, my wife was wondering what had become of me. About 11 o'clock at night a policeman rapped with his club at her door and hollered: 'I'm a policeman come to tell you your husband is in jail

and wants you to come and get him out.'
This was typical of the delicacy of the ordinary cop. It was a shock to her, as she
thought I had been arrested as an ordinary
anarchist. She went to the saloon-keeper and
then they came to the jail and bailed me out.

"I got busy, and found the man I had made
the remark to. He promised to appear as a
witness in the trial on Monday. But the policeman was busy, too. He laid the law down
to this Swede, my witness, and told him not
to come down to testify. Before the trial
came up on Monday I met the young fellow
who had been arrested with me. He had a
card addressed to a detective in that precinct.
The card came from a rich coal-dealer and
said: 'This young man, Mr. ——, is all
right.' The detective told him what to do,
to plead guilty and look sorry. I, however,
would not plead guilty. I was too indignant. When the case was called the policeman made a mild charge against the young
fellow, and he was discharged. When I
came up they handed me a jury-waiver. I
started to read it aloud. That was awful.
The young fellow and the detective pulled my
coat, to no avail. I wouldn't keep quiet. I

signed it, when I had read it. Then the policeman made his charge, stated he had told me to go home three times, and had then arrested me. I pleaded not guilty. The prosecuting attorney asked me if I meant to insinuate that the officer of the law was telling a falsehood. I said, no, that was not my intention, but I had noticed, I said, that on that night the officer of the law was not sober, and his memory therefore might not be entirely accurate. What I said was received with scorn, but the Judge said, as I didn't look like a tough, he would only fine me $5 and costs. I asked him if I was fined because I wasn't tough. He said if I didn't keep still he would fine me $25. They took me away and put me in the Bull Pen. I was indignant and the spirit of protest arose in me. I got to the telephone, and reached the Union Headquarters. The business agent came and paid the fine.

"I went to the saloon-keeper who had bailed me out, and told him the story. He was indignant and said he would fix the policeman, who was under obligations to him. When I applied for work, I was discharged for not appearing on Monday. I had lost my job, had paid a fine, and Maggie was discouraged, all because I had said a sarcastic thing to a policeman. Suppose some capitalist had said the same thing to a cop. Do you think the cop would have arrested him? Not on your life! But a workingman is different. Maggie roasted me for fair; said I could never hold a job because I was too blunt and aggressive. She also said some hot things about the copper.

"The next time the policeman went to the saloon, my friend raised Cain with him; told him I was the President of the Union and a thoroughly honest working man. The policeman said I was to blame for insulting the integrity of the Court by making a defense. But he was sorry, for the saloon-keeper had influence, and that night I met the policeman in the saloon. He said he was very sorry and would get me my job back. He took me to my old employer and told him a lie and the employer said we would have to see the foreman who had discharged me. The foreman 'had it in' for me. He had formerly been a member of the Union and was a great grumbler. When he got the position as foreman he withdrew from the Union. When he asked to have his resignation accepted, I had roasted the living life out of him. I said I was sorry that a man of such independence of character, such an unsuccessful grumbler, should take the position of foreman and therefore lose an opportunity of using his wonderful talents against the employers; he couldn't grumble any more without losing his job: what a hardship!

"So when I came to work under him he took the first opportunity to discharge me. But now, thinking the employer, the policeman and the saloon-keeper (three great powers) were for me, he re-instated me in my position. Then I went to the foreman and called him every name in my vocabulary, and quit. I needed a job, but the spirit of revenge was strong in me and at that time I was all revolt. I knew Maggie would roast me, but I could not help it.

"The policeman was now very friendly and said he would try to get my money back. He called on Maggie and apologized. But the wife gave him her opinion of him, and pictured to him the hardship he had caused. He had a wife and three children and he started to cry like a child. While the wife was satisfied with that, I was not, and started to propagate some of my ideas on him. So I asked him if a police officer ought to make any distinction between one man and another, except the criminal and the law-abiding classes. I asked him if he didn't think that I and other law-abiding citizens were unsafe on the streets as long as there were two or three policemen who did not know them. He admitted that if he had known me, he wouldn't have done it. He grasped at my meaning for he said: 'The socialists are all right, but there are not enough of them.' He arranged to meet me the next night at the saloon and take me to where I could get my money back. We met there a Swedish saloon-keeper, political boss of the Swedes in that neighborhood, who immediately took advantage of the situation in order to get my political support.

"'Why didn't you tell me about 'Anton,' he said to the policeman. 'I have known about him for years, though I have not had the pleasure of meeting him.' I had been his invisible friend, so to speak. The policeman, at the Swede's suggestion, took me to the house of a man who was the boss of the

County Central Committee. When I met him I recognized him as a former President of the Building Trades Council during the lockout of 1900. He was a delegate to the Chicago Federation of Labor and knew me— knew me not so much as a woodworker as in my character of Socialist and a man who knew something of the inside working of the political machine. He was afraid of me, and said if the fine had not been recorded, the action could be rescinded by the same Judge. He was very guarded and made arrangements to meet me at the saloon. There he treated me, but said he could do nothing. He sprung 25 tickets on me for the Carter Harrison Masquerade Ball, at 50 cents apiece. The Union I belonged to was largely composed of Scandinavians, and this Swede boss thought I might be of use, so he gave me the tickets. He said he thought Unions could do more good if they were in politics. I was to get a job as garbage box inspector at $4 a day, if I worked for the cause. I took the tickets to the next meeting of the Union. I told the story before a crowded meeting, told them the politician's game, and tore up the twenty-five tickets, that went around the ward for four or five months. The policeman thought I was unwise, but whenever he met me, he insisted on shaking hands, and on buying me a drink."

"That winter I became a candidate for business agent. I was all emotion and enthusiasm. I had a certain amount of courage and a little scattering of information. I still thought all that was needed was to be honest and sincere. If I had known more about the movement I would have known I had as much chance to be elected as the Lord himself."

All these events strengthened Anton in his emotional anarchism, but also tended to make him see that, when it came to action, it was necessary to make use of the machinery there was at hand. But even then, when he was President of the Union, had a wife and three children and had had much experience with men, he still permitted himself the luxury of losing his job in order to satisfy his temperament. It was about this time that he accepted the offer of a job in Oak Park, rented a house in the neighborhood, and when he went to work, was told another man had been hired in his place.

"I was taken aback and nonplussed at

first, but recovered myself, took my overcoat off, and told the employer I thought he was a —— —— and I could lick him. He said he would give me $5 extra for my inconvenience. I told him to go to ——, packed my tools, and asked him how he would like to be in my position. I said if I didn't have more sympathy for my wife and children than he had for the men, I would blow his brains out. I called his attention to the fact that he went to Church every Sunday, was opposed to lying and yet would place a man in a position where he was forced to lie or go hungry. When I should apply for work in another factory the first question asked me would be, 'Where did you work last?' If I should act according to the Sunday School I would have to tell the truth. The next question would be, 'Why did you leave?' I, being influenced by your religion, would have to say, 'fired for incompetency.' While most of you employers like a truthful man, nearly all of you would let him go hungry under these circumstances.' I made an impression on his daughter, who was in the room. She was a pretty girl and when she looked at me she blushed.

"He finally gave me a letter of reference, which I used against him. I asked him, in front of the girl, if that was his signature. He said yes. I said, 'that signature means the calling of a strike in your own shop. I will present it to the Woodworkers' Council and demand a strike, as you have discharged me in favor of a non-Union man, without other cause, as this letter proves.' He flushed and charged me with ingratitude. He had the nerve to do that, but I went to the next meeting of the Union, told my story and requested them to instruct their delegates to the Council to authorize the walking delegate to demand from the employer a re-imbursement or re-instatement, and I put my bill at $25. It was carried, and taken to the Council, which voted unanimously in favor of it. The next Monday I and the business agent went to Oak Park, and interviewed the employer. The business agent pointed out that the agreement provided for no discharge without cause, and that the employer's letter showed there was no cause. The employer refused to re-imburse me, and then the business agent said he would call the strike. Whereupon the employer shelled out the money and I accepted it."

CHAPTER VIII.

Organizer.

THIS temperamental play on Anton's part meant no work for several weeks, and often nothing in the house to eat. But he was a strong, young fellow, and his wife a strong, young woman, and very competent, and the children were as robust and strong as young oaks, and they all liked to buck the world. And the feeling of solidarity is so great in the Trades-union World, that they knew they had the sympathy and if need be the material aid of thousands behind them. Then, both Anton and Maggie liked so much to talk and talk to one another, that every event, untoward or favorable, gave them food for expressed thought. They are remarkably frank and honest to one another—think aloud. "I could not live with Maggie," said Anton, "if in the long run I could not tell her everything that ever happened to me." And Maggie, for her part, said, "I could not live with Anton if he were like the men they call good husbands, if he always staid home at night, and did not need to work and live and have pleasure among many men and women; when he is home, there is always something interesting to talk about. He is so full of life, always something doing. It is good to live with him."

So the idle time passed without too much hardship, and Anton's next job was an interesting one. One day he saw an advertisement for a "sticker-hand" in West Chicago, which was at that time "a hot-bed for scabs."

There was not a Union shop in the town. Maggie at first objected. She saw that in this "scab" town Anton would agitate and probably get into trouble. So, previous to taking the job, he had a talk with the foreman. He explained that he was a Union man, and that while he was willing to do his duty during work hours, he insisted, after the whistle blew, on talking to his fellow men, in the way he thought was right. The foreman approved of Anton's position. He was in favor of Unions himself, though he did not dare to tell the men so. He liked Anton, and offered him $3 a day, the largest wages he had yet received.

So he moved his family to West Chicago, and began his first important work as an organizer, in a town that knew no union principles and had no Union shop, in any trade.

"An organizer," said Anton, "must understand human nature; and particularly the limitations of human nature. He must be an expert in the art of getting men together without their suspecting why. He must overcome the Idea of 'I-will-if-you-will.' He must be a good speaker, a good fellow and have unlimited patience. He must speak clearly and to the point and inoffensively."

During work and after work and in the evening, Anton talked Unionism to the men in this non-Union shop. He had not been there two months before he began to make an impression.

"I made such good headway," he said, "that I received the earnest opposition of the German Lutheran preacher. One of the firm in my shop was a director in the Church and a large contributor. When he and the preacher saw what my views were and that I was agitating for the Union, they quietly told such of the men as were Church members to be shy of me."

Anton's first convert was the young fellow who worked as his helper. He had been in that shop seven years and then was not a mechanic. The man who had had Anton's place had taught this young fellow as little as possible; and the boy felt it. Anton, however, showed him every thing about the trade he could; but while he taught him the business, he also taught him Unionism and Socialism. "I could not go as far as anarchism with a young fellow like that," he said.

The German Lutheran preacher, however, had fewer scruples than Anton, for, perceiving that this young man was being influenced by the agitator, he gave the young fellow a book "The Greatest Enemy of God Is The Labor Movement." This book was written right after the Haymarket Riots, and was only one of a number of books and pamphlets which represented the Labor Movement as the Arch-enemy of Mankind. The boy immediately took the book to Anton, who read it and "showed the kid the inconsistencies and the abundant fallacies it contained, and gave him other antidotes."

In the meantime, Anton had been working systematically with the other men in the shop. "I got them all to agree with me, individually. Then I got up a discussion at the noon-hour and no one opposed my arguments; for if they had, I could have exposed them, as they had agreed with me individually. After about three months, I called a meeting at my house, but did not tell them why I wanted them. Nine of them came that night. I opened a case of beer and told them my mission. 'There is no use hiding the thing any longer. There is nothing to be ashamed of. I have talked to every one of you and you all agree in the necessity of a Union. All sign your names and give me a dollar.'

"They were speechless, but after talking it over for an hour, and Maggie bearing her share in the talk nobly, one of them finally signed, and then the others did. I immediately sent to Chicago for a charter; so that the Minister would have no show. I made all arrangements for a meeting on Sunday, and in the meantime got the signatures of the other nine men in the shop—there were eighteen in all. I went to the Mayor and asked him to let us have the City Hall for a meet-

ing. I jollied up the Justice of the Peace who
wanted money and needed to make friends
with everybody. He helped me with the
Mayor, but his Honor said the council would
have to act on it. I went to the Postmaster,
who was a politician, who promised to get
us Oddfellows' Hall, and we made arrangements for Monday night.

"When I went to the shop Monday morning I found the Preacher had been at work.
He had called a meeting of the Church
directors and trustees for that night. Three
of my men were trustees in the Church and
in this way he intended to prevent them attending our meeting. They came to me, and
I told them we would put off our meeting
till Tuesday night; I encouraged them and
told them the Preacher would not oppose us
after we were successful; that is the way of
the Church. We had our meeting and I was
elected President and a skunk named Jones
Secretary. Dues were placed at 50 cents a
month.

"This was the first Union ever formed in
this town, and the news spread like wild-fire.
The Secretary wanted the back-room of a saloon for our regular meeting place, but I was

opposed to this; it was not dignified enough. So we hired a nice place at $2 a meeting. Tom Kidd, a big man in our International Union, wrote and congratulated me on forming the Union, and asked me what my expenses for organizing were. I was tickled to death to get this endorsement, and wrote him that my bill was nothing, but if he were so disposed, he could send us two Union-made gavels, of black ebony, one of which I wanted to give to the Oddfellows for lending us their hall and one to the Brotherhood of railroad trainmen, whose good-will we desired. The railroad men were indifferent, but the Oddfellows let me make a speech of presentation, in which I explained the purposes of Unionism."

The effects of organization were almost immediate. It was a ten-hour day shop, but as there were no lights, it had been the custom to work only nine hours in the winter time. A few days after the Union was formed the employers announced a uniform nine-hour day. The men had made no demands, but they already occupied a position of greater prestige. Anton's next step was to get the men to appoint an agreement committee.

His difficuties in teaching the men to act for themselves are thus described by him:

"In the meeting I expected some one to make the motion to appoint the agreement committee. We had talked it all over beforehand. Not a single man took the floor or moved in that direction. I did not feel quite justified in stating the thing from the chair, and when no further business came up, I adjourned the meeting. Immediately everybody wanted to know why the committee had not been appointed. I replied that no one had made the motion. One was afraid of the other and wanted me to bear the burden of responsibility in case of the bosses' discrimination against them. I told them they would have to call a special meeting, as otherwise it would be too late to lay our demands before the employers at the time we had expected. This they did, in the same hall, on the same night. When this meeting was reconvened I pointed out the difficulties in the way of wage workers bettering their conditions, and showed them that their own actions had demonstrated that they were not as free as some of the politicians told them they were. The fact that they feared losing their job was,

I said, a compliment neither to them nor to their employer, as their only crime was to act for a shorter work day. I suggested that some one make a motion to appoint the committee, not because I feared to take the responsibility of doing so, but so that we could be sure it was the unanimous choice of the meeting. That was done, and when they came to nominate their committee, it was a foregone conclusion that I should be chairman. The Secretary of the Union was a great dollar and cent man. He thought more of a dollar than of human life. He emphatically declined to serve on the committee, for a reason that I afterwards discovered. I pointed out to him that he could not constitutionally decline. He appealed and I refused to recognize his appeal, on parliamentary grounds; informed him he could not appeal from the Constitution. He was elected by one vote, and had to serve on the committee, much to his disgust."

The men wanted Anton to "break the ice" in the demand they were about to make—namely that the nine-hour day with the same wages as obtained in the ten-hour day should be adopted. One day, after he had eaten his lunch, Anton went to see the employer, leaving the men "on eggs" in the shop. He presented his credentials, "sat on a chair without an invitation," and said that though the boys had formed a Union, it was not a sign of discontent with their employers; that he thought organization would be for the benefit of both employer and employee. The employer replied that he had no objection to Unions as a principle: he realized, he said, that there ought to be a shorter day, but he pointed out the injury done by strikes, and "pictured the gloomy side in general." Anton replied that while it was true that strikes often did harm, the employers were frequently responsible for them; that this Union was organized to strike only in the last resort and consequently a meeting with the employer was desired by the committee. To this the employer readily consented.

At the meeting the demand of the committee for a nine-hour day with the same wages they had received under the ten-hour day was readily granted by the employers, but they thought that the few men who were paid as high as 30 cents an hour under the ten-hour day, should receive 33 cents instead of 33 1-3

cents an hour under the new arrangement, and
that the 1-3 cent an hour should be added to
the wages of the men who were paid the least.
Anton objected, on the ground that in that
case it was really the more highly paid men
who were paying the others, rather than the
employers. Jones, the man who had objected
to serve on the committee, sided with the employers, and said this proposition ought to be
laid before the Union. This was done, but
in the meantime Anton discovered that Jones
was getting higher wages than was known to
the Union and his objection to serve on the
committee and his sympathy with the employers was thus explained. The men voted to
accept no reduction of wages in any case; and
then the employers maintained that if they increased the scale of wages all around they
would be paying more wages than the shops
in Chicago, on account of the expense of haul-
ing the material.

Anton determined to investigate and see if
this contention was true. But Jones again opposed him and this time Anton lost his temper
and said that if Jones let it leak out that Anton was making this investigation he would
use physical force, that it was the only thing

to do with such a selfish coward. He then went to Chicago, and ascertained that the West Chicago shop was paying less rather than more than the other shops. He had the figures exactly and with these he was soon able to get what he wanted from his employer. It was a complete victory for the men.

The general effect of this victory was marked. There came to the town a general demand for Union made goods. When Anton first went to West Chicago there were no Union made cigars in the place. After the Woodworkers Union was organized, every tobacco store had Union made cigars. Anton was a great man in this city of 2,000. The men were grateful to him for the extra hour of leisure in which they could till their gardens or develop their social natures.

For example, there was an old German common laborer, who got $1.40 a day. He was very religious, and when Anton began his activity, was much opposed to him.

"He was a good old fellow," said Anton, "but he thought I was lost to Paradise. He was afflicted with rheumatism and as his work was to carry large planks I had to help him. I had charge of the lumber and on rainy days,

[178]

when his leg pained him, I arranged for him to work inside. He was very economical. For lunch he had a couple of crusts, a soup bone, or a piece of bologna; and a cup of coffee. Whatever crumbs were left he would wrap up in the same paper and take to his chickens. He thought I was wasteful because I did not save all my bread, so I used to give him my crumbs, to take home to his chickens. After I had succeeded in organizing, the old gent could go home an hour earlier to his chickens. He saw that I was responsible for the change, and began to think well of me. Then I told him how the minister of his church had opposed the forming of the Union. He was dumbfounded at that, and sorry, but told me with tears in his eyes that I was all right and no matter what the minister said the result showed for itself. My object in calling his attention to the act of the minister was to secure his influence in strengthening the unionism of his two nephews, who were not sufficiently in doubt of the infallibility of the Bible and who therefore showed signs of luke-warmness to our organization.

"One of these nephews had been injured

while working for the N. W. R. R. company so that he was 'laid up for ten weeks and his efficiency lost for life. The minister made the settlement between him and the company —$200 when it ought to have been $5,000. After paying his own doctor's bill he was $90 in debt at the end, and unable to get a job. This is what the minister of God did for him. I showed up to the old uncle the hypocrisy of ministers and the greed of corporations when I heard of this injustice. I also went to Chicago and consulted Mr. Darrow, and asked if the matter could not be re-opened. He said the claim was outlawed, but he made use of the case in his articles in *The American* on the injustice of the great corporations and their puppets the lawyers. I was a great admirer of these articles: they were so sarcastic: he always took a dig at the lawyers, although he was a lawyer himself."

In the fall, following the victory of Anton's Union, there was a State election for governor, and also a village election, and the politicians started after the Labor vote. The man who ran the railroad station lunch counter was an alderman.

"One day," said Anton, "this man came to

the factory in a buggy with a saloon-keeper who was also a deputy-sheriff and the prince of gamblers of West Chicago, and cunning to obtain the dollar. They sent in a box of cigars to the foreman and asked him to pass them around to the men, with their compliments. I was opposed to politicians of that kind, and I also noticed that there was no Union label on the cigar-box. I went to the boys, who each had received a cigar. Their minds had been sufficiently agitated against non-Union goods and also against the cheapness of the politicians. I pointed out to them the fact that their intelligence had been underestimated, and each man took his cigar and nailed it on the wall.

"That went like wild-fire all over the town. It was their own idea, that's the beauty of it. Their political opponents made good use of this story. The next day the candidate for Mayor came to the factory with Union made cigars, and boasted of it. When I told him we were opposed to politicians, he said he gave the cigars not to get votes but just to meet the boys. The following Saturday, just before election, the saloon-keeper came around, to get our good-will in favor of his candidate for Mayor; told us how kind the man was and how much he had done for the laboring class. I told him I was not convinced that this man was friendly to the working men, but that if he could prove it, I would acknowledge it. So I and three of the boys met the alderman in the gambler's saloon. Mr. Alderman was half-drunk, bought drinks and cigars and started to apologize for his blunder in the matter of the Union cigars. He thought I was 'it' and that he had to convince me. When he was through with his talk I said it was difficult to believe that a man had such an awful strong feeling towards the workers and so seldom showed it, and when he did show it, did it just before election. I asked him if he did not think the Unions had done much towards raising the standard of living for the workingmen, and in abolishing the sweat-shop, etc. He answered, 'most assuredly, of course, most undoubtedly,' and put about fourteen emphases on it. The sheriff was on to my game, but he could not butt in. Then I asked the candidate if he did not think Union labor represented the certainty of greater cleanliness in the material than non-Union. This he admitted frankly and with tremendous drunken emphasis.

" 'Then,' said I, 'if you really sympathize with the cause, why is it that you didn't assist the Workers by purchasing Union made cigars?'

"He thought I had reference to the particular cigars that were nailed on the wall, and started to apologize again, but I interrupted him and said that I was willing to admit it was only a mistake provided he could take us to his lunch counter and show us one box out of the twenty-four that bore the Union label.

He realized partly that I had him, but he was so drunk that he took us to the lunch counter. Sure enough he did not have a single Union label cigar.

" 'As far as I am concerned,' I said, 'I am not convinced that you are over-burdened in your interest for the cause of the wage-workers.'

"When election came he got the lowest vote of anybody on the ticket. The City Mayor who had refused to let us have the hall was also badly defeated. He would not speak to me for months. I was tickled to death and filled with glory. The friends of the defeated shunned me."

Anton, although he is a trade-unionist, felt that the interests of the workingmen were opposed to the interests of the employers: although to a certain extent he felt that the labor situation was the crux of a class struggle, yet he has never carried this feeling as far as the Socialists. He oftens makes fun of the "class conscious" man and is as fully alive, or almost so, to the weaknesses of the workingman as he is to those of the employer. Though he is belligerent and fiery, he can see good in a man, even though he be an employer. This was shown during his life at West Chicago, when he was apparently the big man of the town.

One of the employers of the shop where Anton worked, the shop he had organized, was told by his doctor that he would have to live on a farm, on account of his health. One day, at the lunch hour, he went to the men and told them he was going away.

"He was a kindly man," said Anton, "and he began to cry. He told about how hard he had worked to build up the business and said that if the men had not treated him so well, he could not have been so successful. His emotion touched the feelings of the men. They could hardly make a reply. After work I called a shop-meeting of the boys and we arranged a surprise party for the employer, took up a collection and bought a diamond stud as a present. We had enough money left for beer and cigars. Then we all marched together to the man's house. He was completely surprised and much moved. I had been appointed to speak, and I said: 'Mr. Toastmaster and friends: No one is more responsible for our presence here to-night than you, Mr. Skinner. Therefore I shall direct my remarks to you in particular. Neither the millions of a Rockefeller nor the wisdom of a Shakespeare coupled with the experience of a Darwin could obtain for any man that feeling of fraternity that bounds within the breasts of all who are here, for you, Mr. Skinner. Neither was it because you were an employer, for employers have gone out of business before and the men have been glad of their departure, but rather because your daily avocation in life and your attitude towards your fellow men were consistent with that principle that is so lofty, equal rights to all and special privileges to none. Whether consciously or unconsciously you have demonstrated the philosophy of Tom Paine when he said: 'The most formidable weapon against error of all kinds is reason.' We are pleased to have worked with you, to have associated with you and I feel sure that your spirit of toleration will ever remain an influence with all of us and make us more considerate to our fellow men. Though you have risen far above the average in the industrial world, yet you have always abstained from that dignity clothed in hypocrisy which fails to have any sympathy with those who perhaps are more unfortunate. We have never known you to discriminate against any man because of his religious beliefs, nor because of his political affiliations, and it is men of your character and temperament who are the forerunners of the ideal society, where man's inhumanity to man will be reduced to the minimum and human happiness elevated to the maximum. This has ever, in all ages, been the song of the poet and the dream of the philosopher. You can rest assured that while we regret to have you leave us, yet it would be extremely selfish on our part not to be cheerful under the circumstances, since it is better for you to go. As an evidence of our appreciation we give to you a small token of our affection; may it be a sign to you and to your friends and family, when you have left this village, that they who knew you best, your employees, can say truthfully: 'He has gone, but he was a man.' "

"He cried like a child before I got half through. Then we sang songs and drank beer. I really loved that man. He was exactly what I said. My speech was printed in the West Chicago paper and went all over town. Maggie was as proud as a peacock when she saw it in the paper, and sent it home to Clinton. Then they thought in Clinton I was not so much of a hobo after all. Everybody thought it was a fine speech to be made by a man who worked in a factory. *The Woodworker* printed a mere statement that I had presented a diamond stud to the employer and my radical friends in Chicago were horrified at the thought that I had turned a complete summersault in my attitude towards the bosses. The radicals are in some ways as narrow-minded as the majority of the capitalists."

In that little gathering at the employer's house a great deal of humanity was represented. There were Germans, Swedes, Irish, Scotch, English, Americans, Bohemians, Catholics, Lutherans, Methodists, Baptists, Congregationalists, a Salvation Army man, Democrats, Republicans, Socialists, People's Party men and an anarchist. The anarchist was Anton, the most important figure on that occasion, and the most tolerant. They all differed in everything except in the need of Unionism, and even the employer agreed with them on this point; and in the essential feelings of kindness and of human solidarity.

CHAPTER IX.

Delegate to New York.

"NOTHING on earth," said Anton, "could stop the workers, if they were active in their own interests. Only about thirty per cent of them are organized, and of this thirty per cent only about four per cent are active; and of these four per cent only about one per cent are really aggressive. If one-third of those who are now organized were active, the eight-hour day would be universal in four years. It would be as irresistible as an earthquake."

Anton's feeling for the need of activity accounts for a good deal of his anarchistic, as well as of his general trades-union agitation. The laboring masses, he feels, are inert and need constant prodding and pricking. The great thing is to make them morally uncomfortable, if not with the truth then with exaggerations of the truth; to rouse them to a sense of their opportunities and excite them with a prospect of more abundant life. I often found him in a mood when he would express himself very one-sidedly and extremely and unjustly; but it was due quite as much to his desire to "get a rise" from the phlegmatic mass as to his balanced conviction; for in calmer moods he would think and talk more justly. He never seems, however, to enjoy himself so much as when he throws a moral bomb, so to speak, either at a conservative capitalist, a politician, a minister or a timid or slow-going laborer.

He was, apparently, especially aggressive during his West Chicago experience. "In the meetings," he said, "I went the limit. I used to attack government on every occasion. I wanted to take away the deadening of the routine. When a man has worked in the shop all day, turning out with the help of machinery something that does not interest him, that has no variety in it, he wants a change when he gets out: he wants to express himself, he wants to express anything that has feeling, whether it is logical or not.

"One night I took the insane asylum as my subject. A man was present who was a heavy drinker, a non-resisting character and very religious. It was right after the exposé of the

Kankakee asylum outrage, where the warden had made an insane woman pregnant. This religious drunkard was so touched by my remarks that he began to weep like a child. He felt that he had been partly responsible for his own daughter's insanity. I had tried in my speech to show what the asylum would be in a state of free society where the insane were treated for the benefit of the insane, and not locked away so as not to interfere with money-making and other noble interests of the sane in a state of free society. He induced me to meet his minister, whom he represented as a kind of Christ. So the next Sunday night I went to Church, as I did not feel like going to the Saloon. I was conspicuous in the audience, because my sense of honesty prevented me from rising when the others rose, or kneeling when they kneeled, for I did not want to deceive them.

"After the meeting, the minister shook my hand, and asked me if I was a Christian. I said I would like to answer by asking him a question. 'Are you a Christian?' I asked. I saw by his face and the faces of the women that my question was considered improper. He said he was a Christian, and then I re-

[191]

plied: 'I am a Christian as far as society permits me to be and perhaps to a small degree further.' I called his attention to what he had said in his sermon: he had prayed that there be none within the sound of his voice who would gather in dens of the devil and under the influence of sinners.

" 'It is a little unkind of you,' I said, 'to insist that anyone who associates with sinners is very different morally from the people in the Church. I am not aware that you are running a boarding-house. There are many who have to stop in boarding-houses and hotels which are filled with sinners. I myself have slept in box-cars, and I find the classification there is the same as in hotels, boarding-houses and churches. Will you suggest to me where I may stop to-night, as my family are not in town and I am staying at the hotel, which is full of sinners. Don't you think, sir, that every man and woman is controlled to a very large extent by their environment? To what extent can a common laboring man who receives from $1.50 to $2 a day, and has a family of from two to six children, to what extent can he choose the locations of his home? Is he not forced to live in a locality

of so-called vile people, or infidels or unortho-
dox? It is a question of rent, of making both
ends meet. Therefore the income determines
largely the child's environment. It is very
hard for me to accept a religion or a creed
that overlooks these things, and when a child
grows up in such surroundings, the Church
condemns and criticizes it and society sends
it to jail or makes it work for small wages,
because it has not learned anything. The
course of this child in life is sufficiently pain-
ful, but after the end of this miserable existence, the Church sends it to Hell. It is
impossible for you, sir, even faintly to imagine
the great satisfaction I feel in being absolutely
certain that this is mythical, pure and simple.'
That settled him and the audience, too. He
told me to go to the hotel and think it over.
I actually felt like telling him that if most
Church people had to choose between clean
beds and sinners on the one hand; or lousy
beds and Christians on the other hand, they
would take the sinners every time. But I
didn't want to embarrass him too much; especially as I began to see, and had for some
time, that nobody in West Chicago was interested in my line of thought; except the work-

ing people. I could explain to them and they were sympathetic, because they felt my passion for human solidarity in all my talk. But otherwise I was very much alone. Even the more belligerent of the workingmen sometimes joked me. 'The anarchist,' said a Polock once, in the meeting, 'will never get elected.' He reminded me of the policeman who told me he liked the Socialists, but that there were not enough of them."

He "took a fall," too, out of the County Commissioner of Charities. He raised in the Union a subscription of $50 for a laborer with a bad leg, and then went to the commissioner with a petition. That functionary looked glum, and said that the board of charities took care of those cases. Anton replied that the board evidently overlooked some people who were in need. "I have come to the conclusion," said Anton to him, "that if the poor did not look after the county commissioners, those commissioners could not go so often to California on a vacation; the working people support you fellows just as they do the lawyers, doctors, preachers, politicians and all the other grafters, but if you are called upon to help the poor, you regard the matter as pure charity." Anton really seemed surprised that the county commissioner got angry at this and said he had been insulted. "I told him I was sorry he was county commissioner. I sympathized with him to that extent." This conversation was circulated about the town, and at the next election, the county commissioner lost his job.

It was not long after this that Anton, too, lost his job and went back to Chicago. Jones, the obnoxious secretary of the Union, had become foreman and had resigned his position in the Union. With this man Anton could not work harmoniously. "When he became boss," said Anton, "he was tyrannical. He was a dollar and cent man and was not a good mechanic. He had no judgment, not the slightest idea of how to approach men, to get the best results. He was therefore unpopular and I liked to ball him out. On Labor Day I went home to Clinton with my family for a visit, and did not return till the following Wednesday. Then he started to raise Cain; and told me to do what amounted to four days work in one. I told him if he was a mechanic he would know it was impossible. Then I called him everything I could think of in the way of cheapness. The only thing that could influence him besides money, I remarked, was the Pope. 'I have some hope for you,' I said, 'for not even the Pope can move you as far as the dollar, and I have more respect for the American dollar, bad as it is, than for the Pope of Rome.' He got white as a sheet, and I threw off my overalls and quit."

Anton did not have a dollar in the world, when he thus impulsively quit work in West Chicago. Easy as it seemed for him to throw off his overalls, it was not such a simple matter as formerly. He was gradually striking his roots. The influence of Maggie was a steadily regulating one. He had become a good mechanic, thirty years old, and his blood was cooler, so that he felt more and more the responsibility of his family; and of his work in the Union.

He quit work in West Chicago on a Saturday morning; and on the following Thursday he secured the position he has held ever since. It is a good job in every way, the best he has ever had. The wages are good, the foreman is congenial; and the new local he belongs to is composed of some of the most vigorous

men in the labor movement. His work as
an organizer in West Chicago had given him
a reputation among active labor men in the
city; and he had not been in Chicago two
weeks when he was elected delegate from his
local to the Chicago Federation of Labor.   *

It was at the time when the trouble between the Woodworkers and the Carpenters
was to come up before the Federation. "As
I had considerable gift of gab and some policy I was made chairman of the Woodworkers' delegation," he said, "and then there
came a long, technical fight, about jurisdiction." I will not follow him in this fight.
It was very complex and not at all inspiring,
as it involved no general principles and only
small politics and local jurisdiction interests.
Anton, although he was very active for the
Woodworkers, whose organization the Carpenters were attempting to absorb, felt keenly
the routine and ungenerous character of the
proceedings. During the course of his three
or four years' experience in the Federation he
has often taken the floor to protest against the
tendency of that body to waste its energies
in unimportant jurisdictions fights when so
many broad principles of labor policy de-

manded the most vigorous and united attention.

The President of the Federation at that time was a Carpenter, and the result was that "the machine" was against the Woodworkers, who were finally worsted in that particular phase of the fight which had been going on all over the country between these allied trades. As far as Anton was concerned, his vigorous speeches in the Federation helped materially to bring him into general notice as a rising man in the local labor situation; and not long after he was elected Chicago delegate to the New York Convention of Woodworkers.

"In that convention," he said, "I had a distinct advantage over those delegates who had a political mind. I was not a democrat, a republican nor a socialist, and so I could reason from more than one point of view. If a man is an anarchist and does not carry things too far he has a great practical advantage in debate over everybody else. They put me on the most important committees and I soon saw that my area of thought was broader than most of the men I came in contact with. I had by that time met the promi-

nent radicals, men like Turner and Isaak; and
I had heard Darrow and read his books and
speeches in labor cases, and I found more and
more a narrowness in the trades-unionist
that took away from me my pleasure in the
movement, but not from my interest in it. It
seemed important, but not so exciting as at
first. In several of the committees I sent in
a minority report to the convention; I found
considerable jealousy in the other committee
members, but I had the satisfaction of having
the convention reject the majority reports and
accept mine, the minority report.

"But I made one speech that was a failure.
I had invited some of my radical friends in
New York to hear me. Isaak was there then,
and Emma Goldman. I felt at that time *
that these people were superior to me intellectually, and that thought cast a damper over
me. I can speak best in a mass meeting of
workingmen where none of the speakers are
superior to me. The Union is a great field
for experience in speaking and in debate, and
I afterwards learned to speak before the radicals in Chicago with confidence. But I was
rattled on that occasion in New York and by
my speech almost destroyed the good impres-

sion I had made by my committee reports. Afterwards, I saw a good deal of Emma Goldman, and while I respect her courage and her energy, I think her ideas are too wild and too religious. She is of a very positive disposition and believes that her theory is just right and everything else just wrong. I have my own troubles with this positiveness, too, so I can't be too hard on her."

Anton is interested in almost anything human which shows itself honestly and squarely to him. He is filled, of course, with the criticism of our social organism shared with him by every intelligent workingman. He is interested in many things that seem half-baked, but he is nevertheless not blinded to their limitations or to the charm of other and possibly better things. He is alive in every way. The "radicals" are interesting to him mainly because they express—although generally in an anæmic way—some of the principles which he as an active worker feels are beginning to form in the heart of the people. But personally, when he is among them, he is like a bull in a clover field. They are gentle, quiet, pale, reasonable within their limitations, rather monotonous; he is stormy, aggressive, varied, complex, sometimes vulgar, more often fine and truly delicate, often above their heads though his language is ungrammatical. He frightens and puzzles them. He goes to them largely as a change from the activity of his trades-union life and also because he loves the ideal of freedom.

During this brief stay of his in New York, his character made a keen impression on people whom I afterwards met in that city. One of them, a woodworker, too, and an anarchist in tendency, a heavy drinker, a man utterly careless in habits and dress, and most repulsive on first acquaintance, but afterwards fascinating because of his ideas, never-failing temperament and genuine experience, spoke to me of Anton as "a powerful fellow."

"The real 'radicals,' he said, 'are in the labor movement; those hanging on the outside began with the movement, too, but then became too weak for it. Anton has too many ideas to please the theoretical anarchists who have lost touch with life. My experience is that the radicals make a mistake in neglecting the trades-union movement. If they are trades-unionists they can have a hall to speak in undisturbed by the police. If you can talk sense there, they will listen to you no matter how radical you talk. You can't talk high-falutin, but some men have the gift of saying things simply. Most anarchists get their words from books, so when they talk they are high-falutin; but if they would talk right, they could say everything they want, in the trades-union meetings; for the trade-unionists accept all radical ideas, if they are not labeled, and are not high-falutin.

"It is natural that all radical ideas should start with the working class. Serfs and slaves think more than anybody else. The other people don't need to think. Give a man a job and he generally stops thinking. They think all together because there is solidarity among them. Each man's thought is the thought of all. There is solidarity among them because they are weak. Ants get together, but lions remain alone." Anton is a man who expresses the laboring man at heart, with more energy and intelligence than most of the radicals, partly because he is near them and works with them.

Yet this vigorous-minded workingman felt abashed when called on to speak before people of more education but many of them of far less vitality of thought. His failure in the speech seemed to have impressed Anton more vividly than anything else in his visit to New York.

When he returned to Chicago, he found that his prestige was still greater, and they wanted him to run for business agent. "I had a good position," he said, "but to be business agent would mean a money sacrifice; for a business agent has to spend money like water in the saloons. Maggie was opposed to my running; but I wanted to have the experience, and thought I could be a better agitator if I could spend all my time at it, and not need to work in the shop. So I ran for business agent, and although I was popular, I was defeated, as I had been before, and for the same reason. I was too independent. I was convinced that the office should seek the man. I had a contempt for political tricks. It was repulsive to me to ask for anything.

"Soon after that I was elected President of my local Union, against my wishes. I did not want the office, and nobody else did. I thanked them, in a speech, for giving me an office I did not want. It was in many ways a disagreeable job. The workingman can maintain order in Church or in a lodge-meeting. But in a local Union he thinks he is the whole cheese, and will do as he pleases. It is hard for the President to keep order. My Union was composed of 1,400 men of mixed nationalities; and there is a very rough element among them. There was an Irishman who gave more trouble than anybody else. He was always drunk at the meetings and ill-tempered. He was an interrupter and was willing to vote money out of the treasury to help a friend. He used all kinds of dirty, vile language, and previous Presidents had not been able to manage him.

"This Irishman had an idea he was responsible for my election and asked me to make him door-keeper, who gets 35 cents every meeting. I told him that the first time I presided I would make a statement before the Union on what the conduct of the meeting should be. On that occasion I recommended dispensing with a regular door-keeper, that the chairman appoint a sergeant-at-arms every Monday and that he act without being paid; so much would be saved for the treasury. All agreed, except the old Irishman. Henceforth, he was opposed to me, for he wanted that money for three whiskeys every meeting. I informed the men that I, as President, would forget that I had any personal friends. I thanked them for the honor of electing me to an office that nobody else wanted, but I hoped that time would never come when the President of a local Union would be a salaried officer; they should always select a man who could command their respect, but remember there were times when it was a crime for the presiding officer to have the respect of certain men. I told them I should enforce the laws of the Constitution, bad or good, and then if they did not like them, they could repeal them.

"A certain question was being discussed,. when the old Irishman, who was tipsy, got up and wanted to talk. I banged the gavel, telling him he must confine himself to the question. The custom had been to repeal any fines inflicted by the chairman for actions that were out of order. The Irishman knew that, and would not sit down. He called me Socialist, anarchist and tyrant. I appointed a committee of three to escort him from the hall. They tussled with him, he agreed to behave, and was given another chance. Soon afterwards, he arose and took a similar aggressive and unparliamentary attitude. I appointed the committee again, and they threw him out. Always after that he was very gentle, and the meetings were orderly. One can be an anarchist in theory, as a protest, but when it comes to do the work, there must be order.

"My anarchism helped me to make an impression. I began to meet the big fellows, men like John Mitchell and Sam Gompers, and I found that my acquaintance with radical ideas, slight as it then was, helped me with these men, no matter how conservative they were—and they always seem more conservative than they are in reality. There is no conception so close to trades-unionism as anarchism, for in these Unions there are so many different elements, nationalities, creeds and ideas that there is no common ground except anarchism; provided they don't know it. If the anarchist, that is, the extreme protester, does not call himself an anarchist, he occupies in the trades-unionism a logical and strong position, but he must not advertise it."

Anton's growing importance in the movement was shown by his election as President of the Woodworkers' Council, which represented all the local Unions in the city. In this position he continued to act with his usual independence. Soon he had the walking delegates against him because of his refusal to extend them special privileges on the floor of the council.

"I was strong," he said, "with the rank and file, because I used my sarcasm against the officers who tried to perpetuate their positions. I was weak with the officers for the same reason; and they to the end will always get the victory, for they keep at it, from motives of business or ambition, while the crowd is moved by impulse which soon dies away.

"It was about the time that Darrow's *Open Shop* was published; and it caused many a discussion in our Union. I sold 800 copies of it, and the talk it made did as much good as the actual reading of it. The men like to discuss this question as much as the employers, and they both regard it as a moral issue; and yet that is silly. It is simply a question of power and advantage. The bosses yell that every man ought to have a chance, and that the shops must be closed to nobody; while the men maintain that it is immoral for the men to be so blind as not to organize. The bosses are more hypocritical about it, for they say they want the open shop for the benefit of the non-Union men. It is to laugh, and everybody knows it."

Anton, after the part he took in the Carpenter-Woodworker debate, became active in the affairs of the Chicago Federation of Labor, and was appointed a member of the organization committee and at a later time of the charter committee. His experience as an active worker in this central labor body was not one conducive to a purely optimistic way of looking at the situation. "A great portion of the worst element," he said, "is elected to the offices and committees. Things are better now, but there was a time when the President of the Federation always drifted into a political job. Office in the Federation was a stepping stone to politics. This was largely due to the ignorance of the politicians; to that is due the prestige of the labor grafter, for the average trades-unionist has very little political influence, a thing the politicians are very slow in learning.

"The fear of exposé tends to give certain men influence, the Lily Whites, the reformers who do doubtful good and are often really dishonest. Nearly every politician howls against the graft of the others, so that unless he can mention names, he has little influence as a reformer—he is not dangerous to the crooked politician. I was known to be against the machine element, whether it was a grafting element or a so-called reform element. I was against the machine as a machine. It was not democratic and did not satisfy me as an anarchist."

CHAPTER X.

Chicago Spirit and Its Cause.

IT was at about this point in his career that I first met Anton. He was then President of his local, President of the Woodworkers' Council, and active delegate to the Chicago Federation of Labor; it was just previous to an important strike of the Woodworkers, to
* the Madden reform fight in the Federation, to the personal conflict which led up to Anton's election as Chicago delegate to the International Labor Congress at Pittsburg. The great Teamsters' strike was under way;
* Mayor Dunne was in the midst of his municipal ownership efforts, and "labor" was almost the only topic of talk in the town. The city was bitter in its side-taking; and yet I was impressed with the relative broadness and toleration extending through the social sections; impressed with the way the working-man, the "common" man had imposed his point of view to a relatively great extent upon

[210]

the entire comunity. Here, indeed, the laborer is more at home than is the rule in capitalistic communities. It is the only big city I know where he has made an atmosphere for himself. Here he begins to abound in his own sense, and to feel the excitement of thought. Here he can nourish his personality, can express himself. Here he has his clubs, his centres of activity, and he is filled with democratic hope. More than all, here he has communicated his needs and his ideals to the general community, so that his laws and the laws on the statute books are not always in harmony.

The effect of expressive labor in Chicago was noticeable to me everywhere. In the University, in the newspapers, in the social settlements, in the public charities, in the newest kind of politician, a relative sympathy for the man who works with his hands is in one way very apparent.

Take any Chicago personage of importance, whatever his profession or his position, and somehow or other he has been influenced by the spirit of the intellectual proletariat. One of the younger deans of the University is the most complete anarchist of my acquaintance.

"Sociology," in all its branches, is the great subject of the place. Young literary men like Herrick and Friedman dwell with insistent sympathy upon the emotional and æsthetic demands of the "people." An important young banker is an emotional socialist. A young newspaper man with strong "capitalistic" backing and tradition was put into an important office in the city hall by the wonderfully broad and democratic Mayor: this young man resigned, to follow out the cause of socialism, to which faith he had come during his term in office.

An important lawyer and politician of the city is Clarence Darrow, a man who in his practical activity and his literary work, has been very deeply influenced by the implicit ideas of the working class. He is radical, idealistic and practical at once and because of his interest in human psychology and in the idealistic future often appears as a crank or worse. He is inconsistent with the inconsistency of the struggling, unclear proletariat whose ideas and impulses he sympathetically grasps.

Even the kid glove reformers (Anton would call them "The Lily Whites") are more cognizant of what is going on below than they are in the East. A Chicago reformer is a real, plain man. William Kent is the ideal reformer of the capitalist class: practical, radical, conservative, humorous, whose honesty is so thorough-going that it sticks out with inspiring positiveness in everything he does and says. About him is something of the down-rightness and plainness of the man-in-the-street.

Perhaps the most remarkable illustration of the power and influence of the proletariat in the big western metropolis is given by the personality and the work of Miss Jane Addams, who, in Hull House, has formed a kind of *salon,* an exchange of ideas, where all the surging social conceptions find expression.

The *salons* of history were limited. The ideas of the laboring classes hardly found an expression in them. Philosophers thought for the crowd, who were out of sight and unknown. The fact that the most democratic exchange of ideas which has ever attained respectability centres about the personality of a Chicago woman, is not an accident. I doubt if Jane Addams could have been evolved anywhere else in the world.

She has been an important factor in putting the different social classes in touch one with another. She can do emotional justice all around. She understands the troubles of the rich as well as of the poor. Her instinctively psychological insight gives her sympathy even with the morally outcast. Wonderful, indeed, is her emotional tact. She is curiously and delightfully free of sentimentality. It is as a rule difficult to talk of oppression and moral degradation without a show of indignation. But she carefully refrains from any snap-shot moral judgment. She is not, in the banal sense, a "reformer," or a worker. Her great function is social: she has established, like the French women of the eighteenth and early nineteenth centuries, a *salon* of a high order; here is established an atmosphere where ideas of importance derived from the interests and passions of many different men and many different sections of society are exchanged.

In her I felt only one interest—in the human being who had something serious to do or say—a never-ceasing helpfulness to all who want to work or live seriously, and therefore at present a great liking for the laboring class. "I am interested in trades-unionism," she said to me, "because it is the only thing which to-day seems to have any religion in it."

Another remarkable woman in this city is less of a public character than Miss Addams, and I shall therefore not give her name. But * she is a woman who on occasions has exerted a strong influence in Chicago. She has an adventurous and investigating turn of mind. She likes to explore life and to delve into the interesting personalities of the town. It was she who acted as a wedge in settling the great butchers' strike, and who discovered the horrible state of things in the stock-yards; the knowledge of which was wielded by her and others as a club to force the packers to send away the disreputable strike-breakers.

She makes her own living in one of the professions. She is clever in her work, but she does not like it. She does it from necessity and grudges every moment that she devotes to it. It takes away from her real interests. It takes away from the amount of time she can give to the strangely keen pleasure of "getting next" to the character, passions and purposes of others.

She is as much interested in the outcast and the thief as she is in the pillar of society and the reformer. But she is particularly interested in the laboring man and his destiny. "These men," she said to me, "are fine fellows, but they all need elbows." She is the elbow, not only of the labor leader, but of the town in general. She tried to work on Shea, at the time of the teamsters' strike, with as much calmness of mind as on the good Mayor. With the latter, of course, she succeeded better, and has been influential in the administration. A member of the remarkable school board, she has worked consistently on almost *ultra* democratic lines. Nothing interests her as much as "the people." And about them she is curiously imaginative.

Her woman's susceptibility to emotional democracy may be due in part to the circumstances of her childhood. Exposure and privation, intimate personal contact with hardship and mere humanity probably rendered her more impressionable to the ideas of a class to which she, in fact, does not belong. She is capable of a great usefulness—as a stimulant, as an expresser—and the ideas she expresses are curiously dependent on the instinctive ideas and emotions of the proletariat.

One of the most vigorous and influential persons in the city is a woman who has made herself into a labor leader, has organized the teachers. She has been a great factor in the political and economic life of Chicago. She carries to excess the virtues and perhaps the faults of the belligerent labor leader—is terribly "class conscious," as Anton would say. But she derives her power from the remarkably widespread influence of the ideas of labor—of the ideas which come from below.

The strongest *feuilletonist,* logically the ablest editorial writer in America, is Louis Post, a Chicago editor. He is also one of the most "radical" men in the country. I heard him denounce, with passion, in a ringing public speech, Judge Holdom's sweeping decision giving almost unlimited power to the employers, through injunctions making organized labor practically illegal. He appealed to the workingmen to go to the ballot, to rid themselves of such utter injustice. "Such tyranny," he said, "can only be opposed with bullets or ballots. In this country, we have the opportunity to resort to ballots." In the East, they would call this cultivated, good

and able man an "agitator." But the sentiment of the laborer is mighty enough in Chicago to estabish an atmosphere in which men
like Post occupy a respectable, almost a conservative position. On the same platform,
the same day, Anton spoke, and showed no
more indignation than Mr. Post, although he
said: "This judicial decision cannot be
obeyed by the workingmen of this city."

While in Chicago, I had the pleasure of attending the meetings of the "Lunch Club,"
composed of men of the best character and
with the deepest interest in "civic" affairs.
An important settlement worker, a leading
Socialist editor, a banker with Socialistic tendencies, the prominent lawyer, politician and
author I have referred to, a young and sound
lawyer, one of the most gifted of the Western
novelists, a newspaper man of high standing,
a progressive priest, the young commissioner of Public Works, these were some of the
members. The talk was always about some
matter of public concern and the general
ideas resulting from such consideration. In
the tone of the most conservative of these men
of good position, and some of them of independent means, there was a marked "radical-

ism," a markedly emotional interest in the people, an inspiring sentiment of democracy.

Wherever I went in Chicago, and I went everywhere, the ideas I heard expressed were preponderantly "democratic," preponderantly on subjects vaguely called "sociological"; expressed with energy and often with distinction. For several months after my arrival in Chicago I saw these "leading" people mainly: it was before I had become well acquainted with the laboring people themselves. When, however, I had met Anton and his friends, whom I have yet to describe, I felt myself to be in the presence of the source of the ideas in which my cultivated friends were so much interested. It seemed that the ideas and feelings most prevalent in Chicago's intellectual and serious circles began with the laboring class, and were expressed best by the intellectual proletariat. Moreover, I found that in this class, where these feelings and ideas originated, the expression of them was more direct and warmer; if less logical and balanced, it was more real, so real that it was fascinating. At this point, therefore, begins my direct observations of Anton and his friends.

CHAPTER XI.

Social Amenities.

A LITTLE while after our meeting, Anton invited me to a Sunday noon-day dinner at his house on the West Side—the first of a long series of visits. There I met Maggie and the three children. I found a house perfectly clean, a garden well-cultivated, the children healthy and well-cared for, a well-cooked dinner, and Maggie, the spirit of it all, without assistance, and yet pretty, young-looking and cheerful. She took intelligent part in the conversation at the table. The talk was frank and full, and dealt with the facts of the teamsters' strike and with labor and social matters generally. I was deeply struck with the vitality and charm of the entire family. I had naturally enough at that time, due to my lack of experience in this direction, a feeling that the conventional education of college and of well-to-do conditions generally puts a wide intellectual difference between the so-called educated man and the vigorous man of the people who learns from experience and observation. But I was soon to find myself so absorbed by my experiences with this family and their friends that it is now a commonplace thought with me that "culture" has many paths by which it is reached, and that it is only the extraordinary person who attains it at all. Certainly many of the American mechanics possess this quality in its essence to as great a degree, at least, as the man of so-called education, though these mechanics do not often think so. They are overpowered with an often baseless sense of inferiority.

"Education," said Maggie, regretfully, "helps you to know anybody you want to." This was a true word, and shows where the real limitation is—social.

Maggie and Anton and their trades-union and radical friends, although they feel the social injustice, are not under the illusion that people who are educated are necessarily thinkers or in any way really superior to themselves. I heard Anton, in one of his speeches before the Social Science League, say:

"I don't know that people who are professional thinkers or philosophers or students do all the thinking; perhaps other people who are at work have an opportunity to think that the other fellows have not got."

Anton, when tired by the routine of the shop and of the trades-union activities, goes to the "radicals," and by the more free and subtle among them is refreshed and encouraged. One night he and I talked till midnight with an æsthetic person about literature and art. On account of Anton's lack of specific education our facility in shades of expression was impressive to him, but not at all discouraging, and it did not need to be; for when there was a connecting point, his ideas came rich and red in response. He seemed to me much nearer to reality than my learned friend or I, and so in a better position to think, if, after the day's work, he had enough energy left over.

Some of the women of Chicago have "taken Anton up," but they are sometimes shocked by his frankness, and as his nature is really a sweet and humane one, the sensibilities of the women do not seem too well founded.

"The women object to my language," he said. "They object to my saying damn and hell. They claim to be interested in the trades-union movement, and yet they often stick on little things. How can they expect to have the workingman use any language but his own? Why, for such a trivial thing, do they criticize? Why not get out and hustle for a cause they claim to be right and forget to be finnicky? It is the same way with some of the 'gentlemen.' If they find the workingman has some bad habits, if he is rough and not refined, or if he is sometimes unscrupulous about money, they lose their interest in the cause. But the cause is just as important, in spite of these things, perhaps more important because of them.

"One time, at a 'radical' meeting, a lady was shocked at my language, and said: 'Now, Mr. Anton, you would be good for the cause if you did not say such words; you say damn, you say hell.' The truth is, I like to shock these anarchists, free-lovers, anthropologists, mystics and cranks who gather at these 'radical' meetings. Some of them are sensible and thoughtful, but most of them are awful faddists.

"At this meeting I thought I would be an irritant, a part I often played in these meetings. In the labor meetings I am serious. I am a tyrant there and try to accomplish things. But in the radical meetings I enjoy myself and try to stir people up. On this occasion, I defended cigarette smoking against the speaker of the evening, and also attacked the Church. He said that cigarettes had a tendency to confuse the mind and destroy the morals.

I got up and protested in the name of humanity and decency against Mr. Sercombe putting together in his argument the cheap politician, Carter Harrison, and the great philosopher, Tom Paine, both of whom he quoted as against cigarettes. I also remarked that it was singular Mr. Sercombe should have so great a horror of cigarettes and at the same time so great an admiration for Clarence Darrow, who was a cigarette fiend. Under another heading, I remarked that religion was tyrannical; as it was preached in the pulpit, it was the author of vice, crime and vulgarity, and that Christ was responsible. This was an extreme statement, and I made it only to irritate the anthropologists. As they were studying Man, I thought I would give them one to study. A lady got up, red with horror, and said: 'I respect the rules of this society, so I refrain from answering one of the critics,' meaning me.

"The next Sunday I seized an opportunity in the meeting of the Anthropological Society to say that I also respected the rules of the society, provided they did not come in contact with my psychology and individuality. 'In that case,' I said, 'while some may prefer others, I prefer myself.' In that society they always hold their breath when I get up to speak. They don't know what I am going to say next.

"The same lady who objected, said, at another meeting: 'I am very much pleased to be able to get up to speak in behalf of the workers. It pleases me very much to say that I, in my youth, was a hard-working girl, and ever since I met my beloved and was married by the laws of God I have given much attention to workers in and out of Unions; I have felt that the poor non-union man who is cut off from society needs more consideration even than an ordinary criminal.'

"I got up at this point and said: 'Mr. Chairman, for *Christ's* sake how long have we got to listen to this stuff?'

"Even a freak can speak before this society

[225]

or before the Social Science League. In both these societies they have some good speakers, and the purpose of the gathering is a good one, namely, the education of the workers to a sense of their rights; but the trouble is few workers go there, while the chairs are taken by a lot of long-haired cranks instead. I liked to put them to a test to see how much they believed in free speech, which they were always shouting about. Maggie, being a woman, is softer than I, and didn't like the way I swore and talked in the meetings. So she put them next to the reason I did it, just to get a 'rise,' and after that they took me more coolly.

"But I could always get a 'rise' out of the lady I have spoken of. One night a wood-worker, a friend of mine and an anarchist of the thoughtful kind who have read and who do not talk nonsense, made a speech before the Social Science League, in which he tried to show that many great men of the past and many cultivated men to-day have been, and are, imbued with anarchistic ideas. The lady was tickled to death that the speaker could define anarchism in such a way as to make it seem nice and respectable, and so she said:

'I am very glad to-night to say to you that I also have been an anarchist unconsciously. I accept anarchism, if so defined, and I thank God for it.'

"That gave me my opportunity. I got up, and said: 'I have met many men and women who have blasphemed the Deity, but I never until to-night met anybody willing to undergo the responsibility of thanking God for creating anarchists. If anarchism is what it is, and if there are any people who have become anarchists, God is the last man who is entitled to any credit for it. I for one would prefer to give the credit to the devil, who has done some things that are good.'

"She thought that was awful. She and the others think they understand poetry, society and philosophy. Why can't they understand me? Why get angry?"

Anton goes everywhere in his flannel shirt. He presides at his own table in one, goes to the meetings in one, and takes pride in it as a symbol of his class. He is most at home with his coat off, a suspender·strap around his robust body, no necktie, and on the point of hurling some bomb-like words at an opponent. On the subject of dress, he said:

"I acquired a bad habit when I was a hobo —the desire to dress well. At that time I was obligated, for I had to make the best appearance, or I would not have been able to beg or get a job. But now it is different. I am independent and don't need to dress. I am independent of all but my employer. If he wanted me to wear a tie in the shop, I probably would. Capitalists and clerks have to dress for business reasons, but I don't have to. All really civilized people from Tolstoi to Wagner believe in the Simple Life. I always preside over the Union meetings in a blue flannel shirt."

Anton likes his joke, and has his moments of workingman's downright lightness. He added, on this occasion: "You made a great impression on Maggie, the other evening, when I had gone out, but you wore a flannel shirt."

At these "radical" gatherings there are many free-lovers, and anti-free-lovers, and they often take one another by the hair, figuratively speaking.

"Some of these women," said Anton, "liked me. They thought I was handsome, vigorous and had nice ways, but they wondered

why I swore. I promised them to give a reason some time. My opportunity came once
when a woman spoke on license versus liberty. I got up, after her speech, and said
some of my friends had corrected me on various occasions about using profanity. I did
so, I said, in order to please both my ultra
radical friends and also my ultra conservative
friends. I had been raised, I said, more than
a Christian, but had been surrounded by infidels, that I had a marriage certificate, but a
free-love inclination; I therefore knew that if
I conducted myself in the conventional manner and did not swear, that all the goody-
goody women would fall completely in love
with me; and, as my capacity was limited, I
could best introduce moderation in their
hearts by using profanity and thus checking
them."

Anton, in spite of the joking tone of the
above, is in reality very attractive to women.
His temperament, energy, idealistic vehe-
mence, and even his rough sincerity, appeal to
them. I had opportunity to see how many
of the "radical" women pursued him. He
was not too offish, and would sometimes yield
gracefully, but Maggie, who knew everything,

always knew that she had the best of Anton's heart, mind and temperament So she forgave not only the trades-union activity that took him from home at night, but even his interest in other women.

"I told her nothing at first," said Anton, "but I learned better, and when I told her everything, she had become more radical, and she understood better and did not mind when I was out. At a later time she went further than I did in radical theory, but her natural, womanly conservatism and our frankness together kept her from putting her ideas into practice. Once she asked me if she ought not to make an experiment. She had been hearing so much free-love talk that she began to feel that she was out-of-date. I told her she was a fool to do anything she did not want to do, just because of a lousy theory that was going the rounds. So she didn't.

"Maggie used to wonder why I did not notice this and that, why I did not pay her little attentions and talk polite to her. But I leave that for conservative men who stay at home. I talk to her, instead, and she likes it."

Maggie was there, as Anton and I talked, and she said, at this point:

"If I have to marry again, I don't know where I can find another like you; and I couldn't stand a home man."

"She is a wise woman," said Anton, "and she knows the best way of managing a restless fellow like me. The other night I had been to a Union meeting and something came up about policy I wanted to talk over with Maggie. That evening I dined in town, and Julia, one of the free-love ladies who are prominent at the radical meetings, wanted me to take her to hear a Pentecost lecture. When I told her I had an engagement with Maggie, she sneered, and said: 'You are a slave to your wife. You only pretend to be a free-lover.' 'I am not a slave to you, anyway,' I said, and I went home.

"This lady, whom I call Julia, has quite an important position among some of the radicals. She is not pretty—you have seen her, and you know—and she is not original or amusing. It is by virtue of her free-love that she gets her position. That is an easy graft with some of these people. For instance, a young machinist asked me one day to take him to a free-love meeting. He is a regular buck, and I knew that he did not care about the principles of freedom. It was license he wanted. So I said to him: 'I don't want to force potatoes on people who want oranges.' "

I saw "Julia" several times, and found her very serious and much interested, though in an unillumined way, in all social problems, and particularly in everything that touched upon the welfare of the working class, to which she belonged. She worked in the factory, and in the evenings improved her mind by going to the radical meetings and listening to the lectures. Her "free-love" was partly induced, no doubt, by her temperament, but it was also influenced by the general "spirit of protest" against all capitalistic institutions, including marriage. She was not at all seductive, but she took herself so seriously, and was taken so seriously by the people with whom she associated, that she seemed a person of the utmost respectability.

"I was conservative," said Anton, "for a long time about sex. These ladies used to get mad at me on that question. But no matter how conservative I was, what I said was no more ridiculous than what they said. I began to feel more broad and tolerant on this subject after I came to know Isaac and his wife and family well. Maggie and I found these people so refined and gentle and good that we came to be tolerant to their theories of anarchy and free-love. They were wild about children, and that went straight to Maggie's heart."

"They talked," said Maggie, "so frankly and so sweetly about things I thought ought not to be talked about that I got to feel they and their ways of seeing things were right, at least in part."

When one takes into account the narrowness of the ordinary laborer's life; how lacking in it are the elements of "sweetness and light" in the intellectual sense, one cannot wonder at the eagerness with which the more energetic among them grasp at any opportunity to broaden their mental horizon. Their method of thinking often seems crude and anti-social, and yet even the extreme anarchistic activities are educating and refining in their influence. Certainly one has abundant opportunity of observing that those laborers who have come under Socialistic or anarchistic influences are much more "civilized," more interesting, more alive and progressive, than those who live exclusively the routine and unstimulating life of the wage-worker. Who can wonder at the fact that the need of excitement, if nothing else, forces many of these men and women to adopt ways of feeling and thinking which are not without danger to the present organization of society?

CHAPTER XII.

Argument With Boss.

THE agreement between the Woodwork-ers' District Council and the planing mill operators of Chicago expired in February, 1905. Anton was at the time President of the Council, and in the negotiations tending towards a new agreement which ensued, he took a leading part. The general method of procedure on the part of the men was for a committee to draw up an agreement, present it for approval to the Council, and then refer it to the referendum for the approval of the rank and file; and it would then go to the employers. On this occasion no demand for increase of wages was made, except in the case of one shop, where the wages were lower than in the others. A continuance of the closed shop agreement, which had been in force, was insisted upon by the men, while the employers made a stand for the "open shop," which at that time was "epidemic" among them.

In previous years the men's committee selected to present the agreement to the employers consisted of the board of business agents, four salaried men; but as the employers' organizations became more general, the employers in many instances complained that the board of business agents did not represent the wishes of the rank and file. So of late the policy has been for a committee of five men, working at their trade, to accompany the business agents in the negotiations with the employers.

On this occasion, however, as it was known that the men "stood pat" for the closed shop, the first meeting with the employers was held by the business agents alone. "The bosses' chairman," said Anton, "wanted to know immediately why the rank and file was not represented. He was sure that the open shop idea would meet with the approval of the men.

The business agents reported the matter to the Council, and a committee of five men, working at the trade, was appointed. This committee, on its return from the meeting with the bosses, recommended to the Council a compromise, but the Council "sat on" the committee and "stood pat" for the closed shop.

"I was not on that first committee," Anton said, "and I severely criticized them for their timidity. One of the committee resigned, and I was put in his place. In the committee meeting, before we went to the bosses, they made me spokesman, and I laid the law down. A business agent tried to tell me what to say, but I cut him short, and said that I would accept the responsibility of my own words, but would not use his.

"When we got before the employers' committee, I began my remarks by saying that we had no authority to enter into a final agreement without referring the matter to the organization, but that the men stood for the closed shop; we felt it was reasonable in itself, and that to change it at this late day, after it had been in force for several years, was unreasonable. I quoted two recent court decisions sustaining the legality of the closed shop.

"The Chairman for the bosses replied, said that if the agreement must be referred back to the Union, they could accomplish nothing; he insisted that the closed shop was illegal, and that the employers might have damage suits on their hands, and he laid stress on what he called the moral point of view: said the closed shop was immoral. In answer, I said that the employers were responsible for taking away the autocratic power of the business agent in making agreements; that the employer, through the press, had continually fulminated against the business agent, or, as they called him, the walking delegate, whom they claimed would do as he pleased without reference to the wishes of the rank and file in bringing about a settlement. And now they inconsistently objected because the committee must refer to the organization. In regard to the alleged illegality of the closed shop agreement, I showed them two distinct decisions rendered about the closed shop, one in New York and one in England, and then I referred them to that part of President Roosevelt's message to Congress where he says, in effect: 'There can be no question of the legality of organized workers refusing to work with such men as are not members of the Union. This may or may not be a moral right, that depends on the conditions in the special case.' So said the President. 'I, personally,' I added, in support of the moral right of the closed shop, 'should reasonably be the judge of whom I shall work with, as far as I have the power. Will you deny me the right of refusing to work with an anarchist or with a brute negro, or any other undesirable character?' I challenged them to show one instance where the law compels a man to work with such associates. I pointed out many cases where employers had discriminated against men by reason of their color: porters on trains are all negroes, section men in some parts of the country are all Chinamen. No man questioned the employer's right to hire whomsoever he pleased or discriminate against anybody he wanted to.

" 'I assure you,' I added, 'our organization has no particular objection to your hiring non-union men. We want to be fair, however, and to notify you in time, that if you do hire non-union men, you cannot hire us. To us, non-union men are undesirable associates, and we will not work with them.'

"The bosses' spokesman interrupted me at this point and said he would waive the legal right, but asked me if I did not think there was a moral question involved.

[239]

" 'Yes,' I replied, 'there is a moral question involved. I quite agree to that. I hope you will pardon me if I try to show you the light. Ninety-nine out of one hundred workingmen, when talking among themselves, are favorably inclined towards Unionism. But they have two objections to joining the Union. One is the fear of incurring the disfavor of the employer, and the other is the cost, fifty cents a month in dues and sometimes assessments which may not directly benefit them. The result is that, after a fair analysis, the principal objection of the workingman to joining the Union is founded on stupid selfishness, ignorance and cowardice.

" 'In view of the fact that human beings are more susceptible to the bad, the mean and the selfish than to the good and the unselfish, it is, in my opinion, decidedly immoral to allow one or two men in a shop to lead eighteen or twenty to become more selfish rather than more humane. For these reasons I quite agree that there is a moral side to this question, and that, morally, the trade-union, and especially the closed shop idea, have been great factors for human good.

" 'The employers' committee have appealed

to my sympathy. Your spokesman has asked me to defend your case. This is an admission of weakness. But for me to do anything on this committee except to reason for the interest of those I represent would be satannical, and I would not be worthy the respect of an honest opponent. I am thoroughly convinced of the justice of our case, and while I would not like to see a strike, I feel I would be a coward and a hypocrite to tell you that I would advise the rank and file in any other direction. I believe the balance of this committee agrees with me, but if they were all opposed, I would still go before the rank and file in their mass meeting and say, like Teddy, 'Boys, you are right; stand pat.'

"I addressed my remarks to the spokesman, and I noticed that, while I corrected him, the other bosses had a smile on their faces. He was too much of a self-appointer, and was not popular. The meeting adjourned, and the next day the secretary of the Lumber Dealers' Association came to the office of the Woodworkers and wanted to know where that young fellow, Anton, worked. He wanted a closed shop, and liked what I had said. The open shop would mean more bother to him. He told me in confidence that my argument had met with the approval of all the bosses, except the spokesman. In our mass-meeting on Sunday every man voted in favor of the closed shop. So at the next meeting with the employers, I told them that we now had the power to act definitely, and would accept the bosses' signature to the agreement we had drawn up. It was in substance an ultimatum, and they agreed to our terms, the closed shop.

"That finished that discussion, and things had been settled without a strike, but soon after a dispute about wages arose in another branch of the trade, interior trimmings. We asked for an increase of two cents an hour for all the men employed, instead of the usual demand to raise the minimum scale. I was spokesman when we presented our request, and the bosses nearly fell dead. They took three hours to picture their poverty, and we came to no understanding. The men, at a mass-meeting, sustained our position, and when we met the bosses again we agreed on a compromise, namely, that the present scale of wages should continue for six months, at the end of that time one cent an hour increase, and another cent increase at the beginning of the second year. This committee recommended this agreement to a mass meeting, but the men rejected it with considerable criticism, as it concerned only the minimum scale and did not apply to all the men. One old Scotchman made the charge that the committee was polluted.

"So we had to report to the bosses that the men would not accept the compromise agreement. Then the bosses insinuated that it had been their intention of giving this increase all around, instead of merely applying to the minimum scale. That was a lie, and it made me raving mad. I got up before the committee of the bosses and said: 'In the mass-meeting our committee has been accused of being polluted, and here the bosses accuse us of being fools. I am absolutely certain that the bosses' chairman stated most emphatically that they would not, and could not, make the increase apply to all the men. Personally, I feel that our committee should now stand pat on the original demand, so that we cannot be misunderstood, either by the bosses or by the rank and file.' I was awfully angry. But the chairman of the employers apologized, and they agreed to make the raise apply to all the men. This we submitted to the mass-meeting, but without recommending it, and it was carried by one vote. So that settled that dispute.

"There was one member of our committee who had an ambition to be a walking delegate. He was a demagogue, who always appealed to the rank and file. He sat in the discussion with the bosses and did not say a word, but in the mass-meeting he got up and supported the demands of the employers; but, when he saw how the men were feeling, he switched around. I made up my mind to give him a good flaying, and in the next Council meeting I showed him up, balled him out for fair, showed his cowardice for a whole half hour. That killed him completely in the movement. He has never been heard of since. In the Council he could not play to the galleries, as he could in the mass-meeting.

"The next negotiations we had with the employers led to a strike, which we lost. It was in another branch of the trade, the bar fixture workers. Their agreement with the bosses expired July 1st, 1905. Their committee demanded an increase of ten cents an hour all around. It was in reality a stiff thing to ask, as in other cities no such wages were given as those we demanded, and the bosses maintained that, if they gave these wages, they could not compete. But the men were in a peculiar frame of mind. Two years before that time the bosses stood pat and said they could pay no more wages, but the men, after being on strike ten days, gained what they demanded. So the men thought the present attitude of the employers was also a bluff, and that they could turn the same trick again. Some of the leaders, of course, knew better, and that it was foolish to strike at that time; and many of these leaders did what they could to affect the mood of the men, but to no avail.

"We had seven meetings with the employers and could not make them yield an inch, so we called a mass-meeting of the men. It was jammed, and disorderly, and there was a large majority in favor of a strike. So the committee returned to the bosses, and I said: 'You cannot blame the rank and file for being sceptical when they are told by their employers that, for competitive reasons, wages cannot be raised. This is, at all times, the contention of the employer, and his manner of reply to the Union, regardless of wages, hours or conditions. It is always the same old story: you cannot compete. If you would say this only at times when it was true, you would find the men ready to believe you. But you always say it, true or not. You are like the boy that yelled wolf too often.

" 'The employer in Milwaukee,' I continued, 'pay twenty-five cents an hour, and yet, if the Union asks for a cent an hour more, which is five cents less than you pay in Chicago, his objections are based on the same grounds as yours: he cannot compete. If we point out to him the fact that the Chicago employer pays twenty-eight cents, and the men in Milwaukee ask for twenty-six cents only, he replies that the Chicago employer has three distinct advantages,—facilities for transportation, an enormous lumber market, and access to labor and to the best mechanics. If, therefore, conditions are so much better in Chicago, according to the employers in other cities, it is reasonable to assume that woodworkers would be immigrating here from time to time, while as a matter of fact, and according to the report of the labor statistician at Springfield, there are not a hundred woodworkers in two years who came to Chi-

cago from these other woodworking centres.'
Then I pointed out the advantages of working in small cities. The bosses bluffed that
they would move their business to places
where the men were more reasonable. I said
we would move there, too; that we also did
not like high rents and the nervous turmoil of
the city.

"I added that I would like evidence supporting their contention that they could not
compete. The biggest employer on the committee arose majestically, and asked me to
come to his office, and he would show me doc-
umentary proof. I said, if I went alone, it
would look rather suspicious. But, previous
to the mass-meeting, I went to his office; he
gave me a cigar, and then showed me his
books and price lists, and claimed he had reduced his prices twenty per cent. I discovered from the books that eighteen per cent
of the twenty per cent reduction was in plate
glass and mirrors, and I pointed out to him
that we had nothing to do with the manufac-
ture of glass: we were woodworkers. He
gave me an economic business talk, which
meant everything or nothing, and then said:
'Now, Anton, there is no use talking. If the

boys insist on this advance, there is going to be a strike.'

"Then, in a low tone, he added: 'I believe that if this matter was properly explained to the boys, they would not want to strike. I'd give a thousand dollars if I could address that mass-meeting and state the case from our point of view; or, if some one else would do it for me.' He had previously emphasized my influence with the men. I took him up, to see how far he would go. 'Personally,' I said, 'I am in favor of giving you the floor to explain your side, provided, of course, that one of our men answer by showing our side. 'Who would that man be?' he asked. 'I think I shall be the man,' I replied. 'My God, Anton,' he exclaimed, 'you are not going to take the floor and encourage the men in these demands?' 'I can't be expected to do anything else,' I said. 'I am a woodworker, and I represent the men. Besides, I don't think a strike will be detrimental in the long run. The rank and file can learn only through experience, and perhaps this experience is necessary at this time.' He then said that he could not speak before the mass-meeting, as he had no authority from the other employers. What he meant by all this I shall not explain. It would be guessing, though it might be guessing pretty shrewdly.

"At the mass-meeting the men voted to strike. Everything possible was done to prevent it, but when the rank and file become passionate there is no use trying to argue with them, as long as the organization is democratic and there is such a thing as the referendum. The mass often acts foolishly, and this whole matter of organization is at bottom only a question of education. It is educating the working people, and the fact that they make mistakes is no argument against it. It is an argument for it, for it shows how much in need they are of experience.

"The machinery got to work and put forth every effort to prevent the actual calling out of the men. Tom Kidd used his big influence, and the State Board of Arbitration did what it could. In this board I had very little confidence. I was President of the Council, and the Board of Arbitration invited me and others to a swell dinner at $10 a head. This made me suspicious. I felt it was a reflection against my manhood. They tried to get me to use my influence against the calling

[249]

of the strike. I stood pat and would not do it. There was no guarantee that the bosses would submit to arbitration. So this matter fell through. Then a shop meeting in every factory involved was called, the object being to get an expression from every man, an absolute referendum. The total vote was 1,858 out of a possible 2,000. Sixteen hundred men voted in favor of striking, so there was nothing else to do. The strike was called July 1st, 1905, and every man of the 2,000 went out. The men were so enthusiastic that they voted no strike benefits should be paid for the first two weeks.

"After the strike had been on for a couple of weeks, the State Board of Arbitration made an effort to get the employers' committee and our committee to confer in reference to a settlement. Both committees were willing to meet, but did not want to admit it. So the State Board arranged a meeting with diplomacy. It did not appear that either side wanted it. The lawyers of the employers were at the conference, the special reason for the lawyers is that they never commit the employers to anything, and the employers are so busy that they cannot meet men who have more than the average information in the economic field, for labor is generally right, so they employ the lawyers, who can harp on technicalities.

"I was spokesman of the committee. There were six employers present, one of whom wore a star, indicating that he had been sworn in as a deputy sheriff. He was the meanest of the bosses. There were not enough chairs, and I sat down in the only rocking chair, feeling that I was able to make myself at home in a foreign land. The employers' lawyer began to speak, but I interrupted him, and said I wanted to speak first in order to put our committee in a light that would not be misunderstood.

" 'While we have no particular objection,' I said, 'to meeting with this deputy sheriff (pointing to the employer with the star), yet we want it distinctly understood that we are no more criminal than the men we are meeting.'

"The employers notified us that unless their terms were met by the men, they would not admit any longer the principle of the closed shop, and would not recognize the Union, and offered to give us a day's grace to think it

over, in the interests of peace, as they put it.
I sarcastically thanked them for this great
concession of a day, and called their attention
to the fact that the Union existed, not because
they wanted it, and that it would continue to
exist, whether they wanted it or not. 'Ninety-
nine men out of a hundred,' I said, 'prefer to
trust to the strength of the organization rather
than to the generosity of the employer, and,
as long as they feel that way, there will be a
Union, whether you recognize it or not.'

"The conference came to nothing, and the
strike went on. It was clear to the leaders
that the strike would be lost; but the temper
of the men was such that it could not be
brought to an immediate end. The men's
treasury was being depleted, and the employers, knowing this, helped the process of bank-
ruptcy by sending the riff-raff of the teamsters' strike to our men to attempt to obtain
money to get home with, claiming they had
been imported, not knowing there was a strike
on, by the employers. But we got on to that
game. Once, eighteen men came to us and
said they had been imported from Buffalo to
come to Chicago, and when they arrived here
they found they were to be used to break the

strike. They wanted $150 from us with which to return to Buffalo. We questioned them closely; asked them how it happened, if they were in sympathy with Unionism, as they claimed, that they did not get suspicious when they saw advertisements for so many men.

We examined them as to their mechanical qualifications and soon saw there was not a mechanic in the whole eighteen. While we were strongly inclined to give them the 'educational test' (a good beating), yet, realizing that their lack of skill made them comparatively harmless, and that only economic deprivation would have made them capable of such an undermining hold-up game, we informed them with a measure of sarcasm that if they would go to work for these employers they would materially help our cause by showing how difficult it was to get mechanics, even from Buffalo. While we appreciated, we said, that they were hard up, and would like to help them, yet we had men of our own on the streets, and in this case we felt charity began at home. Then we let them go, followed, however, by one of our detectives. He traced them to the headquarters of the employers, and left a letter for the bosses, previously prepared by us.

"In this letter we said: 'We thank you for your great consideration in sending us these men. While we woodworkers regret that you are forced to search the slums of foreign cities, yet we realize that mechanical woodworkers are scarce; and to show our good will, and thus to spare you any unnecessary expense, we write this letter to indicate to you the folly of spending more money in that way. Respectfully submitted,

"'MECHANICS.'

"After that the employers sent us no more men, and we were left to paddle our own canoe, a task which grew more and more difficult. During the strike there was very little complaint because of hunger. There were two or three cases where wives came to our headquarters and complained because their husbands did not bring their strike benefits home. In these cases the executive board decided to give the benefit directly to the wives. The men, as a rule, got along pretty well. The business agents provided places where the men could sit, play cards, and drink beer

from the can without giving their pennies to
the saloon-keepers, who would get their pat-
ronage when they went to work again. In
that way, much discontent was overcome. It
required nearly $4,000 to make one strike pay-
ment to the men in our shop. The money
was spread on tables, open to view, and yet
never a penny was lost or stolen. Enthusiasm
and fellow-feeling generally rules during a
strike, even if the men have to look for work
elsewhere. The feeling is so intense that it
is now almost impossible for a leader to sell
out after the strike is on. It is suicidal for
the leaders to show the least sign of weakness.
There is certainly 'graft' at times, but it is exaggerated by the newspapers, which are generally controlled by the employers. The
leader knows that to advise men to give up
while the battle is on is absolutely disastrous
to his prestige. I know of a case where the
board of business agents, four in number, had
decided to go before a mass-meeting of the
strikers, who had been out on strike ten days,
and recommend them to accept a compromise
offered by the employers. In this case I felt
the business agents were justified, both from
the dollar standpoint and from the standpoint

of maintaining the integrity of the Union. The men had demanded an increase of three cents an hour in their wages, and after the strike had continued ten days, the employers offered two cents increase, and the business agents advised the men to accept this proposal. The men rejected the suggestion of the business agents, and three hours after voting it down the employers completely capitulated and signed the agreement. The rank and file are extremely suspicious, not only of the employers, but also of their own leaders, no matter how honest they may be or how long they have worked in the interest of labor.

"The strike went on until one of the business agents reported in the Council that the superintendent of the big plant of Brunswick-Balke had expressed himself as in favor of the closed shop. The superintendent thought it necessary for the employers to win this fight, but he dreaded the idea that perhaps the result would be the open shop; he did not relish the prospect of having in his shop 750 employees whom he would have to discipline through his own efforts, without the assistance of the Union. In the closed shop it is practicable for the Union to check the erratic discontent and the unjust discrimination against one another, among the men, from the purely stupid, selfish point of view. If one employee is unjust to another, redress can be obtained from the organization through the shop steward without recourse to the superintendent. The employer or his representative is thus relieved of the burden of adjusting differences between one employee and another. A man will stand a lot of abuse from another man before he will appeal to the foreman. That is more or less disgraceful, but where the Union rules are in vogue, there is a shop steward, an official of the Union, whose specific business it is to look after such matters, and a complaint to him is considered proper—a complaint against either another workman or against the employer. Experience has shown that, especially where the shop is a large one, the Union is far superior to the non-union shop in harmony and order.

"The superintendent of the Brunswick-Balke concern therefore hinted that if a committee with full power was selected to make some proposition more favorable than the original one, a settlement might be arrived at. This was done; a committee of thirty-six, selected from the various shops on strike, was appointed, the most ridiculous and impolitic thing, in my judgment, that they could have done. The committee was altogether too large. It was like the weakest element of an army going to the strongest element of the enemy and proposing peace. A strong element in a labor union is the man highly skilled in his trade, who has a reasonable measure of information and a fair power of expression. Another strong element is the man who is selected as walking delegate. His strength lies in not being under obligations to his employer. He is paid by the Union.

"But both these elements were absent from this committee of thirty-six, which had full power to act. If the rank and file had any tact at all, they either would have rejected entirely the proposition to delegate the full power to a committee, or else they would have preferred a committee of the strongest character. The only reason for selecting the committee of thirty-six was the suspiciousness always lurking in the rank and file. They preferred the honest fool or simple coward to a strong man whom they suspected, without realizing that men, no matter how dishonest, cannot do worse than a committee of fools.

"It was in reality the fault of the business agents. They were too weak to point out these facts fearlessly to the rank and file, for fear it would not be taken in good grace. It is difficult for the leader to tell the crowd the truth. But it is certainly true that the autocratic labor leader is more likely to get results than the democratic leader. When the power is centralized, as it is, comparatively speaking, in the Miners' and Carpenters' Unions, the employers can be approached more effectively. The delegate is then responsible to a body of men (the Council), who are much superior to the rank and file in observation and the power of initiative. To an office of this kind efficiency rather than good-fellowship generally elects.

"This democratic committee of thirty-six met the bosses' committee and agreed, without a protest, to everything proposed to them. The chairman of this grand committee put his tail between his legs like a whipped cur and said nothing. The strike was called off and the men completely defeated. If, however, this last meeting had been well managed we would probably have secured some concessions. As it was, however, we did succeed in maintaining the closed shop and the organization intact; although, as a general rule, when a strike is lost, the Union is likely to be disintegrated. Funds and hope are gone, and it needs both, and energy in addition, to build the organization up again.

"One great trouble in the calling and managing of strikes is this infernal preaching of the necessity of honesty. It is preached by all the moralists, by all the theorists, and by all the politicians, but not by the real labor leaders—not because they don't believe in honesty, but because of the terrible disadvantage it places the workman in. The rank and file generally recognizes inability as the best evidence of honesty. If you are aggressive and a good speaker, they are suspicious. They are taught that honesty is the most important thing—but it is not the most important thing. They have been hoodwinked so often by everybody that they distrust intelligence. And yet the labor movement is far more in need of intelligence than it is of honesty. Of honesty we have enough and to burn. An honest man, if he is not strong, can get noth-

work he likes to live altogether the life of the temperament. So when he suggested on that night to go out and call on Terry and Marie, * I said, very cheerfully, "All right." Moreover, I had not met Terry and Marie, or as yet any of the more interesting among the "radicals." So I was particularly cheerful in my assent.

He led me to a "slummy" place on the West Side. We groped our way up a dark staircase and into a small, bare apartment, the only furniture of which was three beds, usually occupied, as I afterwards found, by four or five persons; a table and a few chairs. Everything indicated extreme poverty, but the floor was clean and there was a kind of awkward attempt at neatness shown in the general appearance of the place.

On the table in the front room there were three or four books. On this first visit I noticed a collection of Bernard Shaw's plays, a volume of Ibsen and a copy of Spencer's "First Principles." A dark-haired, anæmic-looking, but striking and noble-faced girl was reading "Mrs. Warren's Profession" as we entered. An equally anæmic, but intelligent-appearing man was lying on the bed, smoking a cigarette. They received us with simplicity, offered us cigarettes, and we engaged in talk about literature, and society, and morality. In the course of the evening others came in, of the same kind, and I found this place was a kind of *salon,* where people of a certain sort met and discussed ideas.

They all called themselves anarchists, philosophical anarchists, as distinguished from the violent, bomb-throwing kind. They were a curious, gentle lot, in manner and appearance. Anton and I seemed like barbarians in comparison. They believed to a large extent in "non-resistance," and would not hurt a flea. They were obviously lacking in energy, and altogether seemed like an extremely harmless eddy in the current of social life. They talked about the "conservative" people with mild contempt, but were not inclined, apparently, to carry on propaganda with any force. They did not seem to have the energy for it. They seemed to desire mainly to be allowed to live as they please, with as little social restraint as possible.

"I like to live in the slums," said Terry, the man on the bed, "for there is more freedom there than anywhere else. Your neighbors are neither proper nor inquisitive, and comparatively speaking, you can do as you like."

Terry had been a skilled mechanic, a tanner, and had worked hard at an earlier period. Indeed, all these people belong to the laboring class. They come in contact with economic hardship or injustice and then they go to the extreme of theory and become anarchists. Terry had worked for many years soberly and industriously. He is a man of very unusual intelligence. One day he became aware, he said, that he was being exploited, and he quit; and he has never worked at his trade since. That was about twelve years ago. Before quitting work he had never read, but then he began to read and think. He began with Tolstoi, and Kropotkin, and Tucker, and Spencer, and became familiar with the local turn put to these ideas by Clarence Darrow. He became also a student of poetry and literature, and this instinct and love for the beautiful in expression limits to a certain extent his anarchism.

"There is no such thing," he said, "as the purely economic man. If there were, I would be an absolute anarchist. But man lives not only on food, but on sentiment and on ideas and on beauty. So whatever we may say against government, we must accept a part of the traditions of history and of literature."

He has decided, however, that it is wrong to work for society, so he lives in a garret on crusts, beer and high thoughts. He lives with the dark-haired, interestingly temperamental and passionate girl, whose name is Marie. She is many years younger than Terry, and her life has been typical of the woman anarchist.

She began to work in the factories when she was ten years old—first in a lead factory where the lie burnt her fingers to the marrow. She worked ten hours a day for two dollars a week—money badly needed by her mother, who was married to a drunken mechanic, always out of a job. She worked in other factories, always hard and always at low wages. It hurt her health, and when she was sixteen she became rebellious, was ready for almost anything. She threw herself into the arms of a lover, a young fellow of her own age, and thought she was happy, although she kept up her hard labor.

A year afterwards she met Terry, who had already been an anarchist and garret philoso

pher for many years. He took her to his
salon and read Swinburne to her.

"It was the happiest moment of my life,"
she said. "I saw that life had some beauty
in it, and I loved Terry at once. I left the
young fellow, who meant nothing to me, and
have been living with Terry ever since. You
may think it strange, as I am only twenty-
three now, and that was five years ago, and
Terry is forty-six. I like young men, too,
but Terry has meant life to me."

She quit the factory, and the two have lived
in the garrets of Chicago's slums ever since,
reading, smoking, thinking. But how? may
be a natural question.

There was another woman present at this
gathering when I first met the anarchists of
Chicago, whose life and character explained
how Terry and Marie can live as they do.
Katie is her name, and she loves "Culture,"
though she can satirize it, and has none of it
herself. It is through her love of "Culture"
that Marie and Terry can live as they do.

She is a cook, very witty and lively, but entirely ignorant of literature. She thinks
Terry and Marie are charming,—as they
really are—and great in every way. Katie is

a sport, though an uneducated one, and so she "keeps" Terry and Marie. That is to say, she supports them out of the $9 a week she makes as cook in a Chicago restaurant. She works all day, while they read, smoke, drink and talk; then she comes home, at night, with something to eat, looking forward to a few hours of pleasure, with her two cultivated ones. She is a devoted, willing slave, while they are the aristocrats of the slums—aristocrats who express the philosophy of the rebellious proletariat. That philosophy is anarchism; as it is rebellion against the institutions, not against the ideals, of mankind, they do not like this dependence, this parasitism on another human being. But it is easy to accept devotion.

"I do not like to be a parasite," said Terry, "but I don't see what's to be done about it. I would work if I saw any work worth doing; and if I could work for something except organized society. After all, I live on one person who supports me voluntarily, while your capitalist lives on thousands who are forced to work for him."

He and Marie recognize the inconsistency of their attitude. They do not claim to be virtuous, but they cannot see but what all society is organized on at least an equally unjust and parasitic basis.

On the night of my first meeting with Terry and Marie, he and I talked mainly about poetry and literature and abstract conceptions of justice and I found him, then, one of the subtlest, most self-consciously psychological spirits I have ever known—full of perversity, but wonderfully logical about it all —this man who had never had a school education, but who had thought independently, though often in my opinion wrongfully, about life. He had had not only his experience as a mechanic, his experience as a rebel, but also a career of unusual deprivation and toughness, and the result was not what might have been expected. Instead of finding a rough, uncouth and violent personality as a result of all this, I found myself in contact with a man of excellent manners, of a subtle and experienced mind, of a marked and relatively consistent individuality.

As I saw more of him—and I became, through some weeks, a regular visitor at his *salon*—my impression was confirmed. There, over the beer and cigarettes, I sat often with him and Marie till long past midnight, fascinated by his experience, his character and his expressiveness; and by the girl's emotional nature and untrained capacity for expressing an idea in an artistic way.

Maggie and Anton feel the charm of these two beings, although to their active natures the *far niente* attitude is not agreeable. Said Maggie: "Terry is a fine man, a beautiful character. He talks to everybody so sweetly. He listens to what a child will say, and is very good. There is only one thing I have against him. He won't work. He gets cast-down and drinks; but he never drinks much except when he works. He tried being a drummer for a while, but was a failure because he could not sell things to people when they didn't need them. He don't like to come to our house because I work so hard it reminds him he doesn't work, and he is sensitive about it. Marie doesn't want Terry to work, for then his tongue is violent. Work does not agree with him."

Marie says the same thing; she does not want Terry to work, although she is often hungry and has often to go without her cigarettes. "He is in a bad mood when he works," she said. Once, however, late at night, when Marie's tobacco was all gone, and there was no way of getting more, she burst out against Terry, and said he couldn't even keep her supplied in cigarettes! He seemed cast-down by this and sad, and she repented and explained to me how much Terry really did exert himself.

"It is not an easy thing," she said, "to get along without working. Terry has to be very clever to do it. It takes skill, more skill than to work."

She certainly loves this man who has meant freedom, thought, poetry, refinement to her. She has taken, of course, his ideas, but into them she has put her own individuality and given them a characteristic turn. He has taught her many things—one thing, to be a "free-lover." Though she loves Terry, she likes other men, and Terry encourages her to be what he calls absolutely "free." She carries out his ideas with completeness; and does not find it a hardship. But she is very jealous of Terry, if he shows any inclination for another woman's society.

"Yes, it is inconsistent," she admitted, "but our logic does not count when our fundamental feelings are aroused. Terry does not mind what I do—that is his affair. It is very fine in him, but I don't think it is very wise. Perhaps I would be better if he were jealous. But I mind what he does, I can tell you. Theories don't count in these things. We 'radicals,' in spite of all our theories, are as jealous and human as anybody, perhaps a little more so."

Anton likes Terry and Marie, and he finds it attractive to be with them. But he is aware of their limitations. Going back with him, after this visit to the *salon* in the garret, he said:

"I cannot see how Terry can live as he does. It is true, working for a living is not what it is cracked up to be. It is foolish to work unless one has to or unless one has a higher aim; as the Socialist I met in the box-car years ago used to say: nothing is necessary except the luxuries. And Terry and Marie get the luxuries of thought. They are aristocrats, but they pay too much for it. Terry hates posing. He is not an egotist and he talks about the subject. But I can't afford to be with these people too often—that is, the better ones among them. It would take away from my activity in the trade-union movement. The anarchists are so intellectual, they say, what's the use? And that is discouraging to a man who wants to accomplish things. The anarchists are all right—at least Terry is—when it comes to thinking, but they are practically very unreasonable. They are in this respect like the Socialists. One of them said to me not long ago: 'You are a trade-unionist every day in the year except election day and then you are a scab, for you don't vote with the Socialists.' The trouble with these people is that they think there is no way of doing things but their own. They are always roasting me because I am a trades-unionist. The Socialists shout that trades-unionists are corrupt, and the anarchists say everybody but themselves are corrupt. It's fierce. And yet I must see a good deal of these people. They have free thoughts and some of them think more than the average workingman.

"Many of them feel bitter just because they are superior mentally. Very few of the underpaid, day laborers feel bitter about things. The kickers you will find among the intelligent mechanics. The laborers hope to go to heaven. Their condition of poverty is so abominable that they are busy keeping soul and body together and don't think about economic conditions. They accept God, and don't think."

Anton and I had left the car, and were walking past a church, near his home. He pointed to the building, and said, with bitterness: "Damn that. It was that that kept me back. It was that that said to me it was religious to be poor, that work is a blessing, and contentment is good and all that tommyrot. If we working men don't look after ourselves, nobody will, not even God. We *must* organize, we must fight, to get what men and women ought to have, to make life any good. And we are roasted for this, not only by the ministers but by the anarchists who don't believe in doing anything except being good, except perhaps sometimes throwing a bomb, to draw attention to how good they are. (

"Of course, it is not a question of starving," he went on. "Not for most of us. But it is almost better to starve than not to have a great deal more than what is absolutely necessary. A laborer with a large family generally quarrels with his wife. During the entire day his mind is centred on the dinner hour. No time to think. At least, there is not affection in these homes, as a rule. They have no time to be interested in each other. The man, if a drinker, spends more than he ought to, and that creates discord. Most of the children stand by their mother; but if she puts up with a man who is extremely careless, that has a tendency to make the children think he is not as bad as he really is; and that gives them wrong ideas. So it is bad anyway. Conflicting ideas assassinate the love of man, wife and children.

"It is easy to be an anarchist, if one thinks. But if a man wants to act, he can't be a consistent anarchist. The whole thing can be traced back to economics, to this matter of dollars and cents. The more a man sees the injustice of wealth, the harder it is to work. Terry kicked so hard that he quit work, and is now a leisure-class person. He is now a capitalist without capital. He thinks economics less important than literature, because he possesses literature and doesn't possess money. But you can't get the average man interested in literature.

"You can improve the average man, however, by giving him more money. He then will become capable of better things. When I used to get only $16 or $17 a week and had to support a family, I found life was not what it is cracked up to be. I could not develop my family and social instincts; couldn't ever buy a newspaper. Such a life makes a man stupidly selfish. But these last few years, when I have made a few dollars more, I have developed my social instinct, a desire to read and think. It makes all the difference, I can tell you, a few dollars a week."

A few nights after that, Anton, Maggie and I went to an anarchists' "social"; where I met the whole "bunch" of the more extreme of the Chicago radicals. I found that they all were working people, or had been with the exception of the anarchist poet, an American of *bourgeois* family who had become what Anton calls the "King of the Anarchists."

The social side at this meeting was indeed strong. I had never been to a gathering of people who seemed so much at home together. It was first names everywhere, kisses and embraces. The beer flowed freely, speeches were made about liberty and love, everybody kissed everybody else's girl, and all were happy. The ordinary conventions of conservative society were removed. Extreme naturalness was the note, and yet it all seemed very harmless. They were working people who had decided to have a very good time in their own way; if they could not transcend the social conventions, they could at least cut under them. In spite of all this freedom, however, the women were gentle and intelligent; there was not a suggestion of toughness about the occasion. They were all people with ideas; so much is an idea loved in that society that a man rich in these cerebral concomitants finds himself very popular with the women—it is a surer way to succeed with them than unlimited ducats and gaiety. The men and women genuinely love ideas, temperament and poetry. There is no fake about it, as is often the case in conservative society, if indeed there is any desire for it at all there.

Terry and Marie were present, dressed in their best, which was very simple. Marie was looking for H——, who had not yet appeared. "I wish he would come," she said, enthusiastically. "Why, you know, he is a man who was imprisoned for a long time in

[277]

Austria because of his political ideas. He also escaped from an insane asylum. He is a genius, full of character. I love him dearly. I would rather live with him in jail than with an ordinary man in luxury." Her deep, large dark eyes shone intensely. In her look was the æsthetic side of the fanaticism which brings joy to the revolutionist.

Soon after, H—— appeared. He kissed warmly all his friends, including Marie, who introduced him to me. But at the moment he saw a man dancing with a dark Jewish girl, who worked in the factory and was in love with the Poet.

"Excuse me," said H—, excitedly, "I see a damn fool over there. I must go and kiss him." A little later I asked H—— what he meant by admiring a man whom he thought a fool. "All good men are fools in this world," he said. "They pass for fools with conservative people. I love only those people who do the unwise thing. If a man succeeds, he is not a fool, and is not for me. I never knew a man with brains and sympathy combined who was not a fool. That man is one of them, and that is why I love him."

H— is a journalist woking now on a German anarchist paper in Chicago. He has been a *feuilletonist* in Vienna and other German cities and his talk reminds one in tone of *Jugend* and *Simplicissimus*. He and Terry and I foregathered at the improvised bar, and he spoke of his imprisonment: "My ten years' imprisonment did me great good," he said. "I had a chance to be alone and to think things out. No one has a right to call his soul his own until he has been imprisoned. You treat political prisoners (anarchists) worse in America than they are treated anywhere else in the world. You treat them like common felons. In England, they are treated much better. You get the worst things from England, and leave the best. The English are really tolerant. Their police don't run into jail for disorderly conduct men who are making speeches, anarchistic or otherwise, or publishing papers about sex or government. But here they do. In England, they have no trouble with the anarchists, for they let them talk and write as much as they want. The English are away ahead of the Americans in real toleration and sense of justice. Look at the execution of the anarchists in Chicago. That could not have happened in England.

It is impossible, of course, to be free anywhere. I cannot be free in what I write even
in our anarchist newspaper. I must be a
hypocrite even there. I must write on the
level of the small bourgeois intelligence. It
is a fierce world."

The three of us talked about Anton. I
praised him warmly and said: "He has not
read much, and knows nothing about literature, etc., but he is a real personality, one who
is able to get into life and when in, to think
about it with point." H—— would have embraced me, so enthusiastically did he agree
with this remark. "The real people," he
said, "are among the active workers. There
is no doubt about that. There would be
nothing in socialism or anarchism if it were
not for the workers. There wouldn't be anything, anywhere, if it were not for the workers. Sometimes all this strength, sweetness
and vigor of the class is shown in one man
who can talk. Such a man is Anton."

Then he spoke, rather slightingly, of the
Anarchist Poet, who was present at the social,
very attentive to all the women. This poet,
B——, is sometimes called "King." He is
not of the working class, but goes among the

"radical" people of that class. He likes to eat and drink, perhaps excessively, and in other things of the sense is distinguished. He talks poetry and dresses and looks æsthetic. The women all like him, because they think he represents beauty and idealism. A factory girl is in love with him and follows him around like a dog to all the meetings. He prides himself on his power of capturing women. The real working people look up to him, because he seems to have what they have not—education and a grasp at what they feel are the higher things. But H—— was right when he said this poet was inferior to his admirers. "They like him," he said, "because they are good people, with high ideals, not because he is."

There is no love lost, however, between Anton and the poet, B——. For Anton, although he is an idealist, yet is a shrewd person, made keen in the detection of fakes from his experience in life. He sees through B.'s superficiality as a man, although he is imposed upon by his "genius," and his poetry. He quotes often with approval Katie's way of receiving him, when he comes to see Terry and Marie. Katie is the shrewd cook, and she calls B——, "the potato poet" and always has potato soup for him. She sees, too, that B—— is a mere sensualist, not really interested in the movement, interested only in getting as much as he can from the radical women, whose ideas render them susceptible to poets, and from the "comrades" among the men, and give them only his genius and his egotism in return. This seems to Anton and Katie like a big graft; they are perhaps the two hardest workers in the "radical bunch" and in some ways have the keenest vision; though one is a cook and the other a woodworker; but instead of "through," read "for."

"B—— told me," said Anton, "that his book of poetry would have the union label on it. He said it at least twelve times. If he knew what I think of him he wouldn't say it. He claims to love mankind, but he is an awful sponger on the radicals, who treat him as a comrade. He works them in return, for they all think him great. He will go round to the houses of the working people, eat and sleep with them, and even ask for things that are not in the house. He takes everything, and gives nothing. Once he gave a blow-out, said it was going to be something great.

When we got there we found sandwiches and beer, not enough of that, five cents worth. He had the gall to hold the beer up to the light, to show us how good it was! He thinks because we are mechanics he can treat us as he likes.

"He goes around coolly taking the wives and comrades of other men, and these men are often grateful, he is such a genius. They call him the King of the Anarchists, but I called him the Limit in Gall, the very essence of brass. How jealous he is, too! If the women show any interest in any other man, he is miserable. If he were a better man, he would be a better poet, I believe, though I don't know much about that."

Several devoted slaves of the Poet, besides the factory girl, were there; one man, almost the most idealistic and enthusiastic and unselfish personality I have ever met. He longs to sacrifice himself. His greatest pleasure, I believe, would be to be put into prison for the sake of an emotional idea. He has been, has done, everything; has worked with his hands, in a book-store, has been a publisher; has experienced all the faiths; when a Free Baptist, he was arrested for preaching on a soap-box in Chicago, and spent a night in jail. He gives to all he can, but his emotion is stronger by far than his intelligence, which however is not slight. He married a woman, loves her and her boy, by another man; gives her the freedom which he does not take in any essential way. The result finally is that she now loves a man of stronger, more selfish, more brutal character than her poor husband. There is no need, she thinks, to care for the sensibilities of such an unselfish man—fool, she probably thinks him in her heart. And a fool he is, in H's sense of the word, but he is a fool now who is miserable. The situation is tearing his heart out, but it is against his sense of justice and freedom to object. So he simply suffers. It is a striking case of what frequently happens in this "radical" society.

Men and women try frequently because of their ideas to live "tolerantly," as they call it, but they too often find that their "fundamental emotions"—as Marie puts it—are far stronger than their ideas. And then there is tragedy. On the night of the social, this little man was as gay as a lark. Everybody likes him and he went lightly about, dancing and making himself agreeable; and drinking more than was good for him.

He has a practical turn, in spite of his idealism; makes more money than any of the other extreme radicals. Whenever anything is to be organized, he is called upon. This social was for the benefit of one of the two anarchistic weeklies in Chicago—*The Demonstrator* —"which does not demonstrate," as Anton put it. In this enterprise the little man is an active spirit. He is active, too, in making possible the weekly meetings of the radicals in Masonic Temple—called the Social Science League. He was active in securing a room in that building, and many of the radicals bitterly objected, called him an "aristocrat." They wanted a West Side garret to meet in, thought it more consistent with the cause of the proletariat. Many of the more extreme of the sect refuse to attend the Sunday night meetings. They regard the whole thing as a fake, because of the "swell" surroundings.

One of the most interesting men at the social was like Anton, a woodworker, and worked at his trade. He, again like Anton, had more fibre and calmness and strength than the rank and file of the anarchists. He talks well, and reasons, not emotionally, but coolly; and in character he is balanced, tolerant and kind. He is a learned man among them, school-masterly in look, and talks in a slow, deliberate way. His character has not the emphasis and vigor of that of Anton, but it is steadfast and firm. Jay has led a varied mechanic's life—has been a blacksmith and a carpenter, as well as a woodworker. He is a stow-a-way from Ireland, but has apparently nothing Irish in his character. At one time he was a walking delegate in New York and has written trades-union and anarchistic pamphlets. His anarchism began at the time of the Chicago riots. When he saw the bodies of the eight anarchists who had been hanged, and felt the "organized injustice" of the act, "something happened" to him. He was deeply moved, and he has felt differently about governments ever since.

It was only the other day that I received a letter from Jay. I had written him that I intended to speak at the International Congress of Criminal Anthropology at Turin, and he thereupon wrote me, in part, as follows:

"I must comfess I am greatly at a loss to

know what criminology really is. It does not seem to me there is anything basic in it. Are some men born with a propensity to violate the rules of the game of society; or do they acquire the habit through contact with their environment? I don't think heredity has been modified in the least by society. If the postulates of evolutionary science are correct it took countless ages for man to reach his present state of development. From the standpoint of biology, civilization is merely a check on the natural instincts of man, which lead him to satisfy his desires wherever he can, without regard to conventions, his only question being, 'Can I make it and get away?'

"Every man is born a criminal—born with desires, and cares only that they be satisfied. Heredity says, 'Go and get the things you want wherever you see them!' Society says: 'Hold on, Bill, I have made rules you must observe in the getting.' It is quite clear the only question remains as to whether or not the individual will observe the rules is, how heavily do the rules press upon him. If the beaten path of civilization is level, and has plenty of eating-houses along the way, the chances are many to one that the individual will be a 'law-

abiding citizen.' But if the path is paved
with cobblestones and there is a policeman at
the door of every eating-house who forces the
weary traveler to keep moving, and refuses
him even a 'hand-out,' the chances are strong
that he will wander from the virtuous path
and seek his bread in other ways. He is
caught, clapped into jail, and the criminologist sees at once, in the shape of his ear, of his
head, or what not, signs that tell him this
man has criminal propensities. Of course,
the criminologist can only study the poor,
half-witted or unfortunate 'criminal' who happens to get caught, and he prescribes for him.
If he sees in him a propensity to murder only,
why, get him a job in a slaughter house
—if to be out at night, make a night watch-
man out of him. I believe crime is a social
disease, and should be treated as such. If
your criminologist will go and study the environment that the 'criminal' passed through
on his way to the jail, he will be getting
nearer the cause, not why men are criminals,
but why they do not become honest, law-abiding citizens. I think that in so far as criminology is a part of social science, it is of much
value to mankind, but if it is pursued as a

study of individual characteristics and propensities, it is not worth any more than the study of astrology or palmistry.

"It seems to me the whole question of civilization is one of environment modifying the natural or savage instincts of mankind. I can not see how anyone not a believer in the theory, or rather the poem, of special creation, can take issue with that proposition. If this be true then the duty of the true friends of Humanity is to direct their energies toward making society as serviceable as possible to the individual; that he may be compensated for his change from savagery, and be converted into a true friend of civilization. Get your criminologist to study the causes that make men criminals, and you will have done enough for any one man.

"I didn't intend to say but a few words on this subject, but I feel deeply at the way the subject is being handled by the surface philosophers and wooden scientists. At any rate, since you are going to the conference, the ideas of a criminal upon criminals may not be harmful to you. Esther is busy as usual expounding that which is in her. Her soul is filled to the brim with the joys that are to come when the criminals and criminologists will all be civilized."

This letter is a good example of the kind of speech that Jay makes at the Social Science League, or at other "radical" gatherings. He is of the better and sounder type of the radical agitator. Anton admires and respects him, and often finds him a job at his trade, for Jay is not as active or as resourceful as his friend.

* Esther is what Jay calls his "companion." She is a beautiful Jewess, and was present with her handsome children at the social. She is melancholy and affectionate and gentle and sensual, and has had an unhappy experience with men. She left her husband some years ago, "because we didn't develop together." And Jay and his wife separated for the same reason. Then these two met, and each discovered that the other had "high ideals."

So they very simply began to live together. They have a great respect for one another, and Jay is so tolerant that Esther's "longings" are completely satisfied, even when they lead her away from Jay for weeks at a time. But Jay's soul is fortified and tested:

he is not emotionally vulnerable, like the poor little Free Baptist publisher.

After the social was over, the "bunch" went round the corner to a chop-suey joint, and over tea and the conventional Chinese dish, we talked philosophy, and love, and psychology and scandal until three in the morning. Anton and Maggie, Terry and Marie, Jay and Esther, the Poet and a few others, and in and out of the talk, in the values put on life, in the point of view, in the prejudices, crudities, enthusiasms and hopes expressed, there stalked, in the incoherent background, the silent, though significant figure of the Working Man. His spirit gave meaning to it all.

.   .   .   .

There is a distinct, though rather anæmic charm about these gentle anarchists—these proletarians who develop a consolatory philosophy and work out a natural and intimate social life. In one of his books, Anatole France writes:

"Last week an anarchist comrade visited me. I love him because, never yet having had any share in the government of his country, he has preserved much of his innocence.

He wants to upset everything only because he believes men naturally good and virtuous. He thinks that, freed from their poverty, freed from their laws, they would get rid of their egotism and their wickedness."

CHAPTER XIV.

Politics in the Federation.

ANTON has had enough share in the government of trades-unions, in the workings of politics and in the passionate clashes of ambitions,
to be less innocent in experience than the anarchist friend of Anatole France. It has not
taken from him his ideals, but it serves to
make him very different from his anarchist
associates. He is a *man,* vigorous, tolerant,
passionate, inconsistent, generous, hopeful,
rough, kind and gentle; to a certain degree
practical and cognizant of conditions.

Comparatively recent events in Chicago, in
which he played a part, have served to make
Anton realize that facts have their compul-
siveness, and that the function of the ideal is
often only that of a tonic: that anarchism is
what may be called a tonical attitude towards
life, an emotional cock-tail, so to speak, which
serves to stimulate one's interest in ideal
things and thus exert, on the whole, a useful

influence in reducing the unhumorous seriousness with which many people, given up to routine and convention, regard the fallible institutions of men.

Keen as Anton is to see the limitations of
anarchism, he is equally keen in feeling the
weakness of a merely practical movement if
it is not allied with an emotional idealism. A
high-minded and useful newspaper man of my
acquaintance, one who has worked with distinction for many years on a Chicago paper
and has written every week comment on the
labor news which is invaluable to all students
of the subject, was slugged one day, after attending a meeting of the Chicago Federation
of Labor, the probable cause being that a certain corrupt labor politician did not like the
impartial and critical tone of the writer.
Commenting on this occurrence, Anton, who
is a friend of the newspaper man and respects
his honesty and ability, said:

"He is a fine fellow, but he got his medicine. He is always saying that there must not
be any socialism or anarchism in the movement, that trades-unionism methods, and they
alone, must be strictly adhered to, and of
course he wants trades-union methods without

graft and crookedness. But that is impossible. You can't eliminate graft without ideas, without emotions, and there are no more emotions in strictly trade-union politics than there are in politics in general. There are no ideas in the democratic party or in the republican party, and there are no ideas among the practical men of the trade-unions movement, unless those ideas are put into it by the emotional theorists, as they are called, by the socialists and the anarchists."

I don't think this quite applies to the newspaper man referred to, but it serves to indicate Anton's point of view. That newspaper writer does indeed believe in the need of principle, but he thinks it possible that merely moral principle is sufficient to hold men along the line of ideal action. In connection with the fight in the Federation between the old "graft" element and the so-called "reform" element, the newspaper man wrote me, as follows:

"I thought of you last Sunday and wished you had been at the Federation meeting when the election of officers was stopped by rowdyism for the second time. It was a sight that you would never forget. Another effort will be made to-morrow to elect officers; whether it will be successful remains to be seen. In any event, it is a hopeful sign that we are able to make such fights for what we conceive to be honest and right. As long as men are ready and willing to put up a fight against wrong and injustice, I say it is a hopeful sign whether successful or not. That seems to be the situation in the Federation. Personally I like Madden (the machine politician who has dictated officers to the Federation for * years) better than Dold, but as I told Madden yesterday, I am looking to underlying principles, not to the individuals. I wish the so-called reform element had a stronger man to lead than Dold, for the meeting last Sunday was the best illustration I ever saw that men want to be led. It was really a sight to see a big crowd of men racked and torn with passion becoming calm the moment Madden lifted his finger, and again when he gave the signal, they simply raised hell. Much as I disagree with Madden's methods, I could not help admiring the man during the fight. Cool and smiling he simply swayed his crowd as he pleased, while Dold was hesitating and trembling from physical fear."

Sentiments such as these this reporter put in his paper and probably in consequence of this general attitude, he was at a considerably later time slugged. It was during these political fights, when Madden took around with him his ruffians prepared to use physical violence, that Michael Donnelly, the leader in the great stock-yards strike, was beaten for the second time, and almost killed. His first slugging was due, it is believed, to his attitude of hostility towards the Driscoll-Young machine which controlled the teamsters for so long, and was finally condemned by the reformers in the Labor Federation. Donnelly brought in a resolution severely condemning Driscoll, and it was soon after this that he was slugged and nearly killed. And the second time, it happened probably for very much the same general reasons—a simplehearted and courageous opposition to the corrupt but powerful labor machine. This was also why the high-minded reporter I have referred to, Luke Grant, "got his medicine."

Grant is a shrewd Scotchman, honest and clear, whose heart is thoroughly with the labor movement, but who puts the usual amount of respectable emphasis on the undesirability of violence and "graft." During one of the teamsters' riots, the extent of which was grossly exaggerated, I was with Grant and another Chicago newspaper man; when Grant admitted that he had a strong desire to throw rocks at the "scab" drivers. "I don't believe in doing it," he said, "and think it is all wrong, but yet instinctively I would like to." The other reporter remarked that Grant's words were an expression of the "neighborhood morality," the behests of which were often stronger than law.

And yet Grant, in spite of his strong sympathy with the cause, is deeply affected by the opinion of the settlement workers and of the better element"—such as Grahame Taylor and other good men—which lays stress upon the undesirability of violence and graft—which maintains vehemently that bad is bad and good is good. It is partly this kind of emphasis which gives rise to a misapprehension of the relative values of the whole situation. The wave of "reform" which has swept America for the last few years has no doubt done lasting good, but it has undoubtedly in many cases turned one's eyes away from the forest and riveted them on the trees. And this is particularly true of the labor situation, especially of the distressing events connected with the great teamsters' strike in Chicago which aroused and excited the whole country. The eddies on the surface—"graft" and violence—have been magnified into waves of greater volume than the mass, while the big, underlying and significant facts of the human situation have not always been present in the critical consciousness. Grant was near enough the particular situation to see points of corruption among the labor leaders as well as among the employers, and, naturally enough, on account of his proximity, he sometimes was in a mood to exaggerate the importance of these unpleasant facts. Journalism is more insistent than literature. It deals with the temporary, salient accidents, and neglects the big underlying volume of life; so in the contemporary treatment, in newspapers and books, even when they are honest and unprejudiced, of the labor situation, there has been a harping on the exceptional situation— upon the dishonest labor official, the unjust strike, the walking delegate's arrogance, the "educational committee" and its violence. All these things, to be sure, are undesirable, but it is still more undesirable to allow one's sympathy, because of these things, to fall away from a movement which contains more ethics, humanity and justice than any other movement of our day.

When I first went to Chicago and was slugged in a saloon because I called Sam Parks a thief, I was in a state of mind in which I too believed financial dishonesty and ethical bad taste generally were matters of the very greatest human importance. I still think it is bad to steal, but I now believe that a man who steals may still be of human importance, and that the bulk of his activity may be for good. I have heard many very fine laboring men, who would not steal a penny, defend Sam Parks and men like him, on the ground that these men were really devoted to the cause and had done good work and were full of the milk of human kindness; better men than many of "our best citizens" who obey the law but who are humanly unjust.

The workingmen believe, of course that much of present day law, as it concerns property, is meant for one class only, and they naturally do not feel the same hatred for an ordinary thief as they do for a sheltered or extraordinary one.

It was a feeling very similar to that I have expressed which determined Anton's general feeling towards the grafting machine on the one hand, and the reformers in the Federation, on the other.

"At one stage of the fight against the Madden machine," he said, "the reformers invited me to attend their caucus. They knew that I had always been against the machine, and that I had a strong following among the woodworkers. These so-called purifiers were out to defeat the Madden slate, but had not recommended anybody for President as against Madden's man, Schardt. I suggested the name of a revolutionary Socialist who was Madden's chief opponent. They rejected him as their candidate partly on the ground that if he were elected, it would go out that it was a Socialist election. This seemed to me an unjust and nonsensical reason, although I was not a Socialist, but when they went further and said that if he were elected, they would not be recognized on the committees, they seemed to me to be quite as small as the so-called grafters, and I told them to go to hell, as quietly as I could.

"I consented, however, to watch for them when the ballots were counted. When the polls opened, the judges and clerks, who were Madden men, ruled that we had no right to have watchers, but about 10:30 Schardt, Madden's candidate, came around, and admitted the watchers. By that time, the ballots could easily have been fixed. One of the judges was a prize-fighter, one a bar-tender, two were sluggers, and all were Madden men. But I took a chance, and decided to watch. I was told that the ballots could not all be counted till four or five o'clock in the morning. I thought this was intended to discourage me, and I was more determined than ever. If I had known what I know now, I wouldn't have taken such an awful risk. When I entered, I made a statement to the judges and clerks, for I realized that these men hated the two men who had asked me to watch—for these two men had been the most stubborn opponents of ring rule.

" 'The fact that I am a watcher,' I said, 'need not be taken necessarily as an indication that I suspect the honesty of the judges

and clerks. I disagree with both of these reformers in many respects, but in view of the
rumors that have been circulated in trade-
union circles that there is no such thing as an
honest election in the Chicago Federation of
Labor, I want to learn for myself as well as
for the men I represent, to what extent this
is true or false.' I took a position behind the
man who read off the ballot to be sure
that the names he read had a cross before
them.

I had had no food since breakfast, but the
judges and clerks had all kinds of lunch and
drinks ordered at the expense of the Federation, which was illegal. They asked me to
join with them, but I drank very little, as I
was very suspicious of their motives. After
the lunch, one of the judges pulled out a big
pistol and asked me to hold it for him while
he went down stairs. Another judge laid his
revolver on the table where I could see it. I
thought all this play was meant for me, and
I felt I was up against it. Skinny Madden
came in just then. Everybody knows him as
the Lorimer of the Federation. I quietly but *
persistently asked the judges if Skinny had
credentials admitting him to the counting.

He overheard me, replied that he had no credentials, and left.

"They went on counting the votes. I noticed that the first five names of the candidates for the executive board received two or three hundred ballots all marked alike. It was a cunning scheme, as it meant, 'Vote for the first five,' and would avoid the possibility of confusing names, and would make stuffing ballots easy. About 2 a. m. six hundred and fifty ballots had been counted, and the entire machine had been elected. There was no longer any need for me to stay; the judges and clerks wanted to know what my attitude would be in the Federation. I replied that I would stand by the facts whatever they were.

"At the next meeting of the Federation, the report of the election was given, and no protest was made by anybody. The men for whom I had watched, did not ask me to report, but one of them got up and read a letter from his union charging dishonesty and corruption in the election but not giving an iota of evidence.. I deemed it an insult to me that, after watching all day and all night, my opinion had not been asked, so I took the

floor and roasted the union for making an un-
substantiated charge, and the 'purifiers' for
their cowardice. 'I have no doubt,' I said,
'that Madden is the Lorimer of the Federation, but my observation has taught me that
the main reason the reformers are dissatisfied
is that they themselves are not the Lorimers
of the Federation. I personally and also as
a member of my union am opposed to gang
rule wherever I see it, no matter what flag
it flies under in the Federation, but I am not
willing to make a serious charge without some
definite evidence. I am opposed to many of
those who have been elected, and especially to
the President, but although I watched all
day and all night, I saw nothing that I
could advance as evidence of corruption. It
looks to me as if the man for whom I watched
suspected my honesty, as he did not ask me
my opinion, but preferred to present unsub-
stantiated charges. I voted for him, but if
he has no better judgment than to appoint a
man whom he immediately afterwards sus-
pects of dishonesty, I am glad he is defeated.'

"This speech created a sensation in the
Federation meeting. Some of the Socialists
thought I did not stand by them, right or

wrong, but I am not a 'class-conscious' man, and don't care for that kind of sentiment. They hinted I had not done right. I told them that if the facts would hurt the reform movement, the reform movement ought to be reformed.

"Madden's man, Schardt, when elected President, came to me and asked me to serve on the resolutions committee. He said I was a fair-fighter, but began to tell me what to do when I was on the committee. I checked him and told him I had a mind of my own, and, if on the committee, I would act as I pleased. I would work only as a free lance, I said. He seemed to think that because I had not charged his gang with dishonesty I couldn't prove that I was for them. Needless to say, I was not appointed to the committee.

"These little oppositions of mine did not amount to much, but I kept them all worried. They did not know where I stood. They did not seem to grasp the idea of being independent even from reform. My popularity among the rank and file increased. At every election several would nominate me for some office in the Federation, but I always declined; because, working at my trade, I could not attend the committees regularly, and so would not be in so good a position to criticize. Then, too, a free lance is always in a good position to talk, for men know he is not trying to get anything. As it was, I was the only man in the Federation who was always on the floor to fight anything that came from the administration that seemed to me wrong. The terrible fear of advocating a measure which was likely to be defeated keeps many men in their seats, but I like nothing better than to be in the minority. When you are right, it is very exciting. I dislike those 'reformers' who sit by and see a tyrannical thing done, by the gavel or otherwise, without protesting.

"As time went on, the reformers found it more and more difficult to understand my attitude. When the fight came up between Madden and Dold and the former's bullies made their raids on the ballots, men like Quinn and Fitzpatrick did not understand my lukewarm stand, unless I had gone over to the Madden camp. As I had always fought the Madden machine this looked to them like treachery. I could not be enthusiastic for a man like Dold, and I didn't like the cowardly and tyrannical attitude of the reform machine; and I didn't like their tendency to put their friends in office. If, being against a machine makes a purifier, I am the only purifier in the Federation."

Charles Dold was originally put in office by the Madden machine; and I have it from no less an authority than Samuel Gompers that Dold made Madden a promise not to put a certain vigorous revolutionary Socialist, a "reformer," on any committee. But Dold fell into the hands of the "better element" in and out of labor circles and the result was that he put this man, obnoxious to Madden, on several important committees. Madden, therefore, got out his knife and determined by all legal and illegal methods to defeat Dold at the next election.

"When," continued Anton, "this election was to be held, the Federation was divided into two camps, the Dold faction and the Madden faction. The slugging of Donnelly drew the lines all the sharper, and naturally everybody would be against Madden. But the Woodworkers' delegates had reason to oppose Dold. He had been fighting our organization for a long time, and was in addition a disagreeable side-stepper who liked to avoid responsibility and had no personal courage. Knowing that he would not go very far in defending principle, when by so doing he might be violently dealt with, neither I nor any other woodworker was willing to make a strong fight for him. In addition, the woodworkers were on strike at the time, and needed the support of all the Unions regardless of political factions. So we did not hump ourselves for the "reform" candidate.

"The element of so-called purifiers who had suddenly waked up to the necessity of fighting the machine, took for granted, as I have said, that I was a Madden man looking for favors. They lost sight of the fact that neither I nor any other woodworker had ever occupied any conspicuous official position in the Federation, with the exception of Dick Braunsweig, who some years ago was a member of the executive board, and was a most vigorous fighter against gang rule. Dold at that time was recognized as the most valuable supporter of machine rule; and is quite generally regarded in labor circles as a man not to be relied on too strongly.

"Experience taught me that, if I wanted to be a factor for good in the Woodworkers' organization and the labor movement in general, I must be careful not to recommend a man who I felt would disappoint the expectations of the men behind him, no matter what principle he named as a party measure. I questioned the wisdom of stating with fevered enthusiasm that the election of any man to any office would assure any particular relief to the rank and file. I feared that to be very enthusiastic about the greatness or goodness of any man would divert the attention of the rank and file from the necessity of looking after themselves and of being active from time to time. These were my reasons for not coming out strongly for Dold.

"On the other hand, I knew that the Madden element was certainly not what was wanted in the labor movement. So I was forced to take a neutral position. My anarchism, or in other words my tolerance and the many-sided influence of my radical friends, made it easier for me to take such a position, for I had no great confidence that anything very good could come out of political fights where the factions were looking for advantage; or out of machinery in general.

Great good only comes in my opinion from the educations of life.

"A little while before the slugging of Donnelly and the election I had made up my mind that I wanted to be Chicago delegate to the International Labor Congress which was to meet at Pittsburg in November of last year. I could get off three weeks from my job in the factory, and representing the big labor body in Chicago I would have a chance to express my views on the larger issues of labor and meet men prominent in the movement all over the world. It had been the custom for the President of the Chicago Federation to be the delegate to the National and International Congresses, if he desired to be. I had, previous to the local election, approached the Secretary of the Federation and ascertained that there would be no opposition to my candidacy either from him or from President Dold, who did not desire to be the Chicago delegate.

"When the time for the election of the delegate approached, I found, on account of my luke-warm support of Dold in the local elections, that the 'reformers' were against me, suspecting me to be a Madden man, as I have explained. They all got busy in an effort to defeat me. They knew that I was better qualified than the man who ran against me, but I would not work in favor of their hobbies. That shows the paradox of their position as reformers. The Secretary of the Federation came to me, through their influence, and asked me to withdraw. 'I'm afraid they have got you beat,' he said. 'You can go and tell the caucus of reformers to go to hell,' I said, 'I am in this fight to stay.'

"I determined to beat this gang, if I could, and for the first time I decided to hustle for my election, and play a few cards. The next Monday a convention of street car workers opened, and I as President of the Woodworkers had received an invitation to present to this convention a gavel bearing a Union label. The street-car men have the largest delegation to the Chicago Federation of Labor, and all their strong men were at this convention. That gave me an opportunity to tell them where I stood. I explained to them the situation, and they promised to stand by me in the election. That same night I told my story before my own Union. I had been instrumental in obtaining $2,000 from the Federation for the Woodworkers while on strike, and was generally popular in my Union, and they elected four additional delegates. Another Woodworkers' Union, No. 67, elected five additional delegates and No. 17 six. Every Union instructed their delegates to be present at the Federation meeting when the delegate for the Pittsburg Convention was to be elected. There never was a time when any one organization was so united and determined in any particular purpose, as they were on electing me.

"Every Woodworker delegate showed up at the election. The opposition got very uneasy when they saw how strong I was in my own Union; and adopted the old machine tyrant rule of electing the delegate by motion. It was moved that, since the President was not present, that the Vice-President of the Federation be appointed delegate to the Pittsburg Convention. I immediately jumped to my feet and protested against the autocratic manner of selecting the delegate. Others rose to their feet and joined in my protest, moving that the proper way to elect the delegate was by secret ballot. The purifiers could not object to this, and nominations were made. An old carpenter arose and nominated Steve Sumner, a teamster, a lily-white reformer, on the water wagon and very religious, but only a two-year-old trade-unionist. The financial secretary Hopp then put me in nomination. Tim Quinn and John Fitzpatrick, two stellar lights in the reforming caucus, had been nominated. They got up and declined in favor of Sumner. It was, of course, a put-up game to defeat me. Quinn spoke of the courage and honesty of one of the men already nominated, and heartily recommended Sumner to the Federation. Fitzpatrick in his speech of declination, emphasized the fact that Sumner was on the water wagon and therefore should be elected. A Socialist who had been put in nomination also declined in favor of Sumner 'who was a pure and simple trades-unionist.'

"I got up and demanded that my gray-haired friend inform the Federation whether any one of the candidates was not a trades-unionist, and if so, to point him out. Previously to the balloting, there was much talk among the delegates, and the sentiment against the caucus methods was strong. 'Vote against the caucus,' I heard said everywhere among

[314]

the men. The woodworkers and the street-car men were with me; but they were less than half of my supporters. All the ladies were for me; those representing the Teachers' Union and the Waitresses, whom I used to escort home. Many teamsters voted for me because the other fellow was on the water wagon. The vote was taken, and I was elected, 90 to 67. There was great applause, and I was called on for a speech. That was my opportunity, and I said, 'I am extremely pleased that the chairman possesses the wonderful courage to abide by the decision of the majority. I am sure he would have liked to do otherwise, and if my sympathy was of any use to him, he might have it and I would be satisfied with the votes. As for those who have strenuously defended the slate and done all they could to prevent it breaking, I can assure them that it is sometimes quite as necessary to break a slate that comes from the Masonic Temple as to break a slate that comes from the back-room of a saloon. I trust that no one will misunderstand the utterances of that ungodly man when he resigned in favor of our Christian friend, for I am sure it was not inspired by personal selfishness but merely by the passion he had to submit to the tyranny of a caucus. While I sympathize with the error of their ways, I cannot accept their philosophy, and for those who may have misunderstood the reformer when he spoke of the water wagon, I wish to inform the Federation that it is true I have never been on the water wagon, but I think that may be because I have never been on the whiskey wagon. As for those men who have spoken so feelingly about purity and simplicity, I assure the Federation that I can see the simplicity of their motives, but I'll be damned if I can see the purity.

" 'I can assure the Federation,' I concluded, 'that my attitude in the International Labor Convention will be just as conscientious as it has always been in the Chicago Federation of Labor. I remember a year ago that the delegate representing the Federation was allowed $500 to attend the Convention. I hope in my case $7 a day and car fare will be sufficient to cover the expenses and permit me to be a gentleman. I am at a loss to understand why $500 can make a gentleman out of a man any more easily than $150, but perhaps the caucus people who kept silent a year ago can explain this point to the satisfaction of the Federation.'

"After I had finished, the applause came like thunder, very much to the disheartening of the caucus people. After all their efforts I had defeated them by a large majority. They came around and were very mild and apologetic. I told Fitzpatrick I was sorry he was the caucus candidate for President, but, although he had behind closed doors in the caucus conspired to defeat me as delegate and had shown his willingness to eulogize a two-year-old, yet I was not too small to overlook that weakness and vote for him as President. 'I don't want you to think, however,' I said, 'that I believe in caucuses to elect officers. I have no objection to their being called for the purpose of solidifying the ranks in a common attitude against the common enemy, but when it comes to elect officers, I think a man's character should be sufficiently open for us to judge as to his fitness, without a caucus. I don't want you to feel that I am pledging you my vote, as I can't tell but what a better man may come up before the election, for instance, myself.' He laughed at that, and we were friendly."

In connection with the general subject of politics within the body of organized labor, the attitude of Samuel Gompers, President of the American Federation of Labor, towards this Dold-Madden fight, is interesting. When the fight had become acute, Dold, Fitzpatrick and others of the reformers appealed to Gompers to use his good offices to try to bring about peace between the warring factions. Gompers characteristically delegated the power which he had by reason of the invitation to Thomas I. Kidd, an executive officer of the American Federation of Labor, the most prominent woodworker, and a man whose high character is recognized by everybody. Mr. Kidd heard both sides; in the caucus of Dold's friends it was agreed that Mr. Kidd should preside in the Federation and his decision be accepted as final. Anton, telling the story, said:

"When B——(the anarchist woodworker agitator who has been referred to earlier in Anton's story) heard of this, he threw up his hands, and said to me and Tom Kidd: 'O, Jesus, I knew dot when Foxy Sam Gompers, when he got invitation to come to give one advice in fight of labor against capital, he come right away, but wen he be asked to come to settle a fight between one man and anodder in a Union den he can't come, den he got no time. Gompers ain't no damn fool like you, Dom Kidd. No matter how you decide, no matter how fair you be one way or de odder, dey won't like 'em. You got no right as executive officer of the Amalgamated Woodworkers to act in dat capacity. You make enemies when de woodworkers have to make good. Denn, too, you won't get no hearing. Do you dink dot Skinny Madden allow you to be umpire wen he don't know you are wid him? Not on your life! And Skinny Madden knows, and Charley Dold knows dat Dom Kidd has no use for Charley Dold, and has no right to have any use for Charley Dold, but don't need to make any publicity of it. But you accept and you must do it, but we go and see Skinny Madden.'

"So B——, Kidd and another man went to Skinny's saloon. Madden greeted them cordially and taking B——'s hand said: 'I am glad to see you.'

" 'You be glad to see me,' said B—— 'pecause you tink I have no use for Charley Dold. I remember de time wen you and

your friends were subborting Charley Dold;
I know you be pretty foxy, but Jesus! Charley
Dold fool you, but he deceive everybody else,
too. He no draw the line on you. I know
dat you be crooked, Skinny Madden, and I
know dat Charley Dold be bigger crooked. I
know dat you put up a fight. I know dat
you stick by your friends and I know dat
Charley Dold never puts up a fight, but gets
his friends into de fight and den he gets a
telegram: he has to go away wen tings come
to crisis. I know him in Detroit, in New Orleans, in Philadelphia, everywhere: he always
gets a telegram. So I call him Telegram
Charley.' This was the report which B——
gave me of the meeting.

"Previous to the meeting of the Federation
at which Kidd was to umpire, Tim Quinn and
one or two others called together in caucus
the true and faithful of the reforming flock.
It was called out of respect to Madden's cunning and power. The members of the caucus
were pledged to secrecy, so that Madden
would not learn until too late to act. He
had accepted in good faith the proposition
that Kidd should preside at the meeting, and
therefore made no preparations and did not

get out his friends in force. So when the day came, the reformers were all present and twenty or thirty policemen, but not many of Madden's men. Kidd was there, but the reformers did not want him to take the chair, as they felt they did not need him and could railroad through the thing as they pleased. Madden insisted on Kidd's presiding, and Dold was at first against it. But he came around, and if it had not been for Quinn, perhaps Kidd would have taken the chair. But he saw that there was no united wish for him to act, so he withdrew. The report of the clerks was therefore easily endorsed, and Dold was declared legally elected. B—— was delighted at the truth of his prediction, and Sam Gompers, the old side-stepper, got no blame, but it made Tom Kidd look like thirty cents."

Anton's election as delegate came during the time that I was with him in Chicago. It gave him an enormous amount of satisfaction. He had "played politics" for the first time, and had won. He had beaten an organization which he deemed hypocritical, and that, without allying himself with the grafters. He had made no promises to anybody, and had no debts to pay. He now had an opportunity to satisfy his temperament by a change. Held down as he had been for several years closely to his work, the prospect of a trip to Pittsburg under interesting circumstances was like "hearing the whistles blow in the spring." What was left of the hobo in him contributed to his general joy.

Soon after his election, his Union gave him "a blow-out" and $50 toward his expenses. "Maggie was tickled to death," he said. "She could not sleep for joy. Now that I am going to the Convention, I want her to have a vacation, too. If she didn't, it would spoil my pleasure." So Maggie went with the children to the old home in Clinton, and had a good time "disturbing," as she put it, her old friends, with her "radical" ideas. "Before I had been there a week," she said, "I had three mothers deserting their children at night, to go out and have a good time at some social. And I put a lot of other ideas into their heads, so that before I left they had begun to think some."

CHAPTER XV.

The Intellectual Proletariat.

WHILE Anton was in Pittsburg, I saw a great deal of the "radicals." I came to prefer sitting with Marie and Terry in their simple *salon* and marveling at their sophistication and expressiveness, or talking with the large-passioned Esther or the good, calm and clear-sighted Jay—to prefer this to any of what might be called my more normal occupations. Of Clarence Darrow, too, I saw a great deal at this time. More gifted, more clever, and more able than any other Chicago "radical," he is not as consistent or logical as many of them. He is a friend of the proletariat, a philosopher, a literary man and a dreamer, but he is also a lawyer, a politician, and a money-maker. He has a marvelous inconsistency of mind, but a rich temperament and many "parts." Connected as he is, of course, with the "successful" people, and the bourgeoisie, he is not as clear a case as the rank and file of the radicals. He is a friend of the laboring man, not a laboring man either in fact or by instinct.

But it is this being the real thing, or based upon the real proletariat, as Terry and Marie and Anton and Maggie and Jay and Esther, and many of the others are, which gives them their consistency, their meaning and their eloquence. It is they who get radical ideas, instincts and hopes first hand, and have consequently that freshness of mind and of expression which springs from coming actually in contact with the material of their emotion and their thought. A thousand times I felt myself to be in the midst of a kind of renaissance of labor.

This I felt whether I was in a group of active, hard-working, hard-drinking, practically-minded labor leaders, with their vast physical joy in life and their belligerent hopes of the future, their longing for "velvet," and consequent occasional corruption, their passionate, unconventional habits, rough-house methods and rough capacity for stating their meaning in their own way; or whether I was with the gentle, anæmic commentators on life, those who had been workers and had become

agitators or merely contemplative reflectors—
people like Terry and Marie and Jay and Esther.   What makes Anton so peculiarly interesting to me is that he is both these things—
he is the rough, practical belligerent, idealistic laboring man in the movement, on the
one hand, and on the other he is the reflective
anarchistic, gentle, poetic commentator on the
facts of the labor which he has experienced
so typically.   I have often been at a loss to
know whether he is primarily a practical man,
and a liver, or a philosopher, and an expresser.
What he is without doubt is *Ein Gemuth*—a
temperament—for that accounts both for
practical, rich activity; and for emotional and
full-blooded love for ideas.

I have almost never seen Anton depressed;
but, one night, while he was at the Pittsburg
Convention, I had an opportunity to see how
very far in the moral depths Terry and Marie,
the aristocrats of the slums, the Platonic ex-
pressers of the proletariat, the reflective anarchists, were liable to fall.   I had been at the
salon, had sat for hours over the cigarette and
the can of beer.   Terry had talked about some
of the anarchists in Chicago and other cities,
their weaknesses, their personal traits, with a

fine psychological touch and with an almost never-failing delicacy and originality of expression. He was happy at it, and so were we. But very late in the night we went out and took a walk in the early dawn of a Chicago day, winding up in the back room of a saloon. Terry drank several glasses of whiskey, and Marie, too; that, and the fatigue of the late hour and their accumulated anæmia resulting from bad food, put them in a mood of extreme, though expressive despondency. It was impossible to get cigarettes in that neighborhood, and that, too, was an added burden.

Terry then burst out into a talk of extreme anarchy; said he desired to prey on society, to make himself a complete burden. He rejected the elementary basis of morality, and said that the only reason he did not steal was that he had never seen a really good opportunity. He had known thieves and prostitutes well, and now he spoke of their qualities with affection and seemed perversely to love whatever was rejected by organized society.

Marie referred to one of my books, "The Autobiography of a Thief," and asked me why I had attempted to get the man to "reform." I replied that, aside from conventional morality, this man was a "dead" thief, and had no chance except through reform. Terry then spoke of the advantages of prison life, the opportunity for terrific thought. I objected on the social ground—for a sensitive, developed man, with social instinct and love of woman, life in prison is hell and an inevitable step to the mad-house. "You, Terry," I said, "are too old and too sensitive to be a good criminal."

Then I protested against the cutting off of all morality. Why live among men at all if we are to strip ourselves of everything? The impossibility of his attitude came home somewhat to Terry when I spoke of the deprivations of Marie, of her not having a nice place to live, insufficient food, etc. That night I pointed out to him, she did not even have a cigarette, and there were large holes in her shoes. Marie, who was very tired and a little intoxicated, had been complaining about the lack of the necessary cigarette.

"You don't like me," she said, complainingly, to Terry. "You won't do a thing for me. You even steal my cigarette tobacco."

Terry felt this reproach, and admitted to

me that, if he were in a different mood, he might tell a different story. "But it seldom pays," he said, "to tell one's real mood." Finally, we went sadly to bed.

But it was not always thus, not even generally. I usually found these two people excited, interested and pleased with ideas or with the beauty they were able to find in books. I shall quote here a few of the things they said—only a few was I able to record at the time or shortly after. All records are insufficient: lag behind the reality. The inevitableness of this will easily be recognized by anybody who has ever attempted to record a conversation. Fortunately, Marie has written me some excellent letters, in which she expresses herself characteristically. Some of the ideas no doubt originate with the more philosophic Terry, but the phrase is given its turn by her more artistic personality.

"My ancestral blood has flowed through scoundrels since the flood," is a quotation of which Terry is peculiarly fond.

"It is only in voluntary association that man is fine," is another statement, by an unfortunate man, often appreciatively quoted by the tenement philosopher. William Morris' dictum, "Art was not born in a palace. She was taken sick there"—this is much loved in the *salon*.

From Marie's letters I glean the following:

"I love children, they are such true and fearless rebels. I can't imagine how people, able to take care of them, could ever be blue with such optimistic and anarchistic little ones around them."

Here are some of her literary appreciations:

"Tolstoi has truly a contempt for art, and also a contempt for some of the finest things in life, *love,* for instance. His ideals of love are all very well for septuagenarians, but won't do at all for us young folks."

"What delightful liberties Keats takes with his rhymings, and his quaint expressions, almost cockney, some of them. I noticed one little word he must have been fond of using, which gives a sort of brisky air to his verse.

" 'He was a poet, *sure* a lover too.'

"Perhaps this fondness of mine for these quaint expressions in poetry is because I can't appreciate too much pure poetry. I never could read Milton, and still I can't mush over Whitman. Talking of mushing, I really must get more acquainted with little Sadie.

There is a little girl that likes mushing over poetry all right. I have a complete edition of Swinburne, which I must study some more and then capture little Sadie and see if we both can't have poetic delirium. She has been pensive and interesting, of late, for since the Poet left, she has had 'no one to worry about.' "

Sadie is one of the little "anarchistic" Jewesses of whom there are many in the "movement." She is intelligent and cultivates carefully an air of mystery and the quality of the "baleful." She told Marie that she wanted to be a beautiful woman, merely to be able to make men unhappy, for in that way only can men amount to anything!

"My excuse for not writing before," wrote Marie, "is that I had been reading 'Intentions,' and it has had an irritating effect on me. This would not be so, perhaps, had Terry not been discussing it nearly every day, and brought home the truth to me that I myself was deriving all my emotions from art. And it is true to a great extent. I realize myself that I do not come in contact with life enough to satisfy my emotional nature. Therefore I turn to literature. I've been reading Ibsen's dramas, the more mystical ones such as 'The Lady from the Sea,' 'Rosmersholm,' etc. It seems to me these are almost overwhelming with their moral atmosphere, as you would call it. I sat up last night and read 'Little Eyolf,' and I truly passed through terrible joys and sorrows which were not my own. But after all I believe I would rather satisfy my emotions from life itself, even if I should have to pay a dear price for the joys I might find. But it seems that some of us cannot come in contact with life unless some one else fosters in us the 'life illusion,' to make us believe that we may do something in the world for our good or for the good of others. This life illusion was lacking in me, and consequently I did not participate in the game. But you came along and made me think for a while that I, too, might do something for myself. Terry is so critical of everything that he enjoys nothing. And it is sometimes most depressing to be with him, especially now when he is in a supercritical mood. 'Intentions' is the first book he has seemed to enjoy for a long time, and that book is so much in accord with his own mood at present, and Terry's personality is so strong that it predominates over everyone and everything. Thanks to the gods, Terry is not always as he now is. His moods vary as much as anyone's, only not quite so often. I sincerely hope I shall never become as critical and sceptical as Terry! Just think of losing the faculty of enjoying life and of having to receive only sterile emotions from art!"

"I am often amazed," she wrote, in another letter, "at the density of man, who dreams that he can interpret all our actions and thoughts. It is said that actions speak louder than words, but I believe that silence speaks better than either. If we could only judge others by their thoughts, but alas! how very seldom does it happen that one can express these, or even make any impression on others of having an inner life, which I believe most of us try painfully to conceal. Have you ever noticed how feverishly and restlessly we talk and talk trying to avoid the least approach of silence lest we should therefore reveal our inner life? I believe that more of our real selves could be shown by our silences and not by our words or actions. Whenever a great joy or sorrow touches us deeply we are silent."

Here is a specimen of her humor. I had

written her that I had taken a villa in Italy and told her something of its beauty. She replied: "Terry and I are having quite a strenuous time these last few days fixing up our new home, for we, too, have discovered a little villa of which we occupy three rooms on the top floor rear. We have a small grove of fine willow trees on our right and a lovely view of back-yards and chimneys on our left. Unfortunately, we have no windows, front or rear, which cuts out the view of the railroad track on one side and the street on the other. We have no modern improvements, I am sorry to say, but then we don't care. As it is, a bath-room would be superfluous here, because all we need to do is to wait for a rainy day and then stand or sit at our ease in our own kitchen, parlor or dining-room, to be cleaned by a most excellent shower bath. The roof of our villa is arranged very conveniently for that purpose.

"As for light, have I not always Terry before me? And indeed the light of his genius or personality is almost blinding—at times. If we feel a little chilly, why we get into a hot argument with Kate, for instance. I think if we stay in this villa very long, we shall develop a whole lot, certainly we have a good chance to study certain phases of natural history. We shall also be quite proficient in some kinds of athletics, as our floors all slant towards the centre. It is really quite a climb from the middle of our drawing-room to the west window. It's good exercise, and if we stay here a while I am sure I shall be able to climb up Mount Shasta without an effort.

"Three other families occupy our villa, or, rather, three old women. Their families sink into insignificance when one beholds these three ancients. I am so afraid of them, whenever I have occasion to leave my portion of the villa, I sneak stealthily by their windows lest they see and curse me. They were born old and lived here always, and will continue to forever and ever."

In a less cheerful mood, she wrote: "I used to think that all mothers and fathers whipped their children and were mean to them. But now I think the parents cannot be otherwise. Some things are so terribly true and common and trite that they are not interesting. I know of hundreds of fathers and mothers who hammered and beat their children into nonentities. And they are living

[334]

to-day what they call happy married lives and
have children of their own, which they in turn
hammer and beat into submission, just as they
themselves were. I don't like the atmosphere
of a saloon, [at this time Marie was living
above a saloon] and I don't like the dirty,
common work that I would have to do here.
And yet I'm sorry we are going, in a way.
There is a beautiful grove back of the house,
all full of great big trees. I love trees.
They were all stripped of their leaves, and
as I walked on the ground which was all covered with these poor leaves, I thought of
Keat's poem:

> " ' Too happy, happy tree
> Thy branches ne'er remember
> Their green felicity,'

So for that reason I would like to live there.
It must be beautiful in that grove in the summer time. But I would have to work so hard,
I might not appreciate the beauties of nature
at all. So I think I am more glad than sorry.
I spent nearly all day Sunday exploring this
grove, and all evening I sat in the saloon
drinking a lot of whiskey without getting

drunk, played several games of pool and had to listen to a graphophone playing rag-time until my nerves were all on edge. I have had a black mood ever since. All the sympathy in the world does not help. At moments like these we feel that terrible sadness which comes from the knowledge that each one of us is a separate soul. Though we may love each other, yet there is something in each of us that another cannot know, something that keeps us everlastingly apart."

This expressiveness of Marie is not shared by the remarkable man with whom she lives—not when it comes to the pen. In speech he is subtle of the subtle, but when he writes he attempts the same quality and his manner is labored. He has not the ease and spontaneity which this factory girl of twenty-three shows in a remarkable degree. The only thing of his put on paper that I possess is the following. He wrote, in a note to one of Marie's letters, sent to me to Italy:

"He who finds permanent ground for melancholia, may not be troubled by the shifting scenes of mankind. This nostalgia of the soul is the last resort and retreat of incurables who take their last stand; the forlorn brigade of the Milky Way. You seem to be about that distance from us now, so you give us one more reason for feeling as lonesome as we do. There are so few, I wonder if it would do any good if there were more of us." Then he added, as a matter of "labor" news, in which he knew I was especially interested: "The latest from the coal fields: the stock market is ready for slaughter. Ten thousand troops in the anthracite region await the behest of the Bullionaire. 'On with the dance.' Let 'stock' be unconfined."

This is rather forced; the literary attempt is too obvious. Yet when Terry talks, the effect is just the opposite. Everything he says seems to spring profoundly from his own experience, even when he talks about "literature." His words are generally very sad in their suggestion, far more so than those of Marie, who is younger and more buoyant, has much more of the "illusion of life." Terry is the absolutely self-conscious proletarian: with the utmost logic and consistency he expresses the philosophy of the man who has nothing. There is consequently a most pathetic melancholy in his manner and expression. Intimate as he has deliberately made himself at times with the most absolute "scum" of society, his manner is one of great gentleness and wistfulness.

I have told, in another place, of how, after working steadily for many years at his trade as a tanner, he revolted, because he saw that society was "exploiting" him. The precipitating reason was this. A rich man wanted to start a new business, and, knowing of Terry's skill and practical imagination in the trade, he asked him to get the shop under way for him. Terry, without making a contract —he is by nature singularly confiding and unpractical, as all these anarchists are—set to work and organized the shop, did the whole thing, got the business going, and then was offered by his employer money aggregating what the ordinary wages of a mechanic would have been for the few months' time. He did not accept a cent of this money, but took his coat and left, and has never worked a day since; has rejected the whole system of organized society; has gone so far that, if his ideas were held by any considerable number of men, life in communities would be impossible.

Anton is often impatient at the fact that

Terry and Marie "do" nothing; and yet he impulsively sympathizes with some of Terry's ideas—particularly the impatience at work that is not interesting. Terry has often said: "If society would give me work that interested my mind, I would work harder than anybody." Anton, himself, hates routine. He gets no satisfaction out of his mechanical labor for the reason that the modern differentiation of function and development of machinery has taken all that is individual, all that is truly artistic out of the mechanic's work. The large art of an earlier time was founded largely upon the detailed art, the personal expressiveness of every little object made by the mechanic. But now there is no personal variety, no opportunity for the mechanic to express himself in his work. For this reason the taste of the community in art has been lowered, and the interest of the excellent workman in his work has been taken away. Now he works only because he must. Terry does not see the necessity; the more moral and responsible Anton does. That is the difference between these two men. Neither, however, has any love for labor. And because society and the Church tell them they should love labor, they rebel against society and the Church with all the passion of strong personalities.

While Anton was in Pittsburg, I saw not only a great deal of the "radicals," but also of the more or less hostile critics of organized labor. They, of course, see in these "radicals" only a lot of "cranks." And, indeed, there is no doubt of the absurd character of much of the "radical" body of men and women. Thus far I have given most stress to that side which to me is interesting and sympathetic and based upon real feeling and experience. But that there is much that is half-baked about it all, there is, of course, no doubt.

One sees a great deal of this half-done quality of thought at meetings such as those of the Anthropological Society and the Social Science League, meeting Sunday afternoon and evening at the Masonic Temple. A number of extreme pseudo-scientific thinkers, emotionally free-love females, mushroom commentators, Robert Ingersollian critics of religion, hold forth at these places. Their prophets are men like Pentecost, who announces that Christ was a great fool and that the prostitutes are rapidly freeing society; men who have a little more general education than the mechanics, but not nearly enough, get up and say emotional absurdities, and women from the shops lay bare their extreme crudity of thought in hysterical forms. It is no wonder that Anton cannot resist, in such gatherings, his satirical mood, and as for Terry, he generally "stays away," as Marie puts it. She, however, goes mainly for the sake of meeting a "comrade" or a new and sympathetic man.

In the West Side *salon* or in the domestic tenement one finds the reality, the genuinely intellectual proletariat, but in their crowded meetings is the same *banal* spirit, in a different form, that one finds in crowds everywhere. It is after these meetings that the *élite* gather in some saloon, and there men and women talk freely and often gaily, and the basic ideas of the proletariat are expressed often in form and with considerable beauty. And, in substance, it is never frivolous to the philosopher, for underneath it all is the serious, unsmiling Spirit of Labor; and the great warm feeling of Solidarity, of human love. And it is that which gives even to the absurd meeting its pathos and its significance, and even a kind of sad beauty.

When I first became interested in the labor situation, and began to meet the men, I found very little that interested me. They were lacking in grace, not expressive, not peculiar, not picturesque. It was, at first, only the recognition of the importance of the subject that held me to it. Finally, of course, I became fascinated, as I got beneath the surface and came in contact with some excellent personalities.

After I had once seen the "eloquence" of the thing, I found myself continually surprised and displeased by the hostile critic of organized labor. There are so many men, of good intelligence, who, because of their lack of feeling for humanity or because of the moral astigmatism induced by their personal or class interests, find it very consoling to harp on the crudity and roughness and occasional "grafting" propensities of labor and make of their bad taste a substitute for justice.

I met on one occasion one of the big men in the "beef trust." He is a good citizen, or is so regarded by the world. But as he sat complacently in his office and told of how unjust the strikers had been, as he spoke of his employees in a tone that indicated his belief in their general bestiality, he seemed to me an object totally lacking in attractiveness. "No man," he said, "can stem the striker's unreason." He spoke of the "small margin of profit" in the great beef business, but said that the business, being in a way a public necessity, must be carried on, even at a loss. He made it appear almost a charitable undertaking. One reason the men had given for walking out the second time was that the girls had been insulted by some of the foremen. The trust magnate laughed as he said this. This seemed to him to be the height, or the depth, of sentimentality.

He did not tell me what I knew from another source, and not a labor source, but from an independent investigator, a woman of truly wonderful and penetrating character who had more to do with the final settlement of the great strike than anyone else; facts known to the newspaper men, but never published, because they would have been too shocking to society. The condition of the yards when the negro strike-breakers were there, and the girls from the Tenderloin had been imported in large numbers as a bait to keep the strike-breakers at their work, this cannot be described. I, knowing these facts at the time the comfortable boss was talking morality to me, did not feel deeply impressed with his virtue. I knew the essential moral sweetness of many a rough laboring man; Anton is quite incapable of a cynical attitude towards women—free as he is;—in every way he is the moral superior of the big trust magnate whom I met—the man who sneered at the strikers and at the common working girl, who was willing to make an indescribable place of his workshop and at the same time was "one of the boys about town," might as well leave morality out of his talk.

"Criminals and thieves are preferable to workingmen," said an experienced man of the world to me, who had associated with big railroad men all his adult life. "They are more educated by life, are entertaining talkers and have a kind of cultivation. Laborers when honest are raw, and when clever are dishonest and rawly so. They are in a terrible hurry to get things, and they hate the men who have things. The painter in my hotel room said the other day, at the mere mention of L—'s

name (a rich railroad man): 'The ——
————. He gets \$100,000 a year.' As
he spoke, wolf-like hatred gleamed in his
eyes."

As to unreason, I find it pretty equally distributed between the "classes." The laborers
are often extreme and unfair about their employers; but no more so than is the other side;
while theirs is certainly the balance of morality. Most of the "radicals" are fanatics, to
a more or less degree, but the injustice based
upon fanatical feeling has at least an element
of sympathetic human nature, while that
based upon privilege does not seem to recom-
mend.itself to any disinterested contemplator.

In the great teamsters' strike, which took *
place while I was in Chicago, there is no
doubt that there was money used dishonestly
on both sides; it is likely that in the immediate situation, the men were more at fault
than their employers. But the possibility of
such a situation had largely grown out of the
previous commercial immorality of the employer. Shea, the leader of the strikers, was *
a rough "grafter," in the sense that he deemed
it fair to "get" what he could from the other
side. The revelations about his expenditures,

the "Kentucky Home" episode, and the general ugliness of his moral character, were essentially true; but the newspapers laid bare all these things with a view to turning public sentiment against the men. It was in striking contrast to the way these same newspapers covered up the stock-yards horrors. If the private life of a labor leader is a legitimate thing to expose in reference to his public morality, so is the private life of an employer. But the newspapers of Chicago did not see it that way—for commercial reasons.

I met Shea on several occasions. He sat, more or less like a poisonous toad, in his room at the Briggs House. He seemed a fitting companion to men like Young and Driscoll, whom he was supposed to meet at places like "The Kentucky Home," and settle, over bottles of champagne, the affairs of the city. He was certainly a low representative of the roughest element of labor; but yet there was a certain honesty about him. Though he had every reason to be a hypocrite to me—he took me for a newspaper man—he occupied on one occasion nearly half an hour in defending Sam Parks. He indicated, in a rough way, that everything had not been said when it

[346]

was admitted that Parks had stolen money.

"If," he said, in substance, "you want to write something truthful about the labor situation, take the life of a man like Parks. Don't exaggerate one side or the other. Of course, if you want to howl about dishonesty and graft and all that you may please the capitalists, who want to hang on to what they have stolen, but you won't get all the truth about a man like Parks. If you get all the facts, I think Parks won't seem like such a bad fellow, when all is said."

Shea did not seem to me like the ideal man —far from it. But I liked him better than the hypocritical, sensual and respectable member of the Beef Trust whom I had interviewed.

CHAPTER XVI.

Some of the Big Men.

ANTON came back from Pittsburg full of
the eloquence of "wife, home and family."
Maggie was a day late, and during those
twenty-four hours Anton was miserable. "I
tell you what, Hapgood," he said, "there is
nothing like being away from your wife for
a couple of weeks. It makes you appreciate
her for fair. And I am eager to get back to
the shop, too. I think, after all, a mechanic
who gets good wages, has eight hours' work
and a good home is pretty well off. Saturday night is enough for bumming around. I
am sure I don't know what would become
of me if I didn't have a regular occupation.
If I had your job, for instance, I think I
would be a worse fellow than I am."

This speech showed an extraordinary
change from the character of Tony, the Hobo,
who so often heard the whistles blow and

boarded the box-car. I remarked as much, and he answered:

"Well, if I had been a scab I'd never have got to this. Somehow, working for the rank and file and fighting with your fellow men make you steadier. It makes it seem like good fun to be responsible. That's why it is right almost to force the non-Union men into line. Life, when taken right, forces a man to be a good husband. Why not force a scab to be a good citizen, a good member of his class? It is all a matter of fear, with these fellows. They can't see their own interests. You must make them fear something more than they fear going hungry, and then you can keep them in line."

At the Pittsburg Convention Anton had still further opportunity to meet some of the "big" men in the labor movement. I have often heard him on the floor of the Chicago Federation meeting, and I know him to be a vigorous, forcible and sometimes witty speaker, full of ideas which are sometimes too subtle for the rank and file of his audience; sometimes too radical for them, and frequently too playful. They were evidently too radical for Samuel Gompers, for at the Convention, after one of Anton's speeches, he turned to Tom Kidd, and said:

"I thought you said the Chicago delegate was a sensible fellow. Why, he is a gatling gun. He goes off in every direction." Anton could not resist the opportunity to expound some of the shifting ideas of the practical anarchist, and hence Gompers' remark. After one of the meetings one of the most conservative leaders in the American Federation made to Anton, protesting against some of his speeches, the remark already quoted.

"We are all anarchists, but what's the use of shouting about it?"

"Duncan's remark," said Anton, "is true of the leaders; and it is more true of the rank and file than most people think. The men don't know it themselves, and are frightened at the word anarchist. But they sympathize with a lot of things that conservative people call anarchistic, and if one man is a little more radical than the others he can have anything he wants in the way of an office. That shows what direction they are going in.

"It is hard to say what men like Gompers and Mitchell really think, because they are diplomatists and side-steppers. Gompers is a much abler man than Mitchell, who has a reputation all out of proportion to his ability. There are many men in his Union stronger than Mitchell, who was made by the newspapers. The miners are mainly an ignorant lot. They have all heard Mitchell's name, and they don't know, as a body, any other leader. So Mitchell is bound to be at the head, as long as he wants to be."

I myself have met both Gompers and Mitchell. The former I found very willing to talk facts, but he shied off from opinions with the astuteness of a fox. Mitchell I met over the bar of the Briggs House. The place was full of labor leaders, and they all talked freely, except Mitchell. If he had an idea, he kept it to himself. He is a handsome man, with a pathetic, romantic look, as if he had a mission in life, but didn't want to give it away.

Gompers has a sense of dignity, and the song which the anarchist organizer, several times referred to, sang and was overheard by the President, did not please him:

" Everybody works but Gompers
And my old man."

[351]

A story told me by Anton still further illustrates the character of the President of the American Federation of Labor, whom, by the way, everybody respects, and justly, for he has held his position for many years, and no one who knows him can doubt either his ability or his honesty. The Anarchist Poet desired at one time to write for *The Federationist,* of which Mr. Gompers is editor. Terry, Anton, the Poet and one or two others went to Thomas I. Kidd's office to try to induce that influential man to speak to Gompers about the matter. Among them was the anarchist organizer, who called Anton one side and said to him:

"Anton, I am surprised at you. Do you tink Sam Gompers will allow an anarchist to fight against de Socialists? Wen Sam Gompers can't any longer have de Socialists as his enemies he will lose his popularity and become useless. He wants to do all de fighting against de Socialists himself and don't want no anarchist to help him. Neder Dom Kidd nor all de Kidds can influence Sam Gompers to hang himself. De strength of de anarchist lies in de weakness of de Socialists, and Sam Gompers knows dat and wants to keep dat weakness all to himself so he can show it up in de *Federationist*."

The Anarchist Poet did not get the job. This trait of Gompers is shown by his general sensitiveness to newspaper opinion. When there was an attempt made to get Gompers to help settle the teamsters' strike by publishing the truth, his question was, "What will the newspapers say?"

Anton was struck with the tendency of the Convention to stick to "details," instead of considering general principles or matters of broad policy. "Everybody was there," he said, "to look after his little interests, the interests of his local union, of his city or his trade. No one dared to say anything about bigger things for fear that his little thing would be spoiled. It was mainly about organization matters, questions of jurisdiction, etc., things which are as dry as dust. I wanted to have these matters cleared up quickly, so I recommended that the executive committee be instructd to put through these jurisdiction matters in a certain time. There was, of course, great opposition from the committee, and Vice-President Duncan retorted that   * the committee ought not to be subjected to

[353]

force. 'Why not admit, then,' said I, 'if you object to force, that you are an anarchist?' It was this question of mine that led to Gompers' remark about the gatling gun, and to Duncan's private statement about the prevalence of anarchism among the leaders."

Shea was at the Convention, and Anton said of him: "He is a good representative of the teamsters. He walked into the Convention as he would into a saloon, with his hat on, and spitting to the right and to the left."

Anton's tendency to criticize everything extends quite as thoroughly to the anarchists as to anything else. What he loves most about the theory of anarchy is its individualism: he is consequently dead against the Socialists. And yet he is often exasperated at the lack in the anarchists of practical sense. The Convention passed a resolution combating the alien laws and approving of the admission into the country of all political exiles from Europe. "This resolution," he said, "ought to have been noticed by the anarchists and their newspapers, and ought to have been approved by them. But there was not a word said or written about it. The anarchists lack blood, and in this country are dead. They don't know or

[354]

care what is going on. It is only the opposition of the police that keeps them alive. If they were let alone and allowed to spout, as they are in England, they would all have died of emotional starvation long ago. The execution of the Chicago anarchists in 1886 has been the main-stay of the movement ever since.

"The best thing about the anarchist who calls himself an anarchist—not the practical men with anarchistic tendencies such as I am or other labor leaders—is his emotion. He is a fanatic and thrives when he is oppressed. It would be well for the labor movement if there were more emotion in the American Federation of Labor affairs. Sentiment ought to have some sway in this great movement, but I found no sentiment at the Convention—all dry routine and wire-pulling. All is based on cold, calm reason, but that is not enough. All is based on selfishness, or nearly all. It is the class struggle much more than it ought to be.

"It would be well if there were some men high up in Federation affairs who had sentiment, even sentimentality. A man like Eugene Debs, the famous Socialist, would be

[355]

very useful in that way. His career has been an interesting one. Nearly all labor leaders spring into prominence at a time when it requires courage, determination and more or less extreme radical attitude, but soon after they assume the position of responsibility, they become more conservative, with but few exceptions. Debs was one of those exceptions. In the great railroad trouble of '94, Debs called a general strike. Public opinion was so strong that he showed his hand before he was ready. So that the organization was mainly acting on impulse and enthusiasm. It was only two years old, and was inexperienced and undisciplined, and expected too much from the particular individuals chosen to lead the strike. The result of such hasty action is usually defeat. In this case, it was complete annihilation of the organization; but the strike made Debs so prominent that he became candidate for President of the United States on the Socialist-Democratic ticket. He is a wonderful orator and a splendid organizer, but, lacking in executive ability, is a bad leader in a strike, not because he fears to take an unpopular position, but because his character is emotional and sentimental. He has never been a strong power in organized labor, except among the Socialist enemies of the Federation. If, however, a man of his character were as active in the Federation as he is among the Socialists, it would be of great value in introducing sentiment into the actions of that too practical body of men."

It seems difficult, indeed, for a practical labor leader, engaged actively in the special question of raising wages and shortening hours, to retain the general emotion and imaginative interest in what is called the larger issues. The anarchist organizer seems to be one of the few men who have been able to retain his original enthusiasm. Another man who is as enthusiastic as he was in the flush of his experience in the movement is the President of the Woodworkers' Union, a friend of Anton's, whom I have met and heard speak. He does not appeal to sentiment, is very clear and practical in his talk and in his measures. But away back in his heart lives his one strong interest: the labor movement. He has a strong intelligence, and is singularly simple in his interests. He has never married; he does not believe that a man can do justice to both a wife and the labor movement. Although he has been practically active among men for many years, he is as sensitive as a young girl and far more scrupulous. One day he was with Anton and Tom Kidd, when the latter, who is very fond of a joke, said: "Dinnie is going to see his sister at the expense of the organization." "Dinnie was horribly hurt," said Anton. "He flushed up, and later, when I was alone with him at dinner, he said things which made me see clearly all the tenderness of his nature. Yet Kidd meant it as a joke."

Kidd is another man whom Anton deeply admires—perhaps more than any other man in the labor movement. He is a strong, jolly man—a "good fellow," a capable drinker and a man who even those most unsympathetic to organized labor admit, is thoroughly honest. He did more than any other one man to build up the Woodworkers' Union. "For many years," said Anton, "Kidd worked as general secretary, with responsibility, but no power, a very trying position. There were many calls for assistance, but no financial resources. He is absolutely relentless in character, and pushed along until he built up the organization. For several years, as secretary, he worked at a salary of $15 a month, and also worked at his trade. Then the organization took all his time and gave him a salary of $50 a month. On this he was married. In 1898 came the big woodworkers' strike in Oshkosh, Wisconsin, as a result of which Kidd became famous throughout the country. The men proposed 5 per cent increase of wages, a weekly pay-day, and the taking of women away from the machines. This demand the bosses rejected without even a conference and locked the men out. Kidd was called to Oshkosh to conduct the strike. He took with him the anarchist organizer to furnish the enthusiasm, while he took care of the diplomatic end. There was a street riot, and a little boy was killed. Kidd spoke at the grave of the child, and laid the responsibility of his death at the door of the millionaire employer. The anarchist agitator had spoken a night or two before, and gave a description of what they did to scabs in Chicago. This was credited to Kidd, and he was arrested on a charge of conspiracy. It was conceded that the power of the corporations was not easy to defeat, and so the woodworkers engaged Clarence Darrow to defend Kidd. Darrow's appeal to the jury went throughout the country, and as a consequence Kidd sprang into prominence as a fearless and radical labor leader. Darrow, in the address to the jury, compared Kidd to Christ, and his speech at the boy's grave to the Sermon on the Mount. It did not take the jury long to acquit. After that, Kidd became a prominent man in the American Federation of Labor, and a high officer. Before his election as Vice-President he used to write in his woodworkers' journal serious reflections against Sam Gompers, but after working with the President in the executive council, Kidd became gradually more conservative. This seems the way of the world. But he never lost his individuality, and is still a strong and emphatic speaker, but more cautious in his writings."

I met Kidd a number of times, usually at the bar of the Briggs House. I was always interested in his versatile and witty talk, in his robust temperament and pleasure in vigorous social life. In his way of meeting people he is the man of the world—does not suggest at all the reformer or the emotionalist— seems primarily an active liver; perhaps more so now than formerly. He is incapable of saying a sentimental thing, and regards the trades-unionist in America as at present in some respects well off. Of the "boss" he can say some sympathetic things. One day he said to me that some of the small employers excited his sympathy. "They work hard, and for themselves and their families only; don't have as good a time as the mechanic, and are not interested in any cause. Sometimes they don't even make money. I was a small employer once, and after every pay-day I discovered that my men had more money than I. So I went back to work."

Kidd is an opportunist in life; though he believes that anarchism is the highest ideal. "Men are not good enough to be anarchists," he said. With Socialism he does not seem to have much sympathy: he is too much of an individualist. "The worst things about Socialism," he remarked, "are the Socialists. They are all autocrats in temperament. Their despotism would be worse than what we have."

When I was slugged in the saloon, I thought the episode might prejudice the men against me, and I went to Kidd for advice. That was before I knew Anton or many of the men. I had heard Kidd spoken of by settle-

ment workers, employers,—everybody—as the
wise and good man par excellence in the
Chicago Labor World. He laughed when
I told him of my trouble, and told me to
forget it. "It will make no difference to
anybody," he said. "That was just a man-
to-man affair, easily settled and easily forgotten." Kid has never told me so, but
I yet believe that even a man who is as conservative and good as he is, dare not regard
occasional union violence as altogether a bad
thing, certainly not a very immoral thing. It
is a war measure—mistaken, perhaps, but in
the absence of any great human morality on
the other side, it does not seem like a great
sin. The worst enemy in Chicago of the Labor movement admitted Kidd was personally
honest. "But even Kidd," he said, "lets
vouchers pass for pay for violent work done."
If this were true, it would not surprise me,
and yet I have a great respect for Kidd.

Michael Donnelly, the man who was twice
* slugged, the leader of the great stock-yards
strike, is in manner a great contrast to Kidd,
with whom I have seen him at the Briggs
House. Donnelly has a quiet, sweet way
with him, a good deal of gentle humor and the

reputation of being an eloquent speaker.   He
is another leader generally conceded by everybody as being personally honest; his being
slugged probably helps to prove it.   His calling of the second strike, against his judgment,
is often cited against him by labor men and
others as a proof of weakness.   And yet it is
probable that if he had not called it, the men
would have struck anyway.   This is what he
says, and in view of an exceedingly unreasonable element among the butchers, it is quite
likely the truth.   If he had been a very strong
man, he might have controlled the situation,
but some of the unreasonable ones were of very
vigorous character.

John Joyce, in particular, is as belligerent *
a human being as I have ever met.   He is a
splendid, powerful fellow, and as he paced
up and down his parlor and fiercely talked to
me, I felt that if there were many men like
this strong, aggressive, unreasonable fellow
in the organization, the leader had indeed a
task before him to hold them in line.   He
has a natural hatred of authority, and in espe-
cial of the authority of the foremen.   Donnelly said Joyce is admittedly as good a workman as there was in the yards, but his quarrel-

someness always got him in trouble. He used to insist while at work that every grievance be settled as the aggrieved person wanted. If a boy who was holding gullets saw he would have to hold two more than those prescribed within the hour he would kick, and would always be supported by Joyce and others of the "inflammables." It was no hardship for the boy to hold any number of gullets prepared for him, but when the men got strong, as they were before the strike, they, as often happens on both sides, abused their power. One thing they insisted on was to have twenty minutes twice a day to go to the toilet. This to the calm Donnelly seemed unreasonable.

Before the second strike, when Donnelly and the committee had agreed to a settlement with the packers, Joyce, although he was not on the committee, came into the room and said the men would never agree to the terms. He was a self-constituted boss and had great influence over the foreigners. He is sober and industrious, and has an interesting family, but his spirit is the most untamed and aggressive I have met.

Talking of the superintendent, who it seems had threatened to discharge him, Joyce said:

"He was not sufficiently developed physically to put me out." To this man Joyce always referred among the men and foremen as "Mr. Doughbelly."

Joyce is great at figures: he has spent his leisure time for years in making out lists of the various packing-houses, number of men employed, wages, etc., "so that he can use it as a club over the packers," he said, "if they lie or do wrong."

He denounces with the utmost energy superintendents and scabs, but women are quite as bad.

"A few hen-pecked husbands," he said, "are worse than all the scabs in America. They are chewed up by their wives if they don't come home with money, and if they come home with money, they are chewed up because they don't come home with more. 'What's the use of giving the Union 50 cents?' they say. We are between the devil and the deep blue sea, and the woman is the devil.

"Times are getting worse," he continued. "The employers are getting tired of educated, self-respecting men. They generally want niggers, foreigners and scabs. During the strike they had a prize-fight in the yards every night, and the things that went on there between the nigger strike-breakers and the girls imported to take the places of the girls who had struck is something I am not going to tell you about."

After the strike was over, Joyce was one of the skilled workmen not taken back. "There is no money in the house," he said, "and my son is on strike, too, and he did right. I sleep well, you bet. I'm all right, as long as my family have food. When they don't have it, I'll go out and get it!"

Two or three lion-like strides across the room gave me a vivid impression of how he would "get it."

Our interview closed with his words: "Cowardice is the principal thing in most men."

With many men like this in a union, one can easily see some of the difficulties with which the leader has to contend. The butchers are a more ignorant lot of men, as a rule, than the workmen in older organizations and of more skilled trades. But one of the most inflammable and fire-eating men in the whole Chicago world of labor—and it is not an anæmic, lying-down world—is at present high up in the affairs of the Federation—Tom Quinn, with whom Anton had difficulties when he ran for delegate.

Quinn is an Irishman, of the dynamiter variety, and loves, of course, the opposition. "The movement began with force," he said, "and it will continue with force. At the first great street-car strike in New York, the police interfered with the German strikers who were marching peacefully through the streets. I was one of the Irish boys of the streets, and how we did stone the police! It was that strike and the police interference that started the Knights of Labor—an organization that lasted until it was disrupted by 'conservative' graft. All graft, by the way, is conservative, in or out of the organization."

Quinn is a vigorous fighter and believes in physical force with the same passion as in honesty and love and human solidarity. His love of honesty led him, as a boy, to throw inkstands at the school-master, and to be a leader among the violent street Arabs of New York. "Teddy" Roosevelt was at that time a leader of the rich boys, and he and Quinn, who represented the proletariat, sometimes came in personal contact in the free and open street. One day one of Tim's crowd hit Teddy in the jaw but did no harm except to break his own fist.

"For many years," said Quinn, "I did not see Teddy. And when I presented to him, as President of the United States, the other day in Chicago, the strike petition, I saw that everything was changed in him except that jaw. It was the same old obstinate organ that broke the East Side boy's fist."

Quinn is one of the most democratic people in Chicago, but he believes in bringing about universal justice by violence. He was emotionally interested in the municipal ownership movement, which has assumed almost the character of a religion. Full of personal egotism he did not understand the total lack of personal egotism of a man like Mayor Dunne, or the impossibility of a Mayor of Chicago always acting in the way demanded by an emotional enthusiast. So he was soon as violently opposed to the Mayor as he had formerly been violently in favor of him. Quinn's general note, the underlying trait of his character, is violence. That explains his being.

But in Quinn, this all-pervading violence assumes an attractive form; there is a fascination about a man who is so manly. And most people who meet Quinn have a great respect for him. His brains, however, are not as big as his spirit. He is not as percipient of conditions and does not understand human nature, is not nearly as much of a natural philosopher, as is our Anton; that is the reason he did not understand the latter's attitude towards the Madden machine in the Federation; and the reason why he remained so narrowly by the conventional ideas about the relative value of "graft" and "antigraft."

I do not want to suggest in any way an apology for graft. The reaction that followed the great and beneficent exposures of corruption in business, politics, insurance, trusts, patent-medicine, etc., was based largely, I believe, on the dislike of the grafters in being exposed. It was a natural, but an egotistically motived reaction. We cannot have too much exposure. But, certainly in the labor movement, there is the possibility of a state of mind where a man will on account of his ingrained ideas of property morality, or other current morality, neglect a larger, less defined, less worked out morality. Human good is what we all ought to aim at; and often a passionate insistence upon the degree of value in current morality is an obstruction to moral advance. No real reform is possible without a shaking-up of the current standards of morality and of law.

It is indeed simple and touching to see how moral, in a child-like and unthinking way, many of these laboring men are; and how they think morality is as much of a piece as pure red or pure blue, without shadings. Their enemies shout of "graft" in the movement, but to my feeling, the dominant note is one of almost pathetic morality. Soon after I began my Chicago quest, I met a drunken machinist in a saloon; and, being quite unacquainted at the time, I asked him for some information about the local situation, information which would not involve names or "expcsure" of any kind. Misinterpreting his hesitation, I offered him a little money, in exchange for an effort at expression on his part. To my surprise, he regarded it as an insult. "No," he said, "I'm an honest man, and won't touch your money. And I won't talk to you any more until you can get *The American* to recommend you." *The Ameri-*

[370]

can is the local friend of the workingman. *
Only that endorsement could allay this simple
man's vague supicions.

This simplicity of moral point of view extends from the rank and file to most of the
leaders. One of the prominent butchers,
speaking of a famous labor leader, said that
no man ever said anything against his money
morality. "Everybody thinks he is very honest," he said, "but everybody knows he goes
'on a bat' now and then, and is loose with
women. I believe that any man who is unfaithful to his wife, is unfaithful to the rest
of us and is not the right leader. It is impossible for a man to be honest in one way
and dishonest in another."

A prominent Chicago teamster expressed to
me another very simple view of morality.
I fancy he thinks money morality is not of
much consequence; due no doubt to his experience of injustice and hardship. "I was
a slave for five years," he said. "I worked
three hundred and sixty-five days in the year,
twelve to fourteen hours a day. For this I
was paid $9 to $11 a week. I started to work
at six in the morning, on Sunday at seven,
as a piece of generosity on the part of the

employer. Things like that make me a little unwilling to condemn a man like Parks. I don't want to hear anything against him. Nor shall I say anything against Shea, who has three faults, which I shall not name, but is as able a man as there is in trades-union-ism. He is too frank and outspoken. It is all right for a man to be frank, but if he is, he ought to be honest."

This leader, acquainted with men, and the ways of the world, wonders at the immorality of the employers. "Every boss," he said, "every man who has much money for a long time, is immoral sexually, in my opinion. And that is the great danger of the labor leader. He starts out with enthusiasm for the cause, and for virtue, but often when he begins to have power with the men, the agents of the employers come, give him a good dinner, here in the Bismarck, perhaps, and then take him perhaps to the Everleigh Club, where he comes in contact with a kind of luxury he has never before experienced. When he has acquired the vices of the employers he can no longer serve so well a cause that is hostile to them. So one kind of immorality leads to another kind. Take Al

Young, for instance. I remember when he was a real teamster in spirit. But now his manner of life, even his looks have changed."

A little while after this talk, I was with this leader and Shea in the Briggs House. Said Shea, "Al Young could explain more of the situation here for the last few years than any other man." "But if he did," said the other leader, "it would put him in jail."

It is natural enough that the simple workingman, to whom black is black and white is white, should, when once shaken in virtue, cease to distinguish. But I think the men who yield overtly to this kind of demoralization are in the minority, that the labor leader is in general on a much higher plane of morality than the average man of the well-to-do classes. Many of the prominent leaders have business and executive ability which would have enabled them to make money in any other line of activity. But they have remained poor men, at a low salary, and this shows clearly that the cause has, in part at least, an emotional value to them. I know men who have been offered large salaries by employers—and large bribes—money which they found no difficulty in rejecting, because of their temperamental interest in the work they were doing. Anton himself was offered the position of traveling salesman at a good salary. "I didn't want to leave Maggie for any length of time," he said. "But anyway, I wouldn't have taken it. I feared I might fly off the handle at the hypocrisy of society. And, then, too, I thought I would be bored. I wouldn't have anything to work for except money. And I wouldn't have any men to work with, except tradesmen."

CHAPTER XVII.

Their Points of View.

ANTON and I and Schmidtty—a wood-worker with a ready fist and an honest soul—were sitting in a down-town café, drinking beer and talking philosophy and other things. The talk turned on violence, its ethics, its dangers and its possible excuse.

"Since," said Anton, "the unions have their educational committees, I don't see that Skinny Madden is such a bad one. Arrangements for violence are never made in the committees or in the meetings, but only when two or three gather together, and the rank and file and the Lily Whites know nothing about it. I have sometimes persuaded sluggers not to slug, for I am a philosophical anarchist and do not believe in violence on principle. But people in general believe in force. If the laborers controlled the government, they would not employ slugging, which is now the only force they have. They don't call the

Boston Tea Party a strike, but it was violence and against the law. There are only two real things—genuine humanity and virtue on the one hand, and force on the other. All the rest is hypocrisy and graft."

"Yes," said Schmidtty, who had just been elected as walking delegate, "there is only one thing worth being, and that's a man. I don't feel so much of a man as I did before I was a walking delegate. When you get mixed up with men, its hard to be yourself."

"You are losing your individuality, Schmidtty," laughed Anton. "If you hold your job you won't have any left."

"You don't seem to lose yours," answered Schmidtty. Then, turning to me, he said: "You ought to have heard Anton the other night in the meeting. Someone tried to insult him, and he replied: 'You can't insult me. You have no reputation. Yes, you have a reputation, but it is in the wrong direction.' In this same meeting Anton called another man a liar. An apology was demanded, and Anton said: 'Yes, I apologize. I ought to have been more exact. I called you a liar. What I ought to have done, is to have called you a damned liar?'

"One needs," said Schmidtty, "to develop one's vocabulary. I often advise scabs and I find a good use of the English language is handy. The other day I met a scab and I said to him, 'Why do you attempt to interfere with men who are trying to better their condition? I am willing to admit that you have as much right to the pursuit of happiness as I have. But I have never seen the fellow yet who would ever refuse an increase in wages, and when I and other Union men have taken risks, paid money into the Union, and been blacklisted by the employers, and have at last raised the scale of wages which benefits the non-Union men as well as us, then when we see a man try to get our jobs, a man who has risked nothing but has got a part of the pie, why then I think it is time to argue with him. How much money do you get?' 'Nine dollars,' said the scab. 'I'll get a job for you at $14,' said I. 'Meet me in front of the police station, so you know I won't try to do you.' The scab didn't turn up, but he didn't go back to work."

"Sometimes, though, you meet a scab you can't stand. A fellow that says: 'Sure, I know it's a strike, and that's why I'm here.

I don't give a damn for the Union.' That's the bloke that I'd like to get at. He's the kind that likes a row, always goes where there is trouble, and after the strike's over, goes on to the next place. He don't want a regular job. It isn't exciting enough. He is a perpetual hobo, or a nigger, or something that doesn't want to work steady. The boss, of course, wants as many of these things around as he can get, for they help him to keep down wages. If it wasn't for these immoral scabs, it would all be much easier. But it is a good thing, anyway, to work for something that is good for humanity."

"Schmidtty," said Anton, "is absolutely unselfish. He's a rude fellow that likes to use his fists in the cause of humanity, but he's good."

"Not so rude as you," said Schmidtty, "and not so good."

"You are both rude," said I, "especially Anton. But his rudeness is like a cock-tail. It is a good appetizer."

"That's well put," said Schmidtty.

"I'd like to be an appetizer, as you call it, for the whole labor world," said Anton. "If I had an income of $50 a week, I'd make it the whole business of my life to break down the howl of conservatism, to make the rank and file acquire more initiative, to make the Union so attractive that everybody would want to join, to make it as disagreeable to a man to quit the Union as it is to quit the Insurance Company. To teach men these things, you must be with them constantly. You must teach them to think and talk. I don't think it is necessary to read books. Most books are harmful to the laboring man, for they teach him to see things the way the employers see them, for all books are written by the employers or the men they support. I at any rate can find more satisfaction in talking to men. They sometimes tell the truth. I can talk about books I have not read. I hear Socialists, anarchists, single-taxers talk about the same book, and from what they all say, I can get the essence. I shall subscribe for *The Literary Digest.* That will give me all the reading I need."

Soon after this, I had an engagement with Anton at the Briggs House. I found him with a number of street-car Union men, and a deputy sheriff of Chicago, a politician, who had evidently been drinking too much. Anton had only a few cents in his pocket at the time, and when I entered he was good-naturedly temporizing with a demand made by the sheriff that he should "treat" the crowd.

"Don't apologize," I overheard the sheriff shout. "But buy the booze."

"I never apologize," said Anton, "I explain."

"Don't explain," roared the sheriff, "just go along and holler."

The official seemed to me extremely insolent with pride of office and whiskey, and I called him down as hard as I could; told him he ought to have more sense and decency than to try to force a man to buy drinks. The sheriff began to splutter, but when he found the Union men were all against him, he sullenly subsided; and sat alone, deserted, in the café. His late companions, although they knew that this politician had been useful and might be more so, to the organization, administered a series of rebukes to him by silently departing.

Fearing that I might have "spoiled" something that was on foot, I indicated to Anton some regret at my action. "I sometimes lose my temper," I explained.

"It is not a question of losing your temper," he answered, heartily. "It is a question of taste. He was acting in awful bad taste and you wouldn't have lived up to your character, which is that of a critic, if you hadn't noticed it. It was a good thing. Did you see how the men, as soon as they got the cue, turned the fellow down."

During my intimate association with this workingman, I was frequently struck, not only with the exterior roughness of his manners, but, much more important, with the genuineness and often extreme delicacy of his feelings. He has an unerring way of putting his finger on the weak spot in a man's act; and when the inhumanity or unkindness of a thing is felt, his resulting expression is clear and spontaneous, though sometimes very rough, as on the occasion of his father's funeral. He refused to take his hat off at the services, because the minister had not said anything about his father's personal character.

He told me about this incident the night of my meeting with the sheriff; and also about how on one occasion he treated a man who was making "advances" to his wife.

"Maggie is a woman by instinct," he said,

"and she sees everything that has anything to do with the sex. She came to me the other day and said: 'C——, was here, and explained what a pity it is that you are so busy with your committees, that your work is so hard it leaves no time or energy for your marital duties. He's always saying this to me, and hanging round when you are not there.'

"Maggie likes to keep me guessing. She is enough of an anarchist to know that I must not be too sure of her, if she wants to keep my love, but she didn't like this man and wound up, in her story about him to me, by calling him a few names.

"So the next Sunday I went around to his house, and began to talk to his wife, when he was in the room. I said to her just what he had said to Maggie; told her it was a pity her husband worked so hard he couldn't pay enough attention to his wife, etc. I saw he was uneasy, for he thought I must have been tipped off by Maggie. So when he and I went out together, he began to explain. After he had got in deep, I told him that was the first thing I had heard about it. He felt cheap then for having given himself away unnecessarily."

Maggie and Anton, going as they often do to the meetings of the Anthropological Society and the Social Science League, where all kinds of criticism of society are indulged in, and to the various "socials" given by their anarchist friends, are naturally interested to a considerable degree in the doctrines of free-love. When Anton talks of religion, when he makes a violent anti-culture, or anti-Christian speech, he seems often very crude, for of course, he is not skilled in metaphysical and theological distinctions. But when he talks of love he is dealing with something he knows as much about as he does about the labor movement, and in the same way, from experience. His attitude, and that of Maggie, toward the question of sex, is therefore one curiously civilized, and yet abounding in healthy instinct and common sense.

Maggie's friends, Marie, Esther and the Poet's wife, have been trying to make her what they call a "varietist," but Maggie, although she likes the free talk and opportunity to know men well, shies off from what she feels is a one-sided and merely rebellious attitude. Her "radicalism" in this matter, is of that balanced kind which makes life for her more vivid, quickens her emotions and broadens her sympathy, without detracting her too much from the big stream of conventional feeling in the matter.

When Maggie returned from Clinton, and appeared with the young woodworker Schmidtty, at the Social Science League, Marie, Esther and the Poet's wife came up and congratulated her. "Maggie is now a varietist," they exclaimed, happily. "See how happy she looks, and how bright her eyes are! Maggie has a lover!" It was naive of them, and incorrect, and incorrect because of the fullness of Maggie's life, not because of its poverty. Her anarchist lady friends do not work, and, in comparison, are anæmic physically and emotionally.

Anton encourages this attitude in his wife: he wants her as alive as possible, but he also wants her to be an artist in life, not a propagandist in word or act. He wants her, as he once said to me, to drive swift horses, but he doesn't want the horses to run away with her.

"There is danger in it, Hapgood," he said, "but it's fun."

He has much the same attitude towards Maggie as he has towards his work in the

Unions and his efforts among men. It is interesting and exciting for him to get as much life as he can—to play the game fully, hoping, of course, to win, but risking loss at every turn. He is certainly the man for her, for she enjoys life, and makes others enjoy life. I was at her house often for dinner, and it seemed to me a full, rich place, this working-man's house, with this good and cheerful and active and free-minded woman, her healthy, well-taken-care-of children, clean house, good food and interesting guests,—anarchists, Socialists, Conservatives, but always working people. It seemed always so real to me, the ideas so based upon facts, so instinctively inevitable. Even the thoughts that were crude and violent pointed so forcibly to a social situation. And what optimism and energy and temperament and humanity, what hope!

And yet I remember saying, a few months earlier, "There is no charm about the workingman. He lacks the interest of the thief, the Ghetto Jew, or the strolling actress. There is no picturesque quality, nothing in the workingman but what suggests a hard, passionate clash between the classes; one feels a coming revolution of the proletariat, but its expression lacks charm—it is suffering, hard, sullen, ugly."

But the time soon came when I could hardly take myself away from Anton's house and friends. Passion, poetry, warmth, reality, intimacy; frankness—a thorough acceptance of human attributes, an instinctive way of taking life, very similar to that of the great Walt Whitman. Other people, of so-called "culture," I felt were comparatively anæmic and of a piece. The workingmen seemed more intelligent to me about economic matters and social questions than university students or even university professors. The ideas I heard expressed by the professional economists or sociologists, by the reforming radical politicians or philanthropists, were put with more convincingness if with less rhetoric in the circle of the laboring class. It became clearer and clearer to me that the origin of social ideas was in the society I was then frequenting.

Even superficial culture, many of these people, particularly those who have become out and out anti-social, and quitting work, have been able to devote themselves to the phrase— people like Marie and Terry—have in a marked degree. I shall try to record a more or less typical conversation of the more or less "cultured" kind which took place one day at Anton's house, at dinner and after, when there were as guests, besides myself, Marie and Terry, Jay and Esther, the Poet's wife, Schmidtty and his sister, a robust working girl of the more or less conservative kind.

"Esther," I said, "you are a beautiful woman."

These women do not understand or want compliments which do not go to the soul. Esther did not enjoy my remark, which was sincere, and she said:

"I only care for feeling, for the inside." Esther is so serious and sentimental that Anton, who always fights away from the expression of intense feeling, said, as a diversion:

"Here's to man's freedom and woman's slavery. We were perhaps economically wrong in making women slaves to begin with, for that put them in a position where they can deal men horrible blows. The man feels the woman is his property, and so the woman, if she wants, can injure him in his property feeling and his sentimental feeling at the same time. It is the punishment of the autocrat.

But now we've got them there, we must keep them there to a certain extent. For the most destructive thing a man can do is to take a woman seriously and put her on an equality. She is not capable of it."

"You're talking through your hat, Anton," said Maggie. "You know you don't believe a word of all that. You bet you take me seriously. If you didn't, I'd soon make you."

"I don't blame Esther," said Jay, "for having such a high ideal. That is why I loved her. To be happy we need an ideal. That is why in some ways the laboring class to-day is so unfortunate. Not only is the material result of our labor taken away from us, but also the ideal of work. We must seek our ideal outside of our labor and that is why some of us are anarchists and some trades-unionists, some free-lovers and some Socialists. The employers have an ideal of work, and that takes away from them the need of other ideals.

"You anarchists make me sick," said Anton, aggressively. He was sitting in his flannel shirt, with his collar off, and shoving down Maggie's well-cooked food with great speed. "You are all fanatics, crazy about something.

Esther and Marie are crazy about 'variety,' Terry is crazy about class-consciousness, and about what he calls consistency; the Poet is crazy with egotism, Hapgood is crazy to butt into what doesn't concern him, and Maggie is crazy about monogamy."

"Guess again," said Maggie.

"To show how crazy the anarchists are," continued Anton, ignoring Maggie's remark, "look how they criticize trades-unionism without ever going to the meetings and not knowing or caring what's being done. They jump on the movement as hard as they do on religion or capitalism."

"Well," said Terry, "at the best, trades-unionism is only a makeshift, an amelioration of conditions, and is not ideal. Besides, it is bourgeois, middle-class. Take your worthy President, Gompers, who could be more bourgeois than Gompers?"

"Yes," replied Anton, "Gompers is a side-stepper, I must admit. But it is better than having always a panacea that doesn't work. At the anti-trust meeting the other day, they all had their panaceas, Jane Addams, George Schilling, Tucker—all but Gompers and he in his speech again showed how clever he is

[389]

in saying nothing, in stepping aside. But, after all, we must compromise, to get anything. If we all were as fanatical as the anarchists, there would be nothing but hot air in the world."

"You talk about stupid things," said Marie, "just as if there were no women present. Let's talk about love. By the way, I didn't realize how interesting little Sadie is. But the other night, when she kissed me good-bye after the meeting, I saw there was something in her. Her kiss filled me with surprise and emotion."

"You are about the craziest in the whole bunch," remonstrated Anton.

But Marie had determined the topic for a time, and they talked about love between the sexes with a downrightness and a frankness and at the same time a knowledge of the emotional facts which made me feel that I was associating with people who at least were civilized, and not over-civilized. They had sprung into emotional maturity without the intermediate processes of physical degeneration which are often an accompaniment. The fact that they belonged to the working class was a sweet preservative against the pale anæmia of emotional freedom which one is likely to find in other sets.

Towards the end of the long dinner, Anton addressed me, and said:

"You have been with us now a couple of months. You butted in, but you have made yourself welcome. We have all enjoyed your intelligence, and I particularly have enjoyed your way of putting things. You say rough things so delicately that for working people it is quite a treat. Let's have a speech. Tell us what you think about the labor movement and about anarchism. And don't imitate Sam Gompers and side-step all over the room. It's not a dance, but a talk we want."

It was a large order, but I knew that I was among tolerant friends, so I said:

"I can only repeat the things which you and your friends have either thought or felt about the movement and about society. Left to myself or to books I should never have had any ideas on these subjects. Perhaps you won't recognize yourselves or your ideas in my words. If not, it is only because of my manner of expression. What I say, merely interprets, in my opinion, what you think, and, in

[391]

an inadequate way, embodies the results of your thought and feeling.

"As I have often told you, I have found Chicago wonderfully interesting. Before I became absorbed in you, I saw much of the settlement workers, of the 'smart' people, the young politicians and business men, the journalists and the university professors. And I found them all very broad, for their situation, very tolerant. There seemed to me a wonderful feeling of democracy throughout the city, a lack of snobbishness that I had never felt elsewhere.

"This was interesting, inspiring, but until I came in contact with you, I did not know how interesting it all was. It is you who have given me the key to all the rest. It is the man-in-the-street, the common man, the working man, who is giving tone to all the rest of society. It is your ideas that they are expressing. It is your sentiment that is gradually affecting all classes. It is your philosophy that is affecting the old philosophy, broadening it, giving it a larger human basis.

"Among the newer and better politicians there has been a vital reaction against the principle of special privileges so nicely

worked out by the business class. The last
few years have been years of reform. Behind
this reform has been the working class. Pressure from beneath has forced these social pal-
liatives, such as the insurance investigations,
trust legislation, etc., etc. The feeling for
municipal ownership has amounted almost to
a religion. The back-bone of that movement
has been the laboring class. The President
of the United States is accused by the reac-
tionaries of being a 'radical,' a Socialist. He
is a politician, and he would never have been
forced into a semi-radical attitude had it not
been for the pressure which had its original
impulse in the working class.

"It is natural that the source of radical
thought should be more radical than the results on the established machinery. The remark of your labor leader, Anton, in the Pittsburg Convention, that you are all anarchists,
has some truth. There are very few anarchists like Terry—fortunately—[Perhaps that's
true, interjected Terry, smilingly] but I find
in all of you the germs of a feeling *against,*
if I may so put it. You all distrust, more or
less, the present legal and judicial machinery,
the present law, the present morality. You

all—those who think—believe there is a morality higher than the morality embodied in law. For instance, the law 'thou shalt not be a scab' is for you a higher morality than the law against 'disorderly conduct' and riot in the street.

"This element of anarchism, therefore, goes deep. It is embodied in the very essence of the economic and social situation. I believe, personally, that while it has its abuses, it makes for good. It puts into organized society a distrust of itself, disturbs it, and leads to reform, in self-defense. It can never be realized, in any extreme form—perhaps it ought not to be realized—but it is an excellent tonic: it helps to keep society from being too smug, too routine, too unjust, too uninteresting. We must, in all advance, have a destructive element, and when the destructive element is based upon something as positive, as warm and as humane as the labor movement, it deserves sympathetic attention.

"In the course of my life I have had one deeply anarchical experience. As a student, I thought I could arrive, by the study of metaphysics, to a knowledge of the objects of metaphysics—God, immortality, Free Will, etc. But after reading the history of metaphysics I found that no metaphysician ever arrived at the specific thing he was aiming at—no one ever did or will discover the unknowable. At the same time that I arrived at this negative conclusion, my human experience became richer. I realized the number of beautiful and interesting concrete things and experiences there are. This double situation resulted in my becoming a metaphysical anarchist. With it, came a deeper pleasure in literature, in art, in people, in life. It seemed as a cock-tail before dinner: it made things more interesting.

"This desire for more abundant life, more pleasure, more beauty, more understanding, is at the basis of all sincere anarchical feeling. The great poets and great artists and great spiritual seers have been anarchical in regard to old forms and ideas in their art; that is, they have had an element of anarchism; though at the same time they have felt the beauty of the old.

"So, too, is love. Those anarchists who are free-lovers—sincerely so, for among those are many fakers—are partly right and partly wrong, in my opinion. A husband and wife get along best together when there is an element of uncertainty, of possible change, of growth; when each is interested in some other person or persons of the opposite sex. If their relation is the best, this interest in others helps them to be more interested in one another, and their relation together. It makes it more exciting, more rich.

"Balance seems peculiarly necessary in this relation. Those among you anarchists who are not extremists in this matter seem to me to get the most out of this side of life. There is a monotony in too much freedom that is worse than the monotony of too much conservatism. The ideal is to have one deep and overpowering relation to which all others serve as stimulants and emotional comments. One of your anarchists admitted to me the other day: 'Free-love women have no mystery. The conservative women are the richest. Sin is a luxury, and so it would be a pity to abolish it.'

"That sentiment is really immoral, but there is a moral truth at the bottom of it, more ethically expressed by Balzac, than by your anarchist. He says:

" 'It is an immense proof of inferiority in a

man not to be able to make of his wife his mistress. Variety in love is a sign of impotence. Constancy will always be the genius of love, the proof of an immense force, which constitutes the poet.'

"Anarchism in love should work against the too stolid, and stupid and routine institutional side, not against ideals. Then, indeed, anarchy is bad. If it tends to destroy ideals, away with it. But I feel that with you people the true function of anarchism is to sustain and keep alive the ideal. The life of a man like Kropotkin—almost a saint—shows this to be the case, for his life is like that of many anarchists. It is typical.

"A pathetic and amusing and absurd thing is the ordinary attitude of society, everywhere except in England, towards the avowed anarchists. In England, they are left alone, and no harm is done. But they are persecuted everywhere else, even in America, and yet, if not disturbed, they are entirely harmless. Anarchy, indeed, is a gentle idealism, though that is not the general idea. The popular conception of an anarchist is about as near the truth as the popular conception of a Jew or of a witch. But when I met the anarchists

[397]

among the laboring men I found something unusually gentle, unusually low-toned, and with an avowed and actual hatred of force. The Socialists are like bulls in comparison, and the police and capitalists strong-arm men.

"Anarchism begins with a revolt against economic injustice, but it ends as an æsthetic ideal. It is the fine art of the proletariat. In function, it is stimulating, an attitude of mind. It has a practical side, as it allows a man to be an opportunist in life, while having a high ideal. Of this kind of anarchist, Clarence Darrow is the most prominent among you. It emphasizes individuality and the rights of the soul, as against convention and law. In marriage, it fosters insecurity and therefore love and interest. It is a remedy against snobbishness, as it renders social distinctions insecure. Springing from the people, it finds great things in the people. ·

"Anarchism is something like the Catholic Church. It is tolerant and elastic, and includes everything except intolerance, and sometimes even that, generally that with the declared anarchists, who after all are not the real anarchists, who have no *culte*. The most perfect anarchist I know is one of the deans of a university. It is peculiarly human and makes room even for graft, as part of an imperfect system.

"Although anarchism is an æsthetic ideal, it tends to become fixed, and therefore unæsthetic. Its object is to get rid of prejudice and the routine of institutions, but it often wrongly tends to do away at the same time with the beauty there is in institution, such as marriage, forms of literature, history and art. I find in many of you—not indeed in the most self-conscious—a hatred of poetry, fairy tales, history, a hatred of whatever conservative people like, irrespective of whether it is good or evil. This is the point where anarchism itself becomes routine, founded on narrow laziness of mind, and needing itself to be reformed."

"You express pretty well," commented Terry, "Kropotkin's idea of anarchism, a gentle sweet sort. There is another kind, however, a more egotistic one, that is Tucker's way, and mine. Anarchism is dangerous, even when bombs don't come in. It does tend to destroy the beautiful stability and tranquillity of the bourgeois citizen, and if realized would do harm; but the harm would be

[399]

very slight in comparison with the harm of the present state of things."

"All this kind of talk," said Anton, "would be tommyrot, if it were not for one thing. The important feature of it all is, as Hapgood says, that it is based on the Labor Movement. It is a warning to the world that the conditions under which workingmen live tend to bring about certain ideas. And yet damn fools like you, Terry, sneer at the labor movement, when there wouldn't be any anarchists, if it were not for the labor movement."

But Marie and Esther and Maggie were getting nervous, so they brought the talk around again to Subject Number One.

CHAPTER XVIII.

A Ripe Letter.

THE time for me to leave Chicago came around, and it was with a heavy heart and a feeling of moral wrong that I realized the way things conflict in this world. My farewell evening at Anton's was as interesting as ever, though the coming separation gave it a touch of gloom. When I arrived that evening, Anton was telling his son about some of his hobo experiences—how he swung along the Grand Cañon on the trucks of a passenger train. Schmidtty was there, and noticed in Anton a certain lack of mechanical observation, the thing that had made it so difficult for Anton to learn his trade: he had done it by sheer force of will and energy. Yet primarily, he is a liver, an expresser, and a philosopher.

He spoke, at this last meeting, more seriously than usual, about things connected with the labor situation, marriage and work. "No one can help the men," he said, "except they themselves. It is hopeless from the outside, and difficult from the inside. Education is the great thing, not necessarily from books. Tom Morgan, who for so long was prominent in the movement and afterwards as a Socialist, got his mental start from copying architectural designs while working at his trade. There are many roads, but few results.

"I have enjoyed you and your intelligence and your way of saying things. You represent, in a way, another class, and that, too, I feel, has broadened me."

I explained, with even more sincerity, how he had pleased and influenced me. Maggie said very little, but all these meetings in which there had been so much free talk, so much enjoyment and so much sympathy, had meant much to her, as her tears showed. We talked about marriage, and the great pleasure there is in utter frankness and honesty in life. The latter part of the evening, we three were alone together: I, who had never worked with my hands in my life, much universitied, much becultured so to speak; he, a woodworker, a former tramp and she a workingman's wife, who took in washing and was, as far as "class" went, a most simple girl of German origin. I am forced to remember these distinctions and differences now, for the purpose of this social study that I have made. But I felt no social or intellectual difference between us, essentially, at the time, or now. In them I knew I had met my equals at least; in some ways my superiors, people whom I could love, and as I went away that evening I reflected sadly on the baseless character of snobbishness and the fundamental cruelty and meaninglessness of class.

After I had been some weeks in New York, I received from Anton a letter about Labor politics and also some sentiments about ministers, interesting as showing greater tolerance towards these persons than he was able to show formerly.

"I need not go into details in my excuse for not writing, for you are onto my game. Maggie is out to-night for a good time, so I am alone with the little ones, and as I feel at best, I thought I would drop you a few lines. I had a good report to the Federation, and they had it printed with my picture. We had another election in the Federation Sunday. I was one of the judges and Madden's gang was put down and out. They had a report around town that I was to be Madden's candidate for President. You can bet it made me hot under the collar.

"So on the day of nomination, my name was presented as a candidate for President. John Fitzpatrick and John Levine were also candidates. I arose to the occasion and declared in open meeting that the report of my being Madden's candidate was a damned lie, that I declined in favor of Fitzpatrick, and would always remain a clean-cut trade-unionist without any political intrigue. You can bet I was cheered all over the hall. But I made the Madden gang good and sore, as I gave them hell right on the floor. At the election, about 120 policemen were present. I and many others dislike very much to have the police in our Union affairs, but we could not help it, as we did not want a repetition of the Donnelly's slugging.

"You remember my telling you about Fitzpatrick working against me when I was elected delegate to Pittsburg. He got up in the meeting, you remember, and made a speech in favor of the other fellow. Well,

my time came, and I made a speech in his
favor and when the votes were counted, and
he was elected, I went to him, gave him my
hand, and told him I was ready to assist him
with all my power (if I had any) to conduct
a clean administration. I wish you could
have seen his face. It was a case of my being
a Christian and returning good for evil. And
while he is a strong, robust man, not very sentimental, the tears rolled down his face, and
he asked me to overlook his mistake, in his
misjudgment of me. I was pleasantly affected and told him he could rest assured that
my love for this great labor movement was
strong enough to overcome the desire for re-
taliation, when such action would tend to
check the progress of our movement. 'I trust
and hope,' I said, 'that your talent and ability
will at all times be used in the cause of the
proletariat.'

"I expect that Madden will lie down now *
and admit his defeat. Out of a total of 635
votes cast, Fitzpatrick received 396 and John
Levine, Madden's man, 196. This was in
spite of the fact that Madden had been able
to induce some unions, among them several
of the teamsters' unions, and all the unaffili-

ated bricklayers unions, to join the Federation just before the election; and besides had gotten out phony cards, which we did not discover at first. But as soon as we noticed the illegal cards we put a damper on them. Some men came to vote on bricklayers' cards, but as they looked about as much like bricklayers as the Anarchist Poet looks like a sewer digger, they were challenged, and when it was found they did not know the address of the man whose name appeared on their card, they were promptly denied the right to vote. In one case, a teamster came up to vote with a card which bore the name of a delegate from the cement finishers' union. The tally showed that the cement finisher had already voted.

"We refused to let him vote. He left the hall, but returned with Jerry McCarthy, President of the Truck Drivers' Union, who vigorously protested. He made an attack upon Nockels, and the police immediately threw him out, and also the other teamster. Outside of this little fray there was no sign of violence.

"I don't know if they will repeat these methods six months hence, but the feeling is

so strong against Madden that it is difficult
for one to conceive how they can be foolish
enough to continue in their bulldozing tactics. Yet we must expect very strenuous efforts on the part of the grafter to maintain
his power, when it is slowly waning. You
may expect sarcasm and criticism from him
in one direction and pleading with crocodile
tears in the direction where there appears to
be a faint hope of deception. But when his
power is lost, it makes very little difference
whether it be in the political arena, or on the
economic battle-field, there remains nothing
for him to do but to use bulldozing methods
in the hope that the honest man may fear him.
In the grafter's feelings there is not the slightest conception of morality. His first, last,
and only object, is to regain his lost power,
and in the action of the grafter, the old saying, the end justifies the means, is typical in
its conception.

"I am pleased, however, that with the cen-
tralization of capital, the awakening of the
public conscience becomes greater and
greater. This is especially true in the organized Labor Movement, and I look forward
with more and more hope that the near fu-

ture will show clearly the necessity of removing a system that affords the opportunity for the cunning-minded to accumulate not only millions, but billions, on the one hand, and that deprives honest efforts in millions of cases from the just results, on the other hand.

"I feel extremely thankful that a man like T. Lawson has revealed himself to the world and has made the opportunity more favorable for the little agitators like myself, and thousands of others. To point out, and leave, a lasting impression on the minds of the people as to the sweeping injustice of this condition: this is a great thing. I hope the political arena will produce more Jeromes, and Folks and Johnsons, who although their philosophy seems to me superficial or nothing, and their minds not very deep, yet are good men in action, and the kind we need. They possess the courage necessary to challenge the audacity of the grafter and the ignorance of the partisan voter, in which ignorance rests the real strength of the machine. If we could have one thousand such men, there would be 'something doing.'

"You will perhaps be surprised when I tell you that I was invited to speak at the Olivet

Church. I accepted an invitation to dine with the minister. I assure you that I had an interesting talk with him. You may laugh, but it is true. He is a communist, as far as the ideal is concerned, and in practice an opportunist, but a man who is willing to work for the great army of humanity who need all the best things of life. I spoke on trades-unionism. They appeared well satisfied with my talk, and urged me to speak on the tramp, at another occasion. I don't know what your opinion will be of this incident (and to be frank, I don't care), whether I am going to the bad, or whether the ministers are improving.

"This is all I have to describe, since you went away. I might add that you have left a good impression on our friends and that we miss you very much. I am just at present pacing the floor on Sunday morning (having begun this letter last night) and my dear monogamic wife is making this stenographic report. Maggie says there isn't any use in sending her love, as you have taken away more already than you have kept, but I know that you, having been in Japan and many other places, have the capacity for conserving good things. I remain, yours, for Truth, Liberty and Justice,

"ANTON."

On this note of good-citizenship and social playfulness, I let my dear friend rest, and put before the public his spirit—the spirit of the alive and progressive American workingman of the present day.

Notes.

9   Hapgood had experimented with the concept of a
     "human document" in his *Autobiography of a Thief* (New
     York, 1903), in which he recorded the story of a New York
     City petty criminal. The notion of trying to capture the
     life experiences and the worldview of a common person
     in his or her own terms was not peculiar to his projects,
     however. Between 1902 and 1906 the progressive journal
     the *Independent* published seventy-five short autobiog-
     raphies or "lifelets" of "undistinguished Americans."
     These included the life stories of an Italian bootblack, a
     collar starcher, a miner, a "Chinaman," and a Chicago
     teamster. Some subjects actually wrote their own stories;
     others dictated them and then checked the results. In the
     United States, then, the concept of recording a common
     person's life story developed first among journalists like
     Hapgood. Scholars like the University of Chicago soci-
     ologists later experimented with the personal narrative
     as a way to understand the personalities and social rela-
     tions of the poor, and of people they considered "social
     deviants." On the *Independent*'s autobiographies, see the
     Introduction to *Plain Folk: The Life Stories of Undistin-
     guished Americans,* ed. David M. Katzman and William

M. Tuttle (Urbana, Ill., 1982), x–xii; on the use of personal narratives by Chicago sociologists and social scientists more generally, see Eli Zaretsky, Introduction to William I. Thomas and Florian Znaniecki, *The Polish Peasant in Europe and America,* edited and abridged by Eli Zaretsky (Urbana, Ill., 1984), 26–29; and Louis Gottschalk, Clyde Kluckhohn, and Robert Angell, *The Use of Personal Documents in History, Anthropology, and Sociology* (New York, 1947).

13 **Sam Parks:** Sam Parks, leader of New York City's Housesmiths' Union, became a powerful symbol for the corrupt "labor racketeer" of the early twentieth century. By controlling strikes in the building industry, Parker amassed thousands in income between 1901 and 1903 while earning only $48 per week. Such "labor bosses" ruled their unions and also discouraged strikebreakers through the use of "labor sluggers." In the same period, however, the housesmiths' wages rose dramatically, and this may account, in part, for the attitude Hapgood encountered in the Chicago bar. "Once a workman in the iron trade got $1.50 a day," a member of Parks's union noted. "Parks arose, became our Moses, and led us into the promised land of $5.00 a day. Suppose Parks grafted more or less, and made a bunch of money, he did not get it out off us." Sentenced to Sing Sing prison for extortion, Parks died in a prison hospital in May 1904, about a year before Hapgood's barroom confrontation. (Philip S. Foner, *The Policies and Practices of the American Federation of Labor, 1900–1909,* vol. 3 of *History of the Labor*

Movement in the United States [New York, 1973], 146, 150, 152–53, quotation 150.)

17 Originally a distinctly middle-class suburb on the far west side of Chicago, **Austin** was annexed to the city in 1899. It was becoming more diverse in both ethnic and class terms at the time this book was written. Since the area was characterized by excellent housing and pleasant tree-lined streets, however, Johannsen's home in Austin suggests a modest but solid standard of living.

26 **Schleswig-Holstein:** Originally independent duchies under the Holy Roman Empire, Schleswig and Holstein, on the border between Prussia and Denmark, were disputed territories throughout much of the nineteenth century. Heavily populated by both Danes and Germans, the two duchies were formally annexed as the Prussian province of Schleswig-Holstein in the wake of the Austro-Prussian War of 1866. The region was the source of heavy Danish immigration to the United States in the mid- to late nineteenth century; Johannsen's appears to have been an ethnic Danish family, a group that figured prominently among Chicago's carpenters and wood workers in this era.

35 **Hobo:** Throughout the late nineteenth and early twentieth centuries, hundreds of thousands of transient workers tramped for work. Historian Eric H. Monkkonen estimated that between 10 and 20 percent of late-nineteenth-century families had at least one family member "on the tramp" in search of work. (Eric Monkkonen, ed., *Walking to Work: Tramps in America, 1790–1935* [Lincoln,

Nebr., 1984], 8.) On the hobo subculture at the end of the nineteenth century, see Frank Tobias Higbie, *Indispensable Outcasts: Hobo Workers and Community in the American Midwest, 1880–1930* (Urbana, Ill., 2003); and Roger A. Bruns, *Knights of the Road: A Hobo History* (New York, 1980).

38 **He was a Carl [*sic*] Marx man . . . :** The late nineteenth century socialist movement was populated by several different organizations, the largest of which, the Socialist Labor Party (1877–), still exists. It is likely, however, that this older worker was not a member of any particular organization but simply adhered to the broad socialist program of human welfare over private profit.

85 **Robert Ingersoll** (1833–1899) **and Free Thought:** With deep roots in continental Europe, anticlerical ideology based on Enlightenment rationalism was best represented by Tom Paine's famous tract *The Age of Reason* (London, 1794), which enjoyed great popularity among radical workers in the United States in the late nineteenth and into the twentieth century. Free thought blossomed alongside the labor and socialist movements in the United States among both immigrant and native-born workers. The magazine *Free Thought* (New York) remained the movement's most important English-language organ in this era. Robert Ingersoll (1833–99), Illinois writer, lawyer, orator, and politician, was perhaps the best known American advocate of rationalism and atheism. Politically, he occupied the position of a Radical Republican during the Reconstruction Era and long

after. Although he made his living as a lawyer, Ingersoll built his national reputation as a free thought orator in the late nineteenth century. (Mark A. Plummer, "Ingersoll, Robert Green," in *American National Biography,* ed. John Garraty and Mark Carnes [New York, 1999], 649–51; Frank Smith, *Robert G. Ingersoll: A Life* [Buffalo, N.Y., 1990].)

96 Johannsen, a mill woodworker, was a member at one time or another of both the **United Brotherhood of Carpenters and Joiners of America** (UBC) and the **Amalgamated Wood Workers International Union of America** (AWW). He started out in the latter soon after going to work in a Chicago woodworking factory and served as business agent, delegate to the Chicago Federation of Labor, and president of Local 1367 and of the Woodworkers' Council at the time Hapgood was researching *The Spirit of Labor.* Though earlier efforts to organize the carpenters stretched back to colonial days, the UBC was the first national carpenters' union. Organized in Chicago in August 1881, its leaders took an active role in both the foundation of the American Federation of Labor and the eight-hour day campaigns of the 1880s. Membership stood at about 70,000 at the turn of the century, and until that point the UBC followed a program of broad social reform and strong democratic governance. In the early twentieth century, the Socialist Peter J. McGuire, who had led the union from its foundation, was driven from office and the UBC gradually assumed a more conservative, "business union" stance. In the Chicago district, however, progressive unionism persisted. Throughout the early twentieth century, the UBC carried on a bitter jurisdictional conflict with the AWWIU, created in 1895 and also headquartered in Chicago. The AFL chartered the AWWIU to organize workers producing door frames, window sashes, and other wood components in factories. The union declined quickly from around 1904 as a result of competition from the UBC, and the two unions were finally merged in Chicago from 1911 to 1912. (Gary Fink, ed., *Labor Unions,* [Westport, Conn., 1977], 49–51, 414–15; Richard Schneirov and Thomas J. Suhrbur, *Union Brotherhood, Union Town: The History of the Carpenters' Union of Chicago, 1863–1987* [Carbondale, Ill., 1988], 86–87, 97.)

104 **the hanging of the Chicago anarchists:** On May 4, 1886, in the midst of a national strike for the eight-hour day, members of the anarchist International Working Peoples' Association, which had a strong base in Chicago at the time, called a meeting at "Haymarket," a wholesale market on the city's Near West Side, to protest police brutality against strikers. A person still unknown threw a bomb that killed several policemen. Police killed several more people when they fired into the crowd. In the wake of the event, Chicago authorities cracked down on the city's labor movement. Eight radical trade union leaders with no apparent connection to the violence were tried and convicted of a conspiracy resulting in the Haymarket deaths. Four of the "Haymarket Martyrs" were executed, one committed suicide, and the remaining three were

pardoned by Illinois governor John Peter Altgeld in 1893. The events became a *cause célèbre* for workers around the world. (See Paul Avrich, *The Haymarket Tragedy* [Princeton, N.J., 1984]; Dave Roediger and Franklin Rosemont, eds., *A Haymarket Scrapbook* [Chicago, 1986].)

111–13 Here Hapgood describes the making of labor bureaucrats, activists who rose from the ranks to become union leaders and in the process distanced themselves from their own members as a result of divergent lifestyle and experience. Note that Anton remained working in the shop while he served as an elected union officer. (See Warren Van Tine, *The Making of the Labor Bureaucrat: Union Leadership in the United States, 1870–1920* [Amherst, Mass., 1978].)

140 **Clarence (Seward) Darrow** (1857–1938), radical lawyer and author, may be best known for his defense (1925) of John Scopes, a Tennessee high school teacher charged with teaching the theory of evolution, but his career actually went through several distinct phases. Arriving in Chicago in 1887, he worked first as corporation counsel for the city and then as general attorney for the Chicago and Northwestern Railroad. Active in the left wing of the Democratic Party from the time of his arrival in Chicago, Darrow worked closely with liberal governor John Peter Altgeld and helped to elect reform mayor Edward F. Dunne. Except for a brief term in the state legislature as an independent, he never held office but remained a prominent figure in the political life of the city in the period before World War I. From the end of

the nineteenth century to 1912 or so he maintained close relations with the labor movement and defended a series of activists, including Eugene V. Debs following the Pullman strike (1894) and the McNamara Brothers (see page 375), an experience that badly damaged his law practice and reputation. Darrow rebuilt his practice in the 1920s as a defense attorney in a series of spectacular criminal trials. At his request, Darrow's ashes were sprinkled over the Jackson Park Lagoon on Chicago's South Side. (Ray Ginger, "Darrow, Clarence Seward," in *Dictionary of American Biography,* ed. Robert Livingston Schuyler [New York, 1958], 141–44. See also Kevin Tierney, *Darrow: A Biography* [New York, 1979] and Darrow's memoir, *The Story of My Life* [1932].)

146 **Prince (Petr) Kropotkin** (1842–1921), Russian nobleman, scientist, and anarchist thinker and writer, was a co-founder of the "Black" or Anarchist International in 1881. Kropotkin's philosophy, which emphasized collective organization over individualism and agitation over violence, came to be called "anarcho-communism," the most important anarchist influence in the United States among both native-born and immigrant workers from a wide range of ethnic backgrounds. (Peter Kropotkin, *Memoirs of a Revolutionist* [Boston, 1899]; Martin A. Miller, *Kropotkin* [Chicago, 1976].)

197 **Chicago Federation of Labor** (1896–present): On November 10, 1896, the Chicago Labor Congress and the Chicago Trades and Labor Assembly merged to create the Chicago Federation of Labor (CFL). The CFL

barred endorsements of any particular political party, but the federation immediately immersed itself in the city's progressive reform politics, calling for the nationalization of railroads and telegraph and municipal ownership of all utilities. But the CFL was also soon characterized by extensive corruption and racketeering with "Skinny" Madden's rise to power. (See page 421.) At the time of Hapgood's work in Chicago, the CFL was emerging as the most progressive city labor federation in the United States. (Richard Schneirov, *Labor and Urban Politics: Class Conflict and the Origins of Modern Liberalism in Chicago, 1864–97* [Urbana, Ill., 1998], 353, 355.)

199 **Emma Goldman** (1869–1940): A Russian-born immigrant feminist anarchist writer and speaker, Goldman was a follower of Petr Kropotkin. (See page 418.) She immigrated to the United States in 1885 and embraced anarchism in the wake of the Haymarket events. Best remembered perhaps for her own distinctive contributions to anarchist thought, particularly with regard to sexual freedom and women's rights, Goldman was also a labor activist. She visited Chicago often and developed a life-long friendship with Hutchins Hapgood as part of the Greenwich Village bohemian intellectual scene. She launched the anarchist monthly journal *Mother Earth* in 1906, which she continued to edit until it was suppressed in 1918. Goldman was imprisoned that year for her opposition to the draft and deported to Russia during the 1919 Red Scare. Her Chicago connections were enhanced by her long love affair with Dr. Ben Reitman (1879–1942),

the "Hobo Doctor," a fixture in the city's anarchist circles and another life-long friend of Hapgood's. After a long exile in London, Emma Goldman died in Toronto, but she was buried in Chicago's Waldheim Cemetery near the monument to the Haymarket anarchists. (Lillian Kirtzman Johnpoll, "Goldman, Emma," in *Biographical Dictionary of the American Left*, ed. Bernard K. Johnpoll and Harvey Klehr [Westport, Conn., 1986], 161–67. See also Alice Wexler, *Emma Goldman in America* [Boston, 1984].)

206 **(Sam) Gompers** (1850–1925): A cigar maker by trade, Samuel Gompers emigrated with his family from London and became a leader in the cigar workers' unions between the 1860s and 1880s. He helped to found the Federation of Organized Trades and Labor Unions, later (1886) the American Federation of Labor (AFL). He emerged as the most important figure in the early AFL, serving as its president from 1886 to 1895 and again from 1896 to 1924. Although he was an active socialist throughout his early career, Gompers is remembered as the main architect of "business unionism," the philosophy that American unions worked best where they eschewed all political allegiances and reform activity and concentrated instead on sound business principles and the welfare of their own members. (Fink, ed., *Biographical Dictionary of American Labor Leaders*, 127–28. See also Samuel Gompers, *Seventy Years of Life and Labor* [New York, 1925].)

207 Clarence **Darrow's** pamphlet, *The Open Shop* (Chicago, 1904), which attacked the logic and ethics of employers'

anti-union tactics, was published by the socialist firm Charles H. Kerr and Company in the midst of the open shop drive in Chicago. The sale and discussion of 800 copies of the pamphlet in a union of 1,400 suggests the vigorous intellectual life in a local union at this time.

210 **Martin B. "Skinny" Madden:** Madden, a labor racketeer in the powerful Chicago Building Trades Council, was a major figure in the corrupt administration of the Chicago Federation of Labor when it was established in 1896. Elected president, treasurer, and business agent "for life" of the Steamfitters' Helpers' Union of Chicago, he maintained power through the use of labor "sluggers." Reformers attacked his machine at the turn of the century, replacing it permanently in the 1906 federation elections. (See page 301.) (Foner, *The Policies and Practices of the American Federation of Labor,* 157.)

210 **Edward Fitzsimmons Dunne** (1853–1937): A judge elected mayor in April 1905, as a Progressive Democrat, Dunne had close ties to the labor movement and to the city's strong reform-oriented middle class. He made a commitment to immediate public ownership of public transport and to cleaning up the board of education. Upon his election, Dunne appointed labor leaders and social reformers like Jane Addams and Clarence Darrow to positions in his administration. Extremely popular among voters, Dunne had great difficulty in controlling the city council, and he served only one term. At the time Hapgood was researching his book, however, reform elements in Chicago were riding high. Dunne was elected

governor of Illinois in 1913. (See Richard Allen Morton, *Justice and Humanity: Edward F. Dunne, Illinois Progressive* [Carbondale, Ill., 1997].)

213 **Jane Addams** (1860–1935) . . . **Hull House:** American pacifist, social worker, author, and social reformer, Jane Addams was born in Cedarville, Illinois, and raised in a Protestant, middle-class Republican household. In 1889 she opened Hull-House, one of the first settlement houses in the United States, in the slums of Chicago's West Side, a densely populated immigrant working-class neighborhood. She lived there for the rest of her life. By the end of the nineteenth century, Addams was engaged in a broad range of reform efforts, Hull-House had become a common ground for immigrant families and reformers of all stripes, and some members of the Hull-House staff had developed strong ties to the labor movement. Addams opposed U.S. entry into World War I and won the Nobel Peace Prize in 1931. (See Victoria Bissell Brown, "Addams, Jane," in *Women Building Chicago, 1790–1990,* ed. Rima Lunin Schultz and Adele Hast [Bloomington, Ind., 2001], 139–41. See also Allen F. Davis, *American Heroine: The Life and Legend of Jane Addams* [New York, 1973]; and Jean Bethke Elshtain, *Jane Addams and the Dream of American Democracy: A Life* [New York, 2002].)

215 **Another remarkable woman:** Hapgood is describing **Mary McDowell** (1854–1936). Raised in a middle-class Protestant family, she taught kindergarten at Hull-House in the early 1890s and then established the University of

Chicago Settlement in the heart of the Stockyards community just after the great strikes of 1894. While the university saw the settlement house as a window onto the world of the immigrant working class and a site for its research, McDowell herself became very much a part of the community. She helped to found the Women's Trade Union League (WTUL) in 1903, supported the great stockyards strike in 1904, and served as president of the Chicago WTUL from 1904 to 1907. McDowell lobbied at the city, state, and federal levels throughout the early twentieth century, and she was appointed Chicago's commissioner of public welfare in 1923. (Louise Carroll Wade, "McDowell, Mary," in *American National Biography*, vol. 15 [New York, 1999], 24–25. See also Howard Wilson, *Mary McDowell, Neighbor* [Chicago, 1928].)

217 a woman who has made herself: Hapgood is describing **Margaret Angela Haley** (1861–1939). A sixth-grade teacher at Hendricks School in the Stockyards neighborhood, Haley was cofounder in 1897 of the Chicago Federation of Teachers (CFT). In 1916 the American Federation of Teachers (AFT), a new American Federation of Labor affiliate, chartered the CFT as its Local 1. Haley served the CFT as its full-time business agent from 1901 to 1939, and became the first national AFT organizer. She was active in the Chicago Federation of Labor, lobbying at the state capital in Springfield from the turn of the century on, and she cofounded the Cook County Labor Party in 1918. (Janet Nolan, "Haley, Margaret Angela," in *Women Building Chicago, 1790–1990*, ed.

Schultz and Hast, 338–41; Gary M. Fink, ed., *Biographical Dictionary of American Labor Leaders* [Westport, Conn., 1974], 141. See also Marjorie Murphy, *Blackboard Unions: The AFT and the NEA, 1900–1980* [Ithaca, N.Y., 1980] and *Battlefield: The Autobiography of Margaret Haley* [Urbana, Ill., 1982].)

217 **Louis F. Post** (1849–1928) was a progressive journalist, reformer, and government official. He started his career as a political leader in Reconstruction-era South Carolina and as an editor in New York City, where he supported the radical reformer Henry George. Post and his wife Anna Johnson came to Chicago in 1898 to launch the *Public,* a leading progressive journal of the day. He was appointed to the Chicago School Board by reform mayor Edward F. Dunne and championed academic freedom, sound business practices, and the right of the public school teachers to organize a union. President Wilson appointed Post assistant secretary of labor in 1913 and from that position he opposed the worst of the Red Scare government measures of the post-World War I years. (Charles Howard McCormick, "Post, Louis F.," in *American National Biography,* ed. John Garraty and Mark Carnes, vol. 17 [New York, 1999], 730–31; see also Dominic Lawrence Candeloro, "Louis Freeland Post: Carpetbagger, Single Taxer, Progressive," Ph.D. diss., University of Illinois at Urbana-Champaign, 1970.)

249 **Thomas I. Kidd** immigrated from Scotland to the United States in 1884 and organized woodworkers in Nebraska, Colorado, and Minnesota into the Machine

Wood-Workers' International Union of America in 1890. He served as this union's secretary-treasurer from 1890 to 1895 and as general secretary of its successor, the Amalgamated Wood-Workers' International Union of America, from 1895 to 1904. Kidd also became a vice-president of the American Federation of Labor in 1899 and served in that post until 1905. In 1907 he left the labor movement for a sales job. (Samuel Gompers, *The Samuel Gompers Papers*, vol. 5: *An Expanding Movement at the Turn of the Century, 1898–1902,* ed. Stuart B. Kaufman, Peter J. Albert, and Grace Palladino [Urbana, Ill., 1996], 545.)

263 **Terry and Marie (Carlin)** were the subjects of Hapgood's next book, *An Anarchist Woman* (New York, 1908). They were individualist anarchist followers of Benjamin Tucker (see page 440), less interested in social movements than in personal ethics. Marie left Terry after this second book was published, and she disappears from the record. Terry remained in touch with the Hapgoods and became part of the group of writers and artists at Provincetown in 1916 as the drinking partner of the playwright Eugene O'Neill. An epileptic, Terry developed a drug addiction and mental problems and appeared to have suffered a mental breakdown in the World War I era. (Terry Carlin to Neith Boyce Hapgood, [1916?], Provincetown, Box 2, Folder 40, Hapgood Family Papers, Beinecke Library, Yale University; Christine Stansell, *American Moderns: Bohemian New York and the Creation of a New Century* [New York, 2000], 302–3.)

277 **H____:** Hapgood is describing **Hippolyte Havel,** a
Czech-born anarchist writer and editor. Havel had been
imprisoned for several years as an anarchist in Austria
before coming to the United States around the turn of
the century. In these years, Havel divided his time between Chicago and the New York bohemian scene and
was a close friend of Hapgood and his wife in the latter
setting. He was in touch with Hapgood as late as 1940.
Havel edited a series of anarchist journals, including
Revolt and *Revolutionary Almanac,* in the decade following the appearance of *The Spirit of Labor.* (Terry Carlin
to Hutchins Hapgood, Feb. [1915?], Provincetown, Box
2, Folder 40, Hapgood Family Papers; Hippolyte Havel
to "Hutch and Neith," Aug. 8, 1940, New York, Box 4,
Folder 100, Hapgood Family Papers. See also Stansell,
American Moderns, 98, 152; Paul Avrich, *The Modern
School Movement* [Princeton, N.J.], 121–24.)

286 **Jay (Fox)** (1870–?): Anarchist editor and activist Jay Fox
represented a clear connection between the "Chicago
Idea" of the Haymarket Era, which mixed socialist, anarchist, and syndicalist ideas and strategies, and later
forms of proletarian radicalism. Fox was born near
Chicago's Union Stock Yards shortly after his parents'
arrival from Ireland and joined the Knights of Labor in
1886. He was injured slightly during the Haymarket
events. He joined Debs's American Railway Union and
took part in the 1894 Pullman Strike while working in
the Illinois Central Railroad's repair shops on the city's
South Side. Fox worked with the anarchist collective that

produced *Free Society* and later anarchist publications. A gifted labor organizer, Fox worked on a number of union campaigns in the West. He published *Anarchism and Trade Unionism* in 1908 to argue for a necessary link between anarchist politics and union organization. He remained active in Chicago until 1908, when he left for the anarchist Home Colony near Tacoma, Washington, where he published *The Agitator* on an ancient press he had inherited from the nineteenth-century American anarchist Ezra Heywood. After a period of syndicalist activity with his close friend William Z. Foster, Fox briefly followed Foster into the Communist Party in the 1920s but later resigned and returned to anarchism. (May Carr, "Anarchist of Home: Jay Fox," *Columbia* 3 [Spring 1980]: 3–10; Charles P. LeWarne, *Utopias on Puget Sound, 1885–1917* [Seattle, 1975], 206–11; Carolyn Ashbaugh, *Lucy Parsons, American Revolutionary* [Chicago, 1976], 206–16, 219–21.)

290 Esther (Abramovitz): An immigrant garment worker from a Lithuanian Jewish family, Esther Abramovitz arrived in the United States some time in the 1890s and by the turn of the century was active in anarchist politics, first in New York and then in Chicago. She lived with her lover Jay Fox at the Home Colony, where she met and began a life-long relationship with Fox's friend William Z. Foster in 1909. Along with Fox, Abramovitz joined Foster's Syndicalist League of North America in 1909 and returned with Foster to Chicago in 1912. They married in 1917 while Foster organized workers in the

Chicago stockyards. Esther's own political activity receded in the early 1920s as Foster assumed a leading role in the communist movement. Despite her life-long relationship with Foster, she never played a role in the Communist Party and, remarkably, there is some reason to believe that she remained an anarchist until the end of her life in the 1960s. (Esther features in Hapgood's second book on Chicago, *An Anarchist Woman* [New York, 1909], 153–54. See also Lucy Robins Lang, *Tomorrow Is Beautiful* [New York, 1948], 27–31, 49–78; and James R. Barrett, *William Z. Foster and the Tragedy of American Radicalism* [Urbana, Ill., 1999], 61–63, 203–4.)

296 **(Charles) Dold,** a German immigrant and a cigarmaker by trade, became active in the Cigarmakers' International Union in Aurora, Illinois, and moved to Chicago in 1890. He became active in the Chicago Labor Congress, a forerunner to the Chicago Federation of Labor, in the 1890s and helped to organize the Piano Makers' and Piano Finishers' Local 7143 of Chicago, serving as its general organizer from 1899 to 1904 and as president of that union under a new name, the Piano, Organ, and Musical Instrument Workers' International Union of America, from 1904 to 1921. Dold was elected president of the Illinois Federation of Labor in 1898 and served as chair of the Cook County Labor Party in 1918. He ended his career as owner of a piano store in the 1920s and 1930s. (Gompers, *The Samuel Gompers Papers,* vol. 5: *An Expanding Movement at the Turn of the Century, 1898–1902,* 530.)

297 Michael Donnelly (1898–1916): Sheep butcher Michael Donnelly was elected the first international president of the Amalgamated Meat Cutters and Butcher Workmen of North America when the union was organized in 1897. An early advocate of inclusive industrial unionism and a gifted organizer, he built the Amalgamated through the organization of slaughter- and packinghouse workers between 1900 and 1904 and led a general strike in the packinghouse industry in 1904. As a result of his support for progressive reform elements in the Chicago Federation of Labor, Donnelly was severely beaten at least twice, attacks that affected his mental capacity. He drifted in and out of the labor movement and disappeared for the last time in 1916. (Fink, ed., *Biographical Dictionary of American Labor Leaders,* 81.)

297 Driscoll-Young machine: John C. Driscoll, a former ward politician with strong connections to the city's Democratic Party, became the agent of the Coal Team Owners' Association, which he had organized. Al Young was a Chicago Teamsters' leader at the time of the 1905 strike. In 1899 he had organized his fellow coal teamsters and set up the Teamsters' National Union, a successful rival to the mainstream Team Drivers' International Union. Between them, Young and Driscoll pioneered in the area of union-management cooperation. They brokered a January 1902, agreement that raised coal teamsters' wages from $8 to $15 a week and reduced working hours while doubling the rates charged to haul coal. The association employed only union teamsters and the union harassed any employer who tried to operate outside the association. In the course of 1902, Driscoll spread the system to most other teaming in the city, and labor activists emulated it in other cities. The agreements brought dramatic improvements in the work lives of Chicago teamsters. The working hours for milk wagon drivers, for example, fell from eighty or one hundred hours a week to fifty-two. The Young-Driscoll system, always open to corruption on both sides, was dismantled by reformers in the Chicago Teamsters' Council and the Chicago Federation of Labor in 1903 and 1904. (John R. Commons, "The Teamsters of Chicago," in *Trade Unionism and Labor Problems* [Boston, 1905], 36–64; David Witwer, *Corruption and Reform in the Teamsters Union* [Urbana, Ill., 2003], 16–19; Ernest Poole, "How a Labor Machine Held Up Chicago and How the Teamsters' Union Smashed the Machine," *The World's Work* [July 1904]: 896–905.)

297 Luke Grant: Grant worked as a labor reporter for Chicago newspapers and also published in national periodicals on labor issues.

298 Grahame [*sic*] Taylor (1851–1938): Graham Taylor, a reform-minded minister and educator, arrived in Chicago in 1892 to teach Christian sociology at Chicago Theological Seminary, where he introduced notions of the Social Gospel. He established Chicago Commons settlement house on the city's Northwest Side two years later and spent much of his career at the settlement house and in educating social workers. He was elected president of the National Conference of Charities and Correction in

1914 and the National Federation of Settlements in 1917. Taylor cofounded the magazine *Commons*, which served as a national organ of the settlement movement, in 1896. The magazine became *The Survey* in 1909, and Taylor edited that publication until 1919. When Hapgood was writing *The Spirit of Labor*, Taylor was active in the Municipal Voters' League and writing a weekly column for Victor Lawson's Chicago *Daily News*. (Louise Carroll Wade, "Taylor, Graham," in *American National Biography*, ed. John A. Garraty and Mark Carnes, vol. 21 [New York, 1999], 376–77. See also Louise C. Wade, *Graham Taylor, Pioneer for Social Justice* [Chicago, 1964].)

301 **(William G.) Schardt,** business agent of Local 1 of the Carpenters' Union, served as president of the Chicago Federation of Labor in its early years in affiliation with Simon O'Donnell, "Skinny" Madden, and other racketeers in the Building Trades Council. Schardt was a leader in the 1900 Chicago Building Trades strike and in the struggle against the open shop in the early 1920s. (Schneirov and Suhrbur, *Union Brotherhood, Union Town,* 81, 99; *Chicago Tribune,* Feb. 24, 1922.)

303 **(William, "Blond Billy") Lorimer,** United States senator from Illinois, was head of a powerful and apparently corrupt Republican political machine in the Chicago area around the turn of the century. (See Joel Tarr, *A Study in Boss Politics: William Lorimer of Chicago* [Urbana, Ill., 1971].)

314 **John Fitzpatrick** (1871–1946): Born in Ireland, Fitzpatrick immigrated to the United States as a boy and

settled in Bridgeport, the old Irish neighborhood on Chicago's South Side where he remained until his death. He took up the horse-shoer's trade in the Union Stock Yards and quickly immersed himself in union activity. Allying himself with the reform elements in the Chicago Federation of Labor, he served one term as president in 1901 and was appointed the CFL's first paid organizer the following year. Reelected president in 1906, he remained in that position until his death. A charismatic speaker, a teetotaler, and an ardent Irish nationalist, Fitzpatrick also had a strong reputation as a progressive, though he battled the Communist Party on several occasions throughout his career. Long an advocate of independent labor politics, he launched the Cook County Labor Party in 1918, running for mayor on its ticket the following year, and he helped to found a national labor party movement in the early 1920s. (See John Howard Keiser, "John Fitzpatrick and Progressive Unionism, 1915–1929," Ph.D. diss., Northwestern University, 1965; David Brody, "Fitzpatrick, John," *Dictionary of American Biography*, ed. John A. Garraty, Supp. 4 [New York, 1974], 279–80.)

345 great teamsters' strike: The 1905 Chicago teamsters' strike represented one of two key Chicago labor conflicts in this era and constituted a turning point for labor relations in the city. The Chicago Employers' Association had been preparing for some time for a decisive confrontation with the teamsters and found an opportunity in April, 1905. The conflict started as a sympathetic strike when teamsters refused to cross garment workers' picket lines at Montgomery Ward's department store in the heart of the Loop. The employers' association closed ranks and appealed to the city authorities for help. While Mayor Dunne refused to use the police aggressively against crowds or to employ troops, the courts were more receptive to the employers' association. The association chartered a new corporation and recruited thousands of strikebreakers, while a series of injunctions forced Dunne to flood the streets with police to protect scab wagons. In a related strategy, the association called for a grand jury investigation of corruption in the union and the strike. Ironically, the Teamsters' Joint Council had significantly cleaned up the industry in the city by forcing the team owners' association to fire John Driscoll, but instances of past personal corruption, especially in relation to the union president Con Shea, were easy to demonstrate. The investigation tarnished the reputation of the labor movement and weakened the union. By the strike's end in late July, 21 people were dead and 416 injured. Technically a draw because the employers' association was forced to come to terms with the teamsters, the strike, in fact, represented a significant defeat for the city's labor movement. The teamsters were tamed, and sympathetic strikes dissipated. (Steven Sapolsky, "Class-Conscious Belligerents: The Teamsters and the Class Struggle in Chicago, 1901–1905," unpublished seminar paper, University of Pittsburgh, 1974; Commons, "The Teamsters of Chicago"; Witwer, *Corruption and Reform in the Teamsters Union,* 26–37. For a teamster's own view of the strike, see "The Chicago Strike: A Teamster," in *Plain Folk,* ed. Katzman and Tuttle, 117–23.)

345 **(Con) Shea:** Cornelius P. Shea was the president of the International Brotherhood of Teamsters at the time of the 1905 Chicago Teamsters' Strike. Indicted for bribery in the midst of the strike, Shea managed to retain power in the union, but the most important Chicago locals led a reform movement and eventually established a breakaway from the Teamsters, the United Teamsters of America. (Witwer, *Corruption and Reform in the Teamsters Union,* 34–37, 45–53.)

350 **(John) Mitchell:** John Mitchell (1870–1919), son of an Illinois coal miner and farmer, studied law briefly but followed his father into the mines, working in the industry in Illinois, Colorado, New Mexico, and elsewhere in the 1880s. He joined the United Mine Workers of America (UMWA) when it was established in 1890 and was elected secretary-treasurer of Illinois District 12 in 1895 and appointed international organizer in 1897. After serving briefly as acting president, Mitchell became president of UMWA in 1899 and served in that capacity until 1908. As a vice-president of the AFL from 1898 to 1914, Mitchell advocated mediation in labor disputes and union-management cooperation where that was possible. With this end in mind, he helped to establish the National Civic Federation in 1900 and served as chair of it trades agreement department from 1908 to 1911 and as chair of the New York State Industrial Commis-

sion from 1914 to 1919. Having built UMWA into a powerful union, Mitchell developed a reputation as a moderate union leader and a labor statesman. (Fink, ed., *Biographical Dictionary of American Labor Leaders*, 249–50. See also Craig Phelan, *Divided Loyalties: The Public and Private Life of Labor Leader John Mitchell* (Albany, N.Y., 1994.)

353 **(James) Duncan** (1857–1928): A granite cutter, Duncan emigrated from Scotland in 1880, rose in the ranks of the Granite Cutters' International Association, and was elected president of that body in 1885. He helped to found the Federation of Organized Trades and Labor Unions (later the American Federation of Labor) in 1881, was elected vice-president in 1894, and served on the AFL executive committee, where he was known for his conservatism. Duncan was a close adviser of Samuel Gompers until his death and active in the National Civic Federation from its foundation in 1901, serving on its executive committee from 1903 to 1923. (Fink, ed., *Biographical Dictionary of American Labor Leaders*, 86–87; Gompers, *An Expanding Movement at the Turn of the Century*, 56n.)

355 **Eugene (Victor) Debs** (1855–1926) started his labor career with the Brotherhood of Locomotive Firemen but, deciding that craft distinctions greatly weakened the railroad workers, he organized the American Railway Union (ARU), an industrial union for railroad workers, in 1893. After some spectacular successes, the ARU was largely destroyed in the great Pullman Strike of 1894.

[435]

Jailed for his role in the strike, Debs turned gradually to socialism, running for president on the Social Democratic Party ticket in 1900. The following year he helped to form the Socialist Party of America, the largest socialist organization in the history of the United States; in 1905, he helped form the Industrial Workers of the World (IWW), the nation's premier revolutionary industrial union. Debs ran for president four times on the Socialist ticket, the last time in 1920 from his prison cell in Atlanta Penitentiary, where he had been incarcerated under the Sedition Act for his opposition to World War I. (Scott Molloy, "Debs, Eugene," *Encyclopedia of the American Left,* ed. Mari Jo Buhle, Paul Buhle, and Dan Georgakis, [New York, 1990], 184–87. See also Nick Salvatore, *Eugene V. Debs: Citizen and Socialist* [Urbana, Ill., 1982].)

362 **the great stock-yards strike:** Between 1901 and 1904 the Amalgamated Meat Cutters and Butcher Workmen of North America built a remarkably inclusive and dynamic organization that crossed every line of sex, race, nationality, and skill in Chicago's giant Union Stock Yards on the South Side of the city. On July 12, 1904, 28,000 slaughter- and packinghouse workers walked off the job to demand a minimum wage of twenty cents per hour for any worker in the yards. "Perhaps the fact of greatest social significance," the economist John R. Commons wrote, "is that the strike of 1904 was not merely a strike of skilled labor for the unskilled, but was a strike of Americanized Irish, Germans, and Bohemians in behalf

of Slovaks, Poles, Lithuanians, and Negroes." The stock-yards workers received considerable support throughout the city, but depression conditions made the situation desperate. Sharing the view of the Chicago Employers' Association that a showdown with the unions was inevitable, the packers had prepared carefully. They recruited strikebreakers from outside the city and housed them in the yards. The packers defeated the strike and destroyed the promising organization in the stockyards, but unions reemerged in the World War I era. (See James R. Barrett, *Work and Community in the Jungle: Chicago's Packinghouse Workers, 1894–1922* [Urbana, Ill., 1987], 165–82.)

363 **John T. Joyce** (1863–?): A cattle butcher, John T. Joyce was a well-known figure in the Union Stock Yards by the time Hapgood met him. When he arrived in Chicago in 1884 at the age of twenty-one, he had already been an elected official in the Knights of Labor in the Kansas City stockyards for several years. He was the acknowledged leader of the great 1886 eight-hour strike among Chicago stockyards workers and helped to build the Knights of Labor in the stockyards and surrounding neighborhoods. This impressive organization that embraced workers of all skill levels and nationalities, women as well as men, was smashed by the packers in a second unsuccessful strike against reintroduction of the ten-hour day in fall 1886. Blacklisted at various points in his career, Joyce remained active and emerged as a militant in the 1904 packinghouse strike. He was active in Chicago labor circles as late

as the 1930s. (On Joyce, see *Butcher Workman* 18 [Feb. 1932]: 2 and on the 1886 movement in Chicago, Barrett, *Work and Community in the Jungle,* 122–25.)

370 The *(Chicago) American* was William Randolph Hearst's paper, which tended to be pro-labor, pro-reform, and antibusiness.

372 The **Everleigh Club** was a high-class brothel in the red light district on Chicago's Near South Side. Frequented by leading business, labor, and political leaders, the club often also hosted visiting dignitaries. (Charles Washburn, *Come into My Parlor: A Biography of the Aristocratic Everleigh Sisters of Chicago* [New York, 1936].) For Hapgood's own impressions of the club, a place where he spent a good deal of time while he was teaching English at the University of Chicago in 1896, see Hutchins Hapgood, *A Victorian in the Modern World* (New York, 1939), 135–36.

375 Schmidtty **(Matthew Schmidt and the McNamara Case):** Matthew Schmidt worked as a building tradesman and woodworker and was active in anarchist and labor politics around Chicago. Soon after *The Spirit of Labor* was published, he left for California. In 1911, in the midst of an open shop drive, he was charged in a series of bombings of nonunion bridge and building construction sites, as were the McNamara brothers of the Bridge and Structural Iron Workers Union and David Kaplan, another anarchist worker. Schmidt escaped before the trial and evaded the authorities for about three years before he was arrested and sent to San Quentin prison for the rest of

his life. Hapgood remained in contact with Schmidt while he was in prison. (Hapgood, *Victorian*, 287–92.) On the McNamara brothers and the trial, see Philip S. Foner, *The AFL in the Progressive Era*, vol. 5 of *History of the Labor Movement in the United States* (New York, 1980), 7–31; and Darrow, *The Story of My Life*, 172–91.

389 **George Schilling:** A German immigrant and a cooper by trade, Schilling represented an older generation of labor reformers, but he remained active at the turn of the century. He arrived in Chicago in 1875 and quickly immersed himself in progressive labor and socialist activity. He emerged in the 1880s as a leader in the Chicago district assembly of the Knights of Labor (the largest labor reform organization of the nineteenth century), in the city's eight-hour movement, and in the United Labor Party, by far Chicago's most successful labor party movement. Schilling embraced the reformer Henry George's vision of a single progressive tax on property that would help not only to eradicate poverty but also to solve the problem of class conflict. Schilling long served as president of the Chicago Single Tax Club and wrote extensively on the subject. In the 1890s, he was appointed secretary of the Illinois Bureau of Labor Statistics by Illinois reform governor John Peter Altgeld, and he became an advisor and confidant of Altgeld and an intimate of single tax reformers Henry George and Louis Post. Schilling remained active in Chicago reform politics throughout the early twentieth century, holding a series of appointed and elected positions in city government, and he was a

member of the Women's Trade Union League. As late as the 1930s he was still living on the city's South Side. (*American Labor Who's Who* [New York, 1925], 205; *Chicago City Manual* [Chicago, 1912], 18. See also Schneirov, *Labor and Urban Politics*, 221–22, 244–47, 264.)

389 **(Benjamin R.) Tucker** (1854–1939): An individualist anarchist, Tucker focused much of his career on editing the popular turn-of-the-century anarchist journal *Liberty* and publishing a large number of foreign radical authors, including Tolstoy, Bakunin, and George Bernard Shaw. (Martin Blatt, "Benjamin R. Tucker," in the *Encyclopedia of the American Left,* 786.)

402 **Thomas J. Morgan** (1847–1912): A skilled machinist and a veteran of the Knights of Labor, the Socialist Labor Party, and the Populist movement, Morgan was a founding member of the Socialist Party (1901–) and a spokesman for the party's left wing. He emigrated from England with his wife Elizabeth, also an active socialist, in 1869, settling immediately in Chicago. He became active in the machinists' union and was elected president of his local. A prime mover in the mainstream Chicago Trades and Labor Assembly, organized in the late 1870s, he was also a leading figure in the breakaway left-wing Central Labor Union (1884–96). Morgan read law at night while working in the Illinois Central Railroad shops between 1875 and 1895 and ran for numerous offices as a socialist. In the early 1890s, Morgan drafted a famous program for labor political action, including collective

ownership of the means of production and distribution, which was adopted by the AFL at its 1894 convention. (Fink, *Biographical Dictionary of American Labor Leaders*, 256–57.)

405 **1906 Chicago Federation of Labor election:** After a long struggle, reform elements defeated the machine that had controlled the Chicago Federation of Labor for much of its existence. In a wild election characterized by considerable violence, John Fitzpatrick was elected president and ran a scrupulously clean administration for the next 40 years. The Chicago federation emerged as one of the most progressive labor bodies in the United States, leading the campaigns to organize black and immigrant mass production workers in the World War era, to recognize the Irish and Soviet Republics, and to establish a national labor party in the postwar era. (John Howard Keiser, "John Fitzpatrick and Progressive Unionism, 1915–1925"; Elizabeth McKillen, *Chicago Labor and the Quest for a Democratic Diplomacy, 1914–1924* [Ithaca, N.Y., 1995].)

406 **(Edward) Nockels,** a close collaborator of John Fitzpatrick in various union organizing and political activities, was first a gas-fitter and, later, an electrician. He emerged as an important figure in the Chicago Federation of Labor's reform caucus. Elected secretary of the federation, he served in that capacity from 1903 until his death in 1937. (John H. Keiser, "John Fitzpatrick and Progressive Unionism, 1915–1925," 11–12.)

The University of Illinois Press
is a founding member of the
Association of American University Presses.

———————————————————

Composed in 12/14.2 Adobe Caslon
with Caslon display
by Jim Proefrock
at the University of Illinois Press
Designed by Dennis Roberts
Manufactured by Cushing-Malloy, Inc.

University of Illinois Press
1325 South Oak Street
Champaign, IL 61820-6903
www.press.uillinois.edu